HOLOCAUST
and
REBIRTH

HOLOCAUST
and
REBIRTH

A SURVIVOR'S MEMORIES OF LIFE IN EUROPE
BEFORE, DURING, AND AFTER THE HOLOCAUST

Martin Judovits

URIM PUBLICATIONS
Jerusalem • New York

Holocaust and Rebirth: A survivor's memories of life in Europe
before, during, and after the Holocaust
by Martin Judovits

Copyright © 2016 by Martin Judovits

Typeset by Ariel Walden

Printed in Israel

First Edition

ISBN 978-965-524-237-9

Urim Publications
P.O. Box 52287
Jerusalem 9152102 Israel
www.UrimPublications.com

LIBRARY OF CONGRESS CATALOGING-IN-PUBLICATION DATA
Names: Judovits, Mordechai.
Title: Holocaust and rebirth : a survivor's memories of life in Europe
    before, during, and after the Holocaust / Martin Judovits.
Description: First edition. | Jerusalem ; New York : Urim Publications,
    2016.
Identifiers: LCCN 2016013757 | ISBN 9789655242379 (hardback)
Subjects: LCSH: Judovits, Mordechai. | Holocaust, Jewish (1939–1945)–
    Romania–Personal narratives. | Jews–Romania–Dej–Biography. | Dej
    (Romania)–Biography. | Dej (Romania)–Social life and customs. |
    Auschwitz (Concentration camp) | Holocaust survivors–Biography.
    | Jews, Romanian–United States–Biography. | Immigrants–United
    States–Biography. | BISAC: BIOGRAPHY & AUTOBIOGRAPHY /
    Personal Memoirs. | HISTORY / Holocaust.
Classification: LCC DS135.R73 J83 2016 | DDC 940.53/18092–
    DC23 LC record available at http://lccn.loc.gov/2016013757

Contents

The appeal[1] *appearing in large letters on the facing page is to call attention to a chapter in this book about an urgent Jewish problem, namely the declining Jewish population. The existing situation is intolerable. In that chapter I propose some ideas how to solve this problem.*

---

1. Details of my appeal and proposals are in the last chapter of the book, page 270.
Appeal page design by Susan Rosen.

APPEAL!

An Appeal
From a Holocaust Survivor

To the Jewish Leaders
In every country of the world

To address an urgent problem:
Namely, the declining Jewish population

Let us convene a meeting
in Jerusalem!

Let us propose plans for how to
solve this problem! Please, let us do
something!

In this chapter I propose several ideas how
To solve this urgent problem

Bring your ideas and proposals to this
convention and let us decide what to do.

The goal shall be

6,000,000 more Jews
in the world

Foreword

I AM WRITING THIS BOOK in an attempt to open a window into a time and world of long ago. It is an eye-witness view from the inside – eyes that saw the suffering and endurance of a people during the Holocaust period, and it is also a view of the general conditions in the Shtetel just prior to the Holocaust.

More than that, it is a view of my family and my friends enduring indescribable torture and cruelty. It is a view of a traditional Jewish community that lived in Europe prior to World War II.

No words at my command can adequately describe the horrors of the Holocaust and I apologize at the outset for my inadequacy. However, the story must be told, it cannot be left hidden in the ashes of Auschwitz.

I will attempt to describe what life was like in the town of Dés and in the small village of Naprad where I lived, in the communities I visited, and where I spent my childhood and adolescent years.

Dés[1] is a midsize town in Transylvania, Romania, and the village of Naprad is about sixty kilometers away from Dés. These two communities are the places of my origin.

Auschwitz and the brick factory of Zilah are also places mentioned in the book, but I wish I had never heard of them. When I compare the simple, happy, and sheltered life of my childhood in the small communities of Dés and Naprad to the horrors of Auschwitz or the deprivation we suffered in the ghetto of Zilah, they are as different as heaven is from hell.

After having gone through all those hardships I was finally liberated, and that is a chapter in itself. However the day I arrived in New York,

---

1. Dés is pronounced *Daysh*. This spelling is in Hungarian, and in Romanian it is spelled Dej.

that day I will never forget; it was an exhilarating and liberating experience, both physically and spiritually. When I planted my feet for the first time on American soil I felt finally free in a free country; it was like being born all over again.

My first impression of America, which I never forgot, was the taxi ride from the port of entry at Forty-Fifth Street to Williamsburg, Brooklyn. The taxi took me through the streets of Eastside New York. To my amazement I noticed the display of so many marques in bold Hebrew letters. To my senses it was a breath of fresh air, an expression of freedom that I had never seen before. I could not believe that the Hebrew letters that were not so long ago the object of scorn and derision, are being boldly and proudly displayed in this city, the greatest city on earth; it was an exhilarating feeling and I shall never forget it.

What a contrast to the time spent in the ghetto of Zilah, the horrors of Auschwitz, and the Holocaust experiences; those experiences left an indelible black hole in my soul. They overshadow everything else in my life. In this narrative I will attempt to describe the events as I remember them, the people I knew, the communities I lived in or visited and, above all, my family who perished in the Holocaust during WW II.

I survived Auschwitz, so did my younger brother Mendi for a short time. We had the misfortune to be present in Auschwitz to watch with our own eyes the forceful separation of our parents from their children and the splitting up of the rest of our family. After that separation we never saw our parents or sister again. Both of us were still young boys and we clung to each other in several camps; while we were together we looked out for each other. But even this one remnant of my family was torn away from me a short time later.

I am a descendent of two great families. On my father's side, the Judovits families were landowners in the small village of Naprad. On my mother's side, the Paneth families were rabbis. They were the rabbis of the town of Dés for several generations.

I dedicate this book to my dear wife Helen, *a"h*, who has been my partner for the past sixty-one years, to my dear children: Robert, Lawrence, and Joyce. Also to my dear grandchildren: Mayah, Talya, Amelia, Benjamin, Noah, Emily, and Jonah, and to my great grandchildren: Mordechai and Ari.

Introduction

My name is Martin Judovits[1] ("Mati," for short, and "Morde-chai," in Hebrew). Presently I live in the United States of America, but originally I came from Dés and Naprad, two communities in Romania. My ancestors are the Judovits and the Paneth families. The Judovits family lived in Naprad for four generations and the Paneth family lived in Dés (Dej) for six generations.

The Holocaust is an essential part of this book, and therefore my introduction starts with how the Holocaust began, specifically for our families.

In the spring of 1944 our family, consisting of my parents, my brother Mendi, my sister Lulu, and I, lived in the village of Naprad. My older brother Moishe lived at that time in Dés. We moved to Naprad from Dés for reasons I will describe later.

One day in the spring of 1944 – after we had lived in Naprad for only a few months – the village drummer[2] came to our street corner, beating his drum to call attention to an announcement. He announced that an official order came from the Hungarian capital of Budapest to the gendarmerie;[3] the contents of the order were: "Jews are forbidden to leave their place of residence until further notice."

The Jewish people expected bad news, but it was still a surprise. Before this order, there were all sorts of rumors going around. One of

---

1. The family name is spelled Judovits with a J, but in Europe it was pronounced Yudovits.

2. Being a small village, the custom was that the authorities notified the village population about official announcements by sending out a drummer to every street corner, beating his drum until the villagers gathered around him to listen to his announcement.

3. Local Hungarian police

those rumors was that there are informers watching the Jewish homes; another rumor was that the Jews would be taken from their homes to Zilah[4] to be put into a ghetto. There were also rumors of deportation from Hungary to other countries; Germany and Poland were mentioned as countries to where the Jews will be forcibly deported. Confusion reigned and no one knew for certain what to expect, not even those Jews who supposedly were on friendly terms with the authorities. They tried to find out what was planned for the Jews, without success. One thing everyone was certain of – that something very terrible was being hatched.

The non-Jewish villagers were also asking questions; they were concerned about their own welfare. Their welfare depended a lot on the Jewish professionals and businessmen. Heretofore their doctor was Jewish, the general store was owned by Jews, and some property owners were Jews who gave the village population employment. They wanted to know if it is true that the Jewish doctor would be taken away, and if so, who would tend to their medical needs? Naprad had only one doctor and the same doctor took care of the sick in the nearby three villages. They wanted to know what would happen to the general store and the pub. Where would they buy groceries, hardware, and farming equipment and supplies?[5] They wanted to know what would happen to their jobs. There was talk that the government would confiscate the store and run it. But there was no one in Naprad who knew how to run a store. No one knew where to buy the various supplies for the store.

Notices came, via the drummer, to all the Jews to be ready to leave the village within three days. They were to pack only essential food, clothing, and bedding; everything else is to be left behind. The notices also directed all Jews to turn over to the authorities their Jewelry, gold, silver, and valuables.

On the third day several horse drawn wagons, accompanied by many gendarmes, entered the village and made stops at all the individual Jewish homes. They ordered the families to climb into the wagons, men, women, and children, squeezing in as many as they could into one wagon. Only a few personal possessions – bedding and some bags of food –were permitted to carry on the wagon. When the wagons were

---

4. Zilah was the name of the town where the county seat was located.

5. There was only one general store and pub in Naprad. My cousins, the brothers Shimshi, Hugo, and Erno Judovits, owned it.

loaded, they paraded the wagons through the streets of Naprad with their captives. The villagers were lined up on the sides of the streets watching the spectacle. Some villagers were visibly moved to tears, others had a wide grin on their faces. Some brave villagers dared to call out blessings and "G-d shall be with you!"

But others called out anti-Semitic clichés. My mother was sobbing uncontrollably, holding on to my sister Lulu in embrace. My father, still in great pain from the beatings he received a few days earlier was not able to climb unto the wagon; he had to be assisted. He sat in the wagon silently, hiding his head in his hands. He probably didn't want to see his enemies and tormentors gloat. Mendi and I sat next to each other, scared, confused, and bewildered. Our brother Moishe was not with us; he was in Dej. Mendi and I were talking silently to each other; making remarks about the villagers, whom we recognized in the crowd. Mendi was still limping a little on his left foot, because his wounds from the leg surgery had not healed completely.

Lulu,[6] my sister, who was only fourteen years old, was holding on to our mother, looking sad, but she was not crying. The wagon stopped at another Jewish home and they added another family and their belongings unto the wagon. The wagon was loaded to capacity and there was no legroom. Nobody seemed to be concerned about the discomfort and no one complained. The caravan of wagons drove slowly to Zilah, a distance of about fifty kilometers, passing several villages on the way. The residents were lined up in each village on the sides of the road to watch the exile.

Could it be that the prophecy recited in the morning Tachnun prayers, and in the Psalm number 44, had us in mind when it was crying out? "We have become an object of scorn and derision; we are regarded as sheep to be led to the slaughterhouse, to be killed, destroyed, beaten, and humiliated."

The caravan took many hours to reach its destination. The place we arrived to was an old brick factory on the outskirts of Zilah, which they converted into a ghetto. Here they gathered all the Jews from the entire county. I would estimate that they brought to this ghetto about five to ten thousand Jews. They converted the brick factory grounds into a camp, where hundreds of tents were already set up in rows. The wagons

---

6. The photo of my sister Matel Leah (Lulu) is #5A in the photo section of the book. Lulu is in the middle and our cousins Suri and Rivka are next to her.

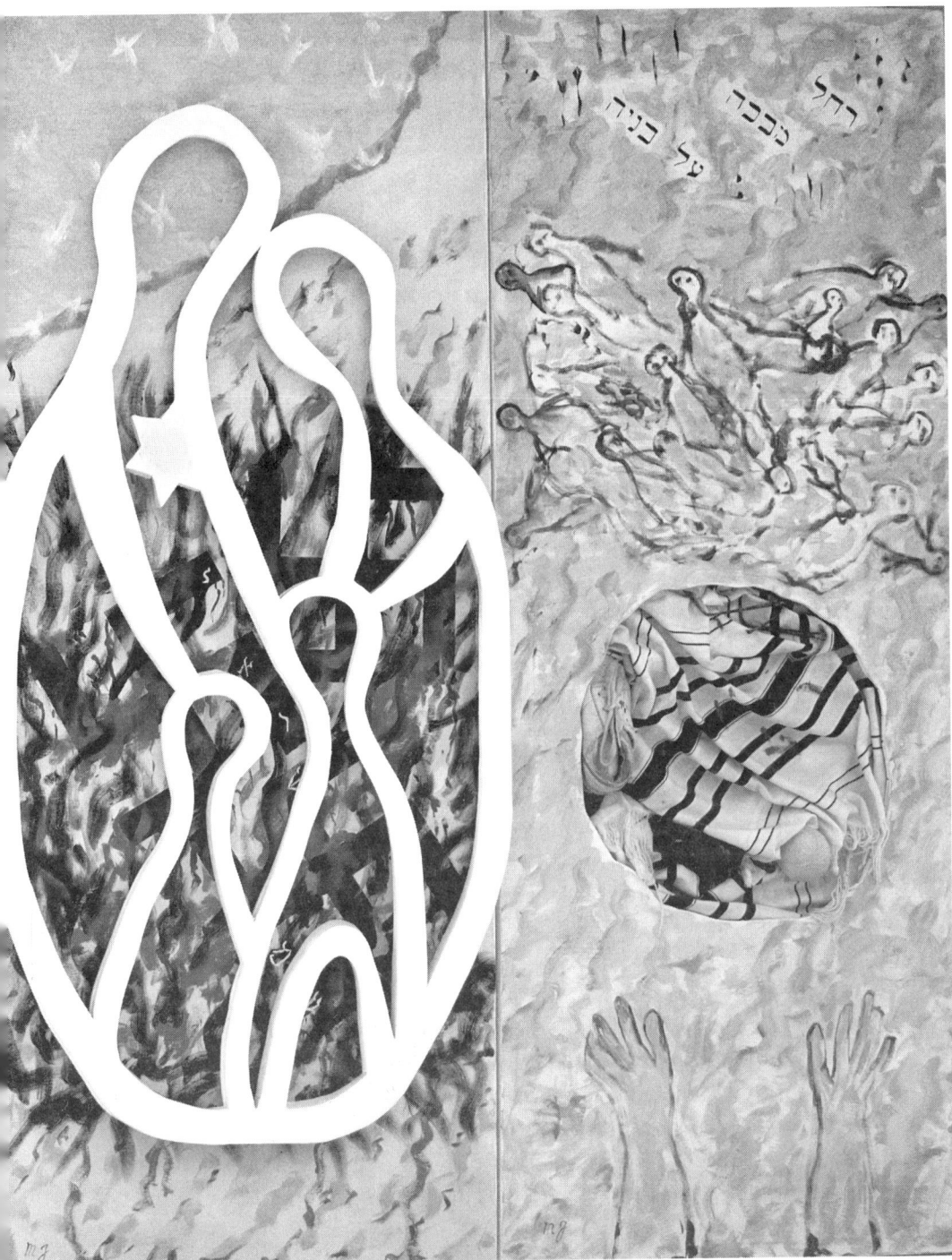

Cover Artwork, painting by Martin Judovits,
photographed by Mikayla McSweeney.

dropped us off at the entrance to the ghetto, and from there we had to carry our belongings to the assigned tent. Our family here consisted of the five of us: my father, mother, Mendi, Lulu, and I. We were allowed to bring with us some pots and pans, other dishes, some bedding and some clothes. We also brought with us some essential food items, like flour, potatoes, and oil. Each tent was assigned to several families. Each one of us was absorbed in our own thoughts and despair. In the days that followed my mother managed to cook and prepare whatever was available. Toilet facilities were nonexistent; however there was an open pit a few feet behind the tents, which was used by men and women as a toilet. Whenever my mother or sister Lulu needed to use the pit, Mendi and I went with them; we were standing guard with our backs turned and holding a blanket to give them some privacy.

New decrees and restrictions were issued daily. They prohibited putting on a Tallis and Tefillin, and anyone caught putting on a Tallis and Tefillin was hanged upside-down until he was unconscious. There were several hangings daily.

I don't know how my mother did it, but she managed to feed us from the little food we had. She cooked potatoes and fried pancakes daily under intolerable conditions.

The guards watching us were drawn from the Hungarian gendarmerie, but a young German soldier – he couldn't have been more than 20–22 years old – was seen strutting around the ghetto. This twenty-year-old seemed to be in charge of the ghetto and the whole operation. The gendarmerie set up an interrogation room near the entrance to the camp. From this interrogation room they summoned the head of each household to come in for questioning. Every day they called in a different group of people for questioning and torture. They wanted the Jewish loot; to this end they questioned every household, asking where they hid their Jewelry and other valuables. Everyone received a beating. The recipients of these beatings were the respected elders of many communities; they were the rabbis, the businessmen. Some came out with bloody faces and broken legs, so badly beaten that they were unable to walk on their broken legs; they had to be carried back to their tent. My father, Reb Shlomo Judovits, who had already received a severe beating from Cserefalvi and the chief of the gendarmes,[7] was also

---

7. The torture and beating of my father by Cserefalvi, while he was still at home, is described in a later chapter.

called in for interrogation. His bruises were still raw and bleeding, but they showed no mercy; they beat him again and questioned him about the valuables he might have hidden. We were waiting for him anxiously outside the interrogation room. When he came out we were aghast at the sight of his condition. He told us what happened, but minimized his pain and suffering; he probably wanted to spare us our suffering on account of him. He endured his suffering with courage and dignity. After this second beating he did not talk very much, he must have given up on life; he just kept to himself. Very often my thoughts flash back and think of his condition in those last days of his life; he must have been in unimaginable agony.

Conditions became worse in the ghetto with every day that passed. There were no sanitary facilities and no place for washing the laundry. The little food the people brought with them was almost completely gone. Even water was hard to get by; people were standing in line for an hour to fill up the buckets at the well. It was the end of springtime and there were some very hot and humid days. Without proper sanitary conditions the place began to reek from foul odors. Some days when it rained, the tent floor became muddy and we had to sit with our feet in the mud, but luckily it didn't rain constantly, otherwise there would have been real floods. For four weeks we suffered the indignities, the physical and mental torture from the Hungarian police in this place, the Zilah ghetto.

Around the first of June 1944 we received an announcement from the authorities in charge to get ready to be transported to another unnamed place. The railroad tracks, which were formerly used to ship out the bricks manufactured in this brick factory, were now converted to roll in cattle wagons to be used to transport us to our new destination. We were watching as they were rounding up the first group of Jewish families to take them to the cattle wagons. For two days, every few hours they took a new group of our people to be loaded onto the cattle wagons. My family was taken on the second day. We were told to take with us only the most personal items. The gendarmerie supervised the loading, but the German soldier was strutting up and down alongside the railroad cars, keeping an eye on the whole affair. They loaded each car to capacity, with men, women, and children all together. People wanted to know where they were being taken; they asked the gendarmes, but they didn't get an answer. In the tumult family members became separated; there was a lot of crying and screaming. Some families were still separated when the whistles were blown for the train to leave; the parents were pleading with the guards to let them find their family, but it was in vain. The gendarmerie ignored the pleas and continued to line up about eighty people alongside each railroad car. There were no stairs to step up to the wagons; older people could not climb up to the wagons. Some empty crates were placed at the door entrance and the young ones helped the older people. There was no resistance; everyone seemed to be resigned to his or her fate. The gendarme chose a captain for each wagon; he just pointed at random to one of the group with a command." You will be the captain of the car for this trip."

Two of the young guys I met in the ghetto approached me and suggested to escape. I told them without hesitation. "No." They had warned us beforehand that if anyone escaped, the whole family of that person would be shot. It could have been a scare tactic, but I had to take it seriously. Anyhow it didn't enter my mind to leave my family and run. I came home from Budapest in order to be together with my family in this fateful hour. I said to the guys, "Wherever they take us I want to be there together with my family."

"Don't be a fool, there is nothing you can do for your family, you can't save them, but you might be able to save yourself. Join us and together we can escape and hide out until the danger is over."

"I would love to escape, but only together with my family; I could not escape alone and leave them behind. I wish you good luck."

I heard rumors that they escaped, but I don't know what happened to them.

There are seven chapters in this book that begin with "✡ נ." The symbols are the Star of David and the Hebrew letter *Nun*. Those symbols indicate that the story described was a miracle. One could say that every day spent in the labor camps or in Auschwitz was very much life threatening, however some happenings were extraordinarily narrow escapes from death, and I consider those escapes miracles. The *Nun* in Hebrew is a symbol for a miracle.

CHAPTER ONE

The Town of Dej[1]

Dej is the town where I grew up; it is a midsize town in Transylvania, situated on the banks of the river Szamos. It is sixty kilometers north of Kolozsvar,[2] the largest city in Transylvania. Prior to 1918, Transylvania was part of the Austro-Hungarian Empire.[3] Every community in Transylvania has at least two names, and sometimes even three. The Hungarians call the town where I lived Dés, and the Romanians call it Dej.[4] Similarly, the Romanians call Kolozsvar Cluj and in German and Yiddish the city is called Klausenburg. Transylvania itself has three names, the Hungarians call it Erdély, the Romanians call it Transylvania and the Germans call it Sieben Bürgen.[5]

The center of Dés consists of a large plaza; where most of the main buildings are located. The plaza is surrounded on all sides with important buildings; on the south side is the Christian reform church, while on the north side there are many retail stores and the entrance to a wide street, which is known as the Corso. This Corso is lined on both sides with substantial houses, most of them two stories high. One of the larger houses is a small hotel called Hungaria; the rest of the houses have elegant retail stores on the ground floors and private residences on the upper floors. The Corso is the main promenade, where people

---

1. Dej was sometimes under Hungarian and sometimes under Romanian occupation, In Hungarian it was called Dés.

2. Kolozsvar is called Cluj in Romanian.

3. In 2015, Transylvania was part of Romania.

4. This author uses both names, depending on the time period.

5. This author is using the name Transylvania throughout the book, because the area is known all over the world by that name.

take leisurely walks and where the parades on national holidays take place. The Corso used to be crowded with pedestrians all the time, be it daytime or the evenings.

The hotel Europa is on the east side of the plaza, next to some textile stores and the police headquarters. On the west side, the plaza was open to the west part of Dés, leading to the Szamos River.

The Christian reform church, mentioned above, was built in 1442, two hundred years before the world-famous Copenhagen church. In both churches, there are inscriptions on the wall written in Hebrew letters, "Hashem Nisi."[6]

Dés is spread out over a wide area, with many of the streets branching out in all directions. The longest street was Vasut Utca, which led to the railroad station, an important junction for the entire region.

There were two promenade parks in the middle of the town, which were greatly appreciated and attended by the inhabitants. The parks played an important role in the social life of the town, because the townspeople considered taking a stroll in the park an important occasion; it was almost a ritual. From early spring until the late autumn, the larger Park was usually full of strollers. Many people would put on their finest and would come to listen to music, meet friends, and bring the children with them. During the summer months the military band would play music four times a week.

The Jewish section was located on the northeast side of the town, with Kodor Utca as its main street. Most of the Chasidic Jews lived in the Kodor Utca area, but Jews lived everywhere in town, intermingled with the rest of the population. When I was a young boy, Dej was teeming with Jews all over the town and in particular Kodor Utca. As a child I took it for granted that it has always been that way, but in truth this was only a recent phenomenon; the settlement of Jews started only after 1848, as will be related in the book later on.

From Kodor Utca several smaller streets branched out in several directions. Three main synagogues were on Kodor Utca: the Great Synagogue, the Beit Midrash, and the Poalei Tzedek. The Great Synagogue was on the east side of Kodor Utca, where it dominated the scenery due to its size and beauty. Next to it on the right side was the custodian's home and some private homes. Then, further to the right was the yeshiva court, with several of its own buildings. The yeshiva had other smaller

---

6. Exodus XVII:15, meaning God is my miracle.

satellite buildings elsewhere in town. In front of the yeshiva court was the house of the late rabbi, Yechezkel Paneth, whose widow[7] still lived there. On the left side of the Great Synagogue was a large court with several community buildings; one of them was the office of the Jewish Community. Across the courtyard to the left was the residence of the present rabbi and in the back of the court was the Talmud Torah School.

In addition to the main synagogues, there were a number of smaller synagogues all over town, among them the Yeshiva Synagogue, where my father used to pray. On the west side of Kodor Utca, opposite the main synagogue was the kosher meat market, which they called, "The Fleish Bank." Next to the Fleish Bank was the Mikvah building and the Beit Yaakov girl's school. The Chasidic Beit Midrash was on the left side of the Fleish Bank. In the Chasidic Beit Midrash one could never be late for the Morning Prayer services, because as soon as one service ended the next one started.

The entrance to the men's Mikvah[8] was in the same courtyard as the Beit Midrash. The men's Mikvah consisted of two large pools, a sauna room, showers, and several private rooms with bathtubs. On Fridays the Mikvah was crowded with bathers. Many men took advantage of the steam room, where they could get the royal treatment from an attendant. He would administer – for a small fee – a beating with aromatic leaves, which were supposed to be a remedy for backaches.

The entrance to the ladies' Mikvah was from Kodor Street and that Mikvah consisted of two pools, showers and private rooms with bathtubs. Next to the entrance to the ladies' Mikvah was the Beit Yaakov School, where most of the Jewish girls attended school, except the very Chasidic. Adjacent to the Beit Midrash on its left side was the Poalei Tzedek Synagogue, whose members were mostly craftsmen. The rest of Kodor Utca was residential, occupied by Jewish residents living in private homes.

Between the years of 1920 and 1944, the Jewish population of Dés numbered about ten thousand strong, or almost half of the total population of Dés. Many Jews of the Chasidic persuasion were attracted to Dés and they settled mostly in the vicinity of Kodor Utca. On a Shabbat day one could see hundreds of men wearing caftans and streimels, as well as ladies wearing wigs or kerchiefs on their heads.

---

7. She was the mother of the present rabbi, circa 1929–1944.
8. Ritual bath house

Kodor Utca was running from north to south through the Jewish section. Then Kodor Utca turned west, terminating at the outskirts of Dés. This southern section had but a few Jewish homes and the buildings were dilapidated. At the edge of the town was an old abandoned salt mine with a large and dangerous open pit. Someone actually fell into this pit and died several years earlier.

All in all Dés was a tolerant community, though occasionally there were incidents of individual anti-Semitic acts.

The first recorded Jewish life in Transylvania was during the sixteenth century in a town called Karlsburg. Later in the nineteenth century, Rabbi Yechezkel Paneth[9] became the rabbi of Karlsburg. Simultaneously he was also the chief rabbi of Transylvania.[10] Many years later his son, Rabbi Mendel Paneth, became the rabbi of Dés, and from then on all the rabbis of Dés were named Paneth. They were all descendants of my grandfather, Rabbi Yechezkel.

Jews have resided in Dés since 1848. Before that year, Jews were not permitted to reside within the borders of Dés, or in any town in the province of Transylvania. However there were exceptions in Karlsburg and Kolozsvar; Jews could live there with special permits, and all other Jews had to live in the villages surrounding the cities. On market days, they were permitted to enter the city limits, but only during daylight hours to buy and sell their merchandise, and they had to leave the city before nightfall. The Jewish merchants would load up their wagons early in the morning and travel to the town markets and then in the evening they would have to leave the town. The next day they would travel to another town, which had the market day on that day. Each town had its market day on a different day of the week; they were coordinated, in order not to conflict with each other. During Christian holidays, Jews were not permitted to enter the towns even during daylight hours. The Jews, who settled in the villages surrounding Dés, were merchants and craftsmen. Some were tailors, glaziers, furriers, and tanners.

The prohibition to live within the city limits was lifted in 1848. During that year there were revolutions all over Europe, mostly against the nobility. The revolution also benefited the Jews; henceforth they

---

9. Rabbi Yechezkel Paneth was my grandfather's grandfather. A photo of his grave is #17 in the photo section of this book.

10. Karlsburg was at that time the capital of Transylvania. Later on Kolozsvar replaced it as the capital.

were permitted to settle in the cities. Dés had the distinction of receiving specific written orders from Emperor Franz Josef of Austria permitting Jews to reside in Dés. Many Jews from the surrounding villages took advantage of this freedom and Dés became a town with a sizable Jewish population.

CHAPTER TWO

───◆◆◆───

The Paneth Family: The Rabbis of Dej

F OR ALMOST 100 YEARS the name of Paneth was synonymous with
Dés, because all the rabbis of Dés from 1862 through the years were
called Paneth. They continued to be the Jewish spiritual leaders of the
town of Dés until the year 1944. In the spring of that year the entire
Jewish population of Dés was deported to Auschwitz, including their
rabbi. At that point Jewish religion and culture in Dés came to an abrupt
halt and Jewish life itself ceased to exist.

The first member of the Paneth family to be ordained as rabbi was
Yechezkel Paneth.[1] Born in 1783, he was the second son of Joseph and
Breindl Paneth. They lived in Bielitz, a small community in the province
of Silesia, in Poland.[2] In later years after he passed away, Rabbi Yechezkel Paneth[3] became known as the Mareh Yechezkel, on account of the
book he authored by that name. He was a child prodigy, even at age five
he was already well versed in Chumash and Rashi.[4] When he became
bar mitzvah he had already mastered several tractates of the Talmud.
After his bar mitzvah he was sent to a yeshiva in Leipnik, and in 1798,
when he was fifteen, his parents sent him to Rabbi Leib Fishels' yeshiva
in Prague. He studied there until 1802. In that year just before Rosh

---

1. A photo of his grave is #17 in the photo section of this book.

2. Sadly, it comes to my mind that I was imprisoned in a concentration camp in
Silesia, not far from Bielitz.

3. See *Encyclopedia Judaica* under "Panet Ezekiel," and under "Alba Julia, Karlsburg."

4. Chumash is the five books of the Torah, and Rashi is the famous commentator
on the Torah.

Hashana he married Chaya Rachel, the daughter of Moshe Henik from Linsk. A year later their first son Chayim Bezalel was born.

At age twenty Rabbi Yechezkel was already a great scholar and many communities were offering him the position to become their rabbi. He was reluctant to accept a rabbinical position, because rabbis in those days were not paid very well. Both he and Chaya Rachel[5] came from wealthy homes and he felt he should not deprive his wife from living comfortably. However his Rebbe, Rabbi Menachem Mendl from Rimenev, with whom he was very close, had other plans for him.

Rabbi Yechezkel and his parents were not Chasidic, but after he met Rabbi Mendl from Rimenev he became a very devoted Chasid (follower) of the Rebbe. Reb Mendel invited him and his wife for a visit. During this visit he convinced them that he is destined to be a leader and a rabbi. They followed their Rebbe's advice, and in 1807 he took on the position of rabbi of Ostryk, Galicia. He served there as their rabbi for six years. Then in 1813, the town of Terczel invited him to become their rabbi and he accepted.[6]

In 1823, his name was already well known in Jewish circles and he was asked to become the Chief Rabbi of Karlsburg. The Chief Rabbi of Karlsburg had a dual role; in addition to being the rabbi of the community, he was also the titular Chief Rabbi of all of Transylvania. He accepted this prestigious position and became the undisputed leader of all the Jewish communities in Transylvania. To his regret, his father Yosef died in 1819 and did not live long enough to see his son become Chief Rabbi. As Chief Rabbi of Transylvania he worked tirelessly, traveling from village to village and from community to community where Jews lived, to speak with the people, to instruct them, and to find out their needs. On his return to Karlsburg from these trips, he dispatched qualified teachers and kosher slaughterers to every corner of Transylvania. His agents saw to it that every community where young Jewish families lived had ritual baths built. He transformed the Jewish populace from ignorant communities to knowledgeable and strictly observant congregations. The government gave him wide authority over all Jewish affairs. They even authorized him to impose jail sentences on litigants who did not obey his judgments. His court had the legitimacy similar to the secular courts, and sentences were recognized as binding.

---

5. A photo of her grave is #18 in the photo section of this book.
6. Terczel is a small town in Hungary, located between Zemplen and Tokay.

It was a paradox that alongside the many anti-Semitic laws, the Jews of Transylvania had autonomy, with Rabbi Paneth as the Chief Judge. Under this rabbinical authority the Jewish community registered their own births and deaths and issued certificates. Rabbi Yechezkel attained fame for his scholarship and saintliness. He was a contemporary of and in correspondence with the Chasam Sofer, who was the rabbi of Presburg.[7] The Chasam Sofer was considered the greatest Jewish scholar of that generation. Rabbi Yechezkel authored many books on Jewish law and several volumes of commentary on the Talmud. Extensive manuscripts, all handwritten, were found after he passed away, but were not published. They were commentaries on the Shulchan Aruch and responsa to many queries from other rabbis. In 1875 after Rabbi Yechezkel passed away, his sons published one of his books. The book by the title of *Mareh Yechezkel* was published in the town of Szigeth, Maramoresh, Romania. He also wrote extensive commentary on the Hagadah, which was published and is still available in some bookstores. Rabbi Yechezkel Paneth passed away on Chol Hamoed Pesach. His grave is in the Jewish cemetery of Karlsburg. He had many followers in Transylvania and particularly in Dej. He was revered even after his death. I was still a young child, but I still remember that every year on Chol Hamoed Pesach there used to be a pilgrimage from Dej to his grave in Karlsburg. They chartered a bus for the occasion, and every year the bus was full to capacity.

Rabbi Yechezkel[8] was born in 1783 and died in 1845. His Rebetzin, Chaya Rachel Henik,[9] was born about 1785 and died in 1863.

---

7. Presburg was called Bratislava in Slovak and Pozsony in Hungarian.
8. A photo of his grave is #17 in the photo section of this book.
9. A photo of her grave is #18 in the photo section of this book.

CHAPTER THREE

Rabbi Mendele Paneth,
The First Rabbi of Dej

Rabbi Mendele Paneth[1] was the first rabbi of the town of Dés. He was born in 1818 as the youngest son of Rabbi Yechezkel Paneth from Karlsburg. Prior to becoming rabbi of Dés he served as the rabbi of Areshor, a small village near Dés. Areshor was the community where most of the Jews lived before they received permission to move into the town of Dés. As was mentioned earlier, there were no Jews living in Dés before 1848. Then in 1862, when a sizable Jewish community established itself in Dés, they asked Rabbi Mendel Paneth to move from the village of Areshor to Dés. In practice he was already the rabbi of Dés many years prior to 1862. He was married to Reizel Rozenfeld.

After residential permits were granted to Jews, the Jewish population of Dés increased exponentially. Under the leadership of Rabbi Mendl the Jewish community of Dés developed into one of the leading Jewish communities of Transylvania.

The very first institution he established was the Chevra Kadisha, which is traditionally a Jewish burial society. He taught a small group of people the ritual laws of burials, which then became the nucleus for a much larger committee. At his urging they also started a tradition of completing a tractate of Talmud every year. The completion was to co-incide with the seventh day of the month of Adar, which is the birthday and yahrzeit of Moshe Rabeinu, the lawgiver. On that day the Chevra Kadisha members were fasting and in the evening they would break the

---

1. Rabbi Mendele was my great-grandfather. A photo of his grave is #19 in the photo section of this book.

fast with a Siyum.[2] People were vying to join the committee; it was a matter of prestige to belong to the Chevra Kadisha. He also established the first Talmudic yeshiva in Dés, which became well known around the country. Many parents from the surrounding areas sent their sons to Dés to study at the yeshiva.

Rabbi Mendel is the author of several books on Jewish law – Maaglei Tzedek, Shaarei Tzedek and Mishpat Tzedek. Rabbi Mendel Paneth passed away on the thirteenth of Tishrei in 1885. His grave is in the cemetery of Dés in an enclosed structure, which the community built around his grave. Later on all the rabbis of Dés, the descendants of Reb Mendele, were buried inside the Ohel.[3] A wooden box the size of a coffin was placed on top of his grave, with a slit opening at the top. His followers would visit his grave and deposit notes in the slit of the box with personal petitions. On the day of his yahrzeit people would come from distant places; they would also come to his grave at all times when they were troubled.

When Rabbi Mendele passed away his son Rabbi Moshe[4] became rabbi of Dés. Rabbi Moshe was born in 1843. His first wife was Rebetzin Malka Kahana; she died young. His second wife was Rebetzin Chayah Sarah Kallus[5].

He was already holding the position of junior rabbi in his father's lifetime. Rabbi Moshe was very well liked by the congregation and widely respected by gentiles and Jews alike. When Franz Josef was crowned emperor of Austria and Hungary, Rabbi Moshe was one of the selected few rabbis to be invited to Vienna to attend the coronation. He traveled to Vienna by coach, drawn by four horses. The coach was bought by the Jewish community of Dés and kept in the rabbi's courtyard for many years after the coronation. At some later date the emperor bestowed upon him a title, which is usually bestowed upon distinguished commoners and is not hereditary.

Under Rabbi Moshe's leadership the Jewish community of Dés grew and developed even further, spiritually and economically. His followers revered him, and many miraculous stories were attributed to him. They

2. A siyum is a ceremony performed when completing a tractate of the Talmud.

3. In Dej they called the enclosure Ohel.

4. Rabbi Moshe Paneth was my mother's father. A photo of his grave is #20 in the photo section of this book.

5. A photo of my grandmother Chaya Sarah (Kallus) Paneth is #3 in the photo section of this book.

called him lovingly, Reb Moishele. His book "Sefer Avodat Hakohanim" was printed in 1894.

Rabbi Moshe Paneth[6] was born 1843 and died in 1903. His grave is in the cemetery of Dés, next to his father's grave. There is a wooden box on top of his grave, slit at the top, similar to his father's, where his Chasidim could drop in notes of petitions to the Almighty. My mother was only twelve years old when her father Reb Moishele passed away.

After Rabbi Moshe passed away, his second son Rabbi Yechezkel Paneth succeeded him. The older son, Rabbi Yitzchak Mechel was bypassed, because the community elders preferred the second son. They felt that the younger brother was more suitable for the job. Both brothers were great scholars, but Rabbi Yechezkel was more polished, more outgoing, and a better public speaker. However this ruffled some feathers of a group that preferred him, and by tradition the oldest son is the heir apparent. In order to mollify this group, the elders of the community elected the older brother to be president of the Kollel.

The Kollel, which was known by the name of "*Kollel of Rabbi Meir Bal Hanes,*" was a charitable organization, providing a livelihood for numerous rabbis, who devoted their lives to the study of Torah in the cities of Tiberias and Tzefat in Eretz Yisrael (Palestine). The administration and the headquarters of the organization were in Dés. Rabbi Mendele, the first rabbi of Dés, was the founder of the Kollel and its first president. His son Rabbi Moshe followed him as president, and it was already an accepted tradition that whoever is the rabbi of Dés is also the head of the Kollel. The removal of the presidency from the rabbi of Dés caused a concern to the officers of the Kollel. They felt that the organization would suffer financially if the rabbi of Dés were not on the letterhead. Therefore they came up with the idea of creating the title of "Nasi." It was only an honorary title, without a salary, and the rabbi of Dés was given this title. Rabbi Yitzchak Mechel, the older brother, was elected president and CEO of the organization. It was a full-time job with a salary. He had already run the office in his father's lifetime.

---

6. A photo of the grave of my Grandfather Rabbi Moshe Paneth is #20 in the photo section of this book.

CHAPTER FOUR

The Great Synagogue of Dej

AFTER ASSUMING IIIS POSITION as rabbi of Dés, Rabbi Yechezkel[1] devoted all his energies to the task ahead with great enthusiasm. Under his leadership, the yeshiva in Dés grew and attracted many new students, and a new building was added. He himself lectured a few times a week and so did his oldest son, Rabbi Yaakov Meilach. His sons-in-law, Rabbi Meisels[2] and Rabbi Grunwald, both of them great scholars, were also lecturers in the yeshiva. Rabbi Yechezkel's son, Rabbi Yaakov Meilach, was appointed as head of the yeshiva administration.

In the meantime, the Jewish population of Dés grew steadily. The main synagogue became so overcrowded, there was no room to accommodate everyone, and some people organized services in their own homes. Realizing that a crisis was looming ahead, Rabbi Yechezkel called a meeting and addressed the congregation. He urged them to start planning a new larger synagogue building. He set an example by contributing a large sum of his own money towards the campaign. That money was put to immediate use; they purchased a parcel of land that was vacant across the street from the existing synagogue. He personally visited many of the congregants to solicit funds for the new building. Within one year he accomplished his goal. The groundbreaking took place amid great excitement. When the building was finished, it was so magnificent that it was viewed as the Jewel of Dés. There was no other building in all of Dés to equal its beauty and magnificence. The

---

1. The photo of Rabbi Yechezkel Paneth is #6 in the photo section of this book.

2. Rabbi Meisels later became the rabbi of Ulyvar, and Rabbi Grunwald became the rabbi of Hust.

synagogue of Dej[3] was erected on a wide-open space on Kodor Street, where it could be admired by tourists and by the locals alike; it was visible from a distance, unobstructed by any other building. The interior was just as beautiful, with the Torah Ark as the centerpiece, a true piece of art. The synagogue was dedicated with pomp and ceremony; many distinguished guests participated, including the leading rabbis from all over Transylvania.

At this point in time there were already many Chasidic Jews in Dés. The community welcomed the Chasidic with open arms; consequently there was a great influx of more Chasidic Jews. Heretofore everyone prayed in the same synagogue, but after the dedication of the new larger building, there was a separation. The Chasidic desired to have their own place of worship, because their order of service was slightly different from the Ashkenazi. Therefore the older building was taken over by the Chasidic, and they named it The Sefardi Beit Midrash, whereas the new building was called The Great Synagogue. Rabbi Yechezkel divided his attendance at Saturday services between the two; the Shacharit service on Saturdays he prayed with the Chasidic and the Musaf service he prayed with the Ashkenazi, whereas for the Torah reading he alternated every other Shabbat between the two. It was the custom in Dés to honor the rabbi every Saturday with the sixth Aliyah,[4] and he was given this honor in both synagogues.

Rabbi Yechezkel Paneth[5] was born in 1870 and died in 1930. His Rebetzin was Rivka Pollack.

Not long after the new synagogue was built another group decided to build their own synagogue. They called it "The Poalei Tzedek."[6] The congregation consisted mostly of the tradesmen of the community and their employers. They were the barbers, cabinetmakers, carpenters, coachmen, electricians, shoemakers, tailors, and upholsterers. They bought a piece of land adjacent to the Chasidic synagogue and built a sizable building. The services were conducted in Ashkenazi. Once in

---

3. Photos #10A and #10B are pictures of the Synagogue in Dej; its exterior and interior.
4. An honor to be called up to the Torah reading
5. The photo of Rabbi Yechezkel Paneth is #6 in the photo section of this book.
6. "Poalei Tzedek" means "The Righteous Workers."

a while Rabbi Paneth attended their services, but they had their own Magid,[7] in the person of Rabbi Bieber.[8]

---

7. Magid is a rabbinical orator.
8. His son Yanki Bieber was one of my best friends.

CHAPTER FIVE

The Judovits Family

MY GREAT-GRANDFATHER, REB SHOLEM JUDOVITS, settled in Naprad sometime around 1830. His full name was Sholem Avruham Judovits, but he was commonly known as Tsule. He migrated to Naprad from one of the Slavic countries. He did what many Jews in those days had to do – resettled in a neighboring country in order to be able to marry and raise a family. Had he stayed in the country of his origin, he wouldn't have been able to be married or to raise a family, because if you were Jewish, the law permitted only one son in the family – usually the oldest – to get married. He chose Transylvania, in spite of anti-Semitism and discrimination against Jews that existed there, because it had no marital restrictions. With the little money he had, he bought a small parcel of land and established a little farm in Naprad; planting on it wheat, rye, and corn. He must have been an excellent farmer, because he brought with him advanced agricultural skills, skills that seemed to be a novel idea in this part of the country. By using his skills and diligent work his land produced twice the crop of the other farms. In the span of a few years he raised a family in Naprad.

Naprad is a small village in the northwest of Transylvania, Romania, about fifty miles east of the Hungarian border. It is an agricultural village with a population of about 300 families. The majority of the villagers were Romanian peasants, who toiled the land from sunrise to sunset. Some toiled the land for daily wages and some were sharecroppers, but very few farmers owned their own land. Many of them had aspirations to own their own land, or at least to become sharecroppers, but to most of them it was unattainable, because they needed their wages that very same day. As sharecroppers they would have had to wait for their produce until the end of the season when the crops were harvested.

Most of the homes in Naprad were built of mud and the roofs were made of straw. The inside of a typical house consisted of three rooms, the middle room was used as a kitchen and dining room, and the two end rooms were used as bedrooms. There were no indoor bathrooms, and there was no running water, indoor plumbing, or electricity in any of the houses. None of the mud houses were architecturally planned; they just copied one house from the other. However, there were a few better homes on Main Street, which were built according to architectural plans. Those were built from bricks or sandstones, and the roofs were covered with ceramic tiles. They were sizable homes, with four or more bedrooms, a large kitchen, a living room, and a dining room. But even these large homes had no indoor plumbing or electricity. Most of them were on properties of several acres, including a barn and a sizable garden next to the house.

Naprad also had a large baronial castle, hidden behind a thick forest, just half a mile from Main Street. The owner of this castle at that time was a nobleman by the name of Baron Huszar. Very few natives of Naprad ever set foot inside this castle. Baron Huszar and his wife owned about a thousand acres of lands around Naprad, but they were absentee landowners. They had other homes in Budapest and Vienna where they lived most of the year. The couple had no children. During his absence, a hired caretaker was in charge of the fields. But the fields were neglected; they did not yield much of a harvest, probably due to the Baron's absence.

The following story was heard repeatedly as recited by the older generation of the Judovits family. I want to stress that I did not hear it from my father; I only heard it from relatives after the Holocaust.

One summer day the Baron came to Naprad for his annual summer visit and he drove out to his fields to inspect them. He was always of the opinion that the soil in Naprad was not as fertile as the soil in other parts of Hungary. Therefore he did not expect a great yield of crops from his farms. This time as he rode through his properties, he found them in the same condition as in prior years. But then he came upon a small farm, which was adjacent to his, and noticed a big difference. The corn on that field was twice as tall as on his fields, and the same was true in the wheat field. He inquired who the owner was of this small farm. His employees told him whatever little they knew about him. He sent one of his servants to invite Reb Sholem to his house for a chat. Grandfather, Reb Sholem was hesitant, but he had no choice; he went to see the Baron. Grandfather was not fluent in Hungarian and he had never been in a baronial castle before. He drove with his wagon from his farm straight to the castle, left his wagon near the stall, and entered the house. Inside, he looked around with amazement at this large magnificent house. The Baron welcomed him and invited him to sit down. The Baron was a thin, tall gentleman, slightly taller than Grandfather. He looked like a healthy middle-aged gentleman, with dark brown hair, a long twisted mustache, stiffened at its tips, which was beginning to gray at the edges. Grandfather's clothes looked shabby compared to the Baron's. He hesitated; he didn't know where to put himself. He was reluctant to sit down with his soiled work-clothes on the elegant silk chair. But the Baron put him at ease and made him sit down; he even offered him alcoholic beverages, which grandfather declined. They had a long discussion about farming and the Baron was very impressed with Grandfather's knowledge of agriculture. The Baron told him how disappointed he is with the crops on his farm and made him an offer to become the overseer of all his properties. At first, Grandfather declined; he argued that he needed his time to supervise his own fields and that he didn't want to take a job away from the present caretaker. The Baron assured him that the present caretaker would not lose his job and that he will remain the caretaker under Reb Sholem's supervision.

When Reb Sholem arrived home, his wife and sons were waiting with curiosity; they wanted to know what the Baron wanted from him. He began by describing the castle, its size and elegant furniture. Then he described the Baron and the nice reception he received from him. He relished telling them the encounter and was dwelling on every detail. Then he repeated in detail the proposal the Baron offered him. Grandmother thought this was a great opportunity for them to plant real roots in the community.

She encouraged him to accept.

After thinking about it for a few days, Reb Sholem decided to accept Baron Huszar's offer. They signed an agreement. As soon as Reb Sholem took charge, he made many changes in the management of the properties. He separated the various properties into individual farms and appointed a foreman for each farm. He met with the foremen and the caretaker once a week on a regular basis and more often when needed. Reb Sholem used to be seen riding on his shiny dark brown horse from farm to farm. He would appear suddenly without notice at this farm or at that field, especially during harvest time. Since the Baron was away most of the time, it was Reb Sholem who was in charge of everything that went on in the village of Naprad. Even the village authorities came to consult with him first before making changes in community affairs. Many villagers, the majority of whom were Romanian peasants, worked on the Huszar farms as field workers or as sharecroppers.

For many years such was the life in Naprad, year in and year out. The farms did very well under Reb Sholem; they exported wheat, barley, corn, and even walnuts. Baron Huszar was very pleased with the management of his estate, especially with the additional income it brought him under Reb Sholem's management. He was extolling his Jewish overseer to the other Barons as a very loyal and honest overseer. Reb Sholem instituted many new rules and conditions on the farm. He built huts in the fields to shelter the workers during downpours, and cooling-off places during the very hot summer days. The huts were open on all four sides with a straw roof overhead. He forbade underage children to be employed on the farms. On most farms it was the normal custom to employ children.

The Baron prospered under his new overseer, and so did Reb Sholem Judovits. As time went by, Reb Sholem bought additional farmland in the village for himself and added them to his property.

All went well until 1848. In that year revolutions broke out all over Europe. The people revolted against the nobility and many of the noblemen were toppled. Some were arrested and tried before a court and some were even executed. Baron Huszar was also arrested and kept in jail in the city of Kolozsvar. His wife, the Baroness, sent word to Reb Sholem, urging him to try to do something to free her husband. Upon receiving the distressing news, Reb Sholem left Naprad immediately and traveled to Kolozsvar. He had acquaintances in Kolozsvar through his business connections and he went to work immediately contacting various people. One of his contacts was a lawyer, who had a leading role in the revolution and who was on friendly terms with all the leaders of the revolution. However, in spite of his influence, he could not get the Baron released, but he was granted more favorable treatment in jail. He was allowed visits by his wife and also by Reb Sholem. The trial was postponed for several weeks; he was promised a fair trial and was allowed to bring witnesses. As soon as Reb Sholem secured a postponement for the trial, he returned to Naprad, where he lined up several favorable witnesses, among them some sharecroppers and field workers. They all agreed to travel to Kolozsvar to testify on Baron Huszar's behalf.

A day before the trial Reb Sholem gathered all the witnesses and together they traveled by wagons to Kolozsvar. It was a long distance trip of many hours. When the witnesses were examined, they all testified that the Baron was a very benevolent employer and that he never took advantage of them. They also gave the court an account of the protective huts in the fields. Upon cross-examination by the prosecutor, it came to light that the Baron did not permit children to work on his farm.

This singular testimony turned the judges around in his favor, and the verdict was "Not guilty." Nevertheless he was penalized with a large sum of money for past inequities.

The Baron was released, but he was not the same person anymore. The imprisonment and the trial itself had an adverse affect on the Baron and the Baroness; it affected their physical and mental health. They returned to Naprad and stayed there all year round. While residing in Naprad they did not receive any visitors, they saw only Reb Sholem. No longer did they travel to Budapest or Vienna; they did not want to have anything to do with the outside world. They became very close friends with Reb Sholem and were very grateful to him for saving his life. It was common knowledge in Kolozsvar and in Naprad that Reb Sholem saved the life of Baron Huszar. Before Reb Sholem intervened, everyone was of the opinion that the Baron would be condemned to the gallows.

For a while they lived contentedly in Naprad, but shortly after they settled down, the Baroness complained of occasional sharp pains in the chest. She went to see the doctor in the village.[1] Upon examination he found that she had a heart condition and he advised her to travel to Kolozsvar to see a specialist. But she didn't listen to him; she never wanted to set foot in Kolozsvar again. He gave her medications and came to see her frequently, but there wasn't much he could do. After a while her condition got worse and she became very depressed; she cried often and didn't want to get out of bed. The Baron stayed at her bedside most of the time and rarely accepted visitors. This went on for a long time. A year later the Baroness passed away from a massive heart attack. They had no children.

---

1. There was only one doctor in Naprad. He provided medical services for several villages.

After her passing the Baron became reclusive and secluded himself even more. There was nothing wrong with him physically, but he had no zest for life anymore. He spent a lot of time with Reb Sholem, playing chess games and talking business. Gradually, as time went by, he came out from his seclusion and started to take a little more interest in life; he took some walks through the village and he seemed to look better. Then one day, all of a sudden in the middle of his supper he had a stroke and died. He left his entire estate to Reb Sholem Judovits.

Reb Sholem was aware of the Baron's fondness for him and he anticipated some small gesture of goodwill, but he was completely surprised at the extent of the inheritance. The village of Naprad was even more surprised; it was buzzing with gossip and rumors for many weeks. But they took it in stride. Reb Sholem was well liked in the village and the people were already used to having Reb Sholem administer the estate and be involved in the affairs of the village.

CHAPTER SIX

Life in Naprad for a Jewish Family

M̲y̲ g̲r̲e̲a̲t̲-g̲r̲a̲n̲d̲p̲a̲r̲e̲n̲t̲s̲, R̲e̲b̲ S̲h̲o̲l̲e̲m̲ J̲u̲d̲o̲v̲i̲t̲s̲ and his wife, were simple, G-d fearing Orthodox Jews. As was mentioned earlier, they moved to Naprad in order to be free to marry and raise a family. However, they had great difficulty raising their children in a non-Jewish environment and without Jewish schools. Their three sons, Mordchai, Moshe, and Yehuda, were unable to make friends with the other children; they dressed differently, and of course, they did not attend church as the rest of the village children did.

Initially, Reb Sholem tried to send them to public schools, but this lasted only a very short time; they didn't fit in. A private tutor was hired for the children from another community; the tutor lived with the Judovits family. Later on when the boys grew older they attended yeshivas in other cities. After finishing their schooling they went to work for their father on the farms of the various properties they owned.

Gradually, as time went by, several Jewish families moved into the village of Naprad. As the Jewish families grew in numbers, the need for a synagogue became a priority. Initially they had their prayer services in Reb Sholem's home. A fund was established and within a short time they raised enough money to build a synagogue and a Mikvah. The congregation hired a Shochet,[1] who doubled as a cantor on Jewish holidays. From this time until 1944, they always had enough Jewish male members to constitute a Minyan[2] on Saturdays. However, in spite of the influx of other Jewish families, they never numbered more than

---

1. Shochet is a ritual slaughterer.
2. Minyan is a quorum of ten Jewish males.

twelve families, which amounted to a very small minority of the total population.

The Judovits families observed Judaism according to strict customs and as Jewish law dictates. They abstained from work on Shabbat and kept a strict kosher diet. Most of the men in the family wore modern western clothes, except Reb Mordchai, my grandfather, who wore dark suits and black hats at all times. Reb Mordchai was leaning towards Chasidism and became a follower of the Déser Rebbe. Reb Mordchai was a familiar figure in Naprad; every morning he was seen riding on his horse to his fields, wearing his dark long jacket with his long pipe dangling between his lips. Once in a while he would travel to Dés to spend the holiday with the Rebbe. Before every Pesach he would send wagonloads of wheat flour to Dés, kosher for Pesach, so it could be distributed to the poor. He was also a generous contributor to many other charities.

Reb Mordchai, my grandfather, followed his father's example and had his children tutored by a private teacher. My father, Reb Shlomo, who was the oldest of Reb Mordchai's children, was sent to Dés at age sixteen to study in the yeshiva of Rabbi Yechezkel Paneth.

CHAPTER SEVEN

My Parents in Dej

MY FATHER, REB SHLOMO JUDOVITS, arrived in Dés as a young teenager of sixteen; he entered an entirely new environment, different from what he was used to in the small village of Naprad, where his life revolved around agricultural issues. But he quickly adapted himself to a yeshiva environment and became an ace student. His father, Reb Mordchai, came to visit him on occasion and he also visited Dés during the Pesach season, as was his custom for many years. On one of these visits a close friend of the Dejer Rebbe approached my grandfather and said to him,

"Mr. Judovits, I would like to have a chat with you about a delicate matter."

My grandfather wondered if there was anything wrong, but he assured him that there was nothing wrong, except that it is a matter that might be of interest to him.

Later on in the afternoon when they met, he sprung a surprise on him by proposing to match up his son Shlomo (my father) with Rebbe Moshe's daughter.

My grandfather wanted to know on whose behalf he was speaking. The answer was that it was on behalf of Rabbi Yechezkel, the present Dejer Rebbe who was the older brother of the young lady Nechama Reizel (my mother). At this point in time Rabbi Moshe, my mother's father, was no longer alive

My grandfather, Reb Mordchai, told him to wait a few years until the children mature, when it will be more appropriate to discuss marriage.

But the friend persisted. He suggested that the marriage can take place at some later date, but it would be advisable that they should get engaged now. Grandfather told him that he has no objection to the idea, that he would consider it a great honor to be related to the Rabbi's family. But he thought the timing was wrong; the children's ages were a problem, both of them were just too young.

My mother was only thirteen years old, and my father was seventeen. Nevertheless after the friend persisted, he promised to discuss it with his son Shlomo.

There were a lot of discussions between father and son. They were both reluctant to have an engagement now, but they did not want to reject the offer outright. Several months later they were engaged and the wedding took place four years later.

CHAPTER EIGHT

My Father's Grain Business

Aᴄᴛᴇʀ ᴍʏ ᴘᴀʀᴇɴᴛꜱ ᴡᴇʀᴇ ᴍᴀʀʀɪᴇᴅ, they settled in Dés in an apartment on Deak Ferenc Street. It was a very nice quiet street, with sidewalks on both sides of the street.[1] The Machzikei Torah School was nearby.

It was a walkup second floor apartment, consisting of a living room, two bedrooms and a kitchen. The extra bedroom was in anticipation of having a room ready for the children. Alas, things didn't turn out that way, because they were childless for many years. At first they did not worry, but when two years went by, they became concerned. She discussed the matter with her mother and their family doctor, who referred them to the finest doctors and the best experts in this field. The doctors recommended several weeks in Karlsbad, a resort place in the Czech region.

They took the doctor's advice and they spent several weeks in the famous Karlsbad resort. They met there many young couples that were in a similar predicament. Most of the doctors recommended the mineral waters of Karlsbad as a cure for couples with infertility problems.

The doctors cautioned her that it might take several visits to the Karlsbad baths before there are results. Other resort places were also recommended. The next summer they traveled to Pöstyen, also a resort place in the Czech region. My mother visited the resort places annually, either Karlsbad or Pöstyen, most of the times with my father, but sometimes without him.

About a year after my father got married he went into the wholesale

---

1. Not every street in Dés had sidewalks.

grain business. Dés was the center of commerce for the surrounding communities in the county. All the farmers and sharecroppers brought their crops to Dés during harvest time, to be sold in the market. In the spring they came to buy their seeds for planting. While the farmers were in town they bought sacks of flour for their bread. My father rented a medium-sized warehouse on the main plaza of Dés. He stocked the warehouse with different grains and a variety of grades of flour. Much of the grain came from his father's farm, but he also bought from other suppliers. It was an immediate success. In a short time it grew from a small business to a medium-sized grain business. He hired additional employees and a foreman to run the warehouse. He extended credit to some of the farmers, especially in the springtime when they needed the seeds to plant. My father occupied himself mainly with finding new customers and was always on the lookout for customers.

After a while he entrusted the running of the business to his foreman. On the surface the business seemed to be prospering; there was a lot of activity and farmers were coming and leaving with loaded wagons. But in reality the business was always short of cash and he had to borrow from the banks to cover the cash shortage. He was already in debt to the banks, because when he started the business he took out a loan from the banks. But soon enough he realized that the problem was more than a temporary cash shortage. The banks made demands for payments on the loan, which he could not meet. For a while he refinanced the loans, but time and again he was short of cash. Within a short time the business had to declare bankruptcy. Later on, to my father's regrets, he discovered that his foreman was the problem. The foreman sold the grain to the farmers for cash at a reduced price, which he then pocketed. The bank auditors discovered the fraud when they took over the assets of the business.

My father was devastated; it was a blow to his pride and a great financial loss. However he did not despair; after a while he tried his hand in another business. Fortunately, he had a wealthy father, who was able to see him through this financial crisis.

After his grain business failed, my father put out feelers in the insurance business. The Fonciera Insurance Company offered him an opportunity to open an agency in Dés. He had to take a four-week insurance course, which was given in Kolozsvar. At first he did business from his own home, but later on he rented a small office near the main plaza. It was a very difficult undertaking, because the people of Dés were not familiar with the concept of buying life insurance or home insurance. The average head of a family earned barely enough to feed his family; insurance was considered a luxury. But my father tried Naprad first; he was well known there. He started with his family, by selling insurance to his uncles and cousins. He also solicited the wealthier Romanian farmers, convincing them that it is a good idea to have insurance against catastrophes. In a small village like Naprad everyone knew about everyone's business. When some of the farmers bought insurance, the whole village knew about it and others followed suit. Then when a fire broke out and the owners were fully compensated for their losses; the villagers took notice. Word got around that insurance is an important protection against a catastrophe. After that he no longer had to call on people, they came to him. However, my father was not content to wait for customers; he traveled from village to village, and opened up new territories for the insurance company. He met with the peasants from the other villages and convinced them that one drink less a day at the pub could provide protection for their family.

After a few years my father became one of the most successful insurance agents in the area. He accomplished this in spite of his Chasidic attire. Language was no barrier, because he spoke Hungarian, Romanian, German, and Yiddish fluently. When tragedy struck he exerted all his efforts on behalf of the insured to affect a speedy settlement and collection. He was very well liked in all the villages by Jews and gentiles alike and was always given a warm welcome when he visited those villages.

CHAPTER NINE

Childless for Thirteen Years

My cousin, Rabbi Yosef Paneth, the last rabbi of Dej, used to remind me frequently that my birth was a miracle and that his father, the Dejer Rebbe, Rebbe Yechezkel Paneth, prayed for the miracle. I also heard parts of the story from other relatives.

Twelve years had passed since my parents were married, but they were still childless. Year after year my mother visited the best spas and resort places, she visited the best doctors, but none of them could help her.

Every year during the holiday of Lag B'Omer, my parents used to be guests at Rabbi Yechezkel,[1] the rabbi of Dés, who was my mother's older brother. That particular year was no different; they went to his house to spend a pleasant afternoon together. It was springtime and the weather was beautiful, as the springs were always beautiful in Dés. My mother[2] had her long hair falling down over her shoulders. The long strands of hair were not her own; she wore a wig over her own short hair,[3] but no one could tell that the hair was artificial. They were having tea and biscuits in the dining room. There was a lot of small talk, and the subject turned to Karlsbad and the other resort places. My mother

---

1. Photo of Rabbi Yechezkel is #6 in photo section of this book.

2. Photo of my mother, Nechama Reizel Judovits, is on page #1 in the photo section of this book.

3. My mother had sheared off her own hair when she got married, as was the custom for all Chasidic women.

was telling them about her visits to the resort places, year after year, to find a cure for her infertility.

Her sister-in-law complimented my mother by remarking that her wig looked stunningly beautiful.

Rebbe Yechezkel spoke up. "My dear sister, I do not want to offend you, but perhaps that beautiful wig of yours is the problem. It is not proper for a married woman to wear such an attractive wig. It looks better than real hair; people might be deceived. It is my conviction that if you would exchange that wig for a spitzel, then you will be able to bear children."

My father did not know what a spitzel was.

Rebetzin Rivka explained to him that a spitzel is similar to a wig, except that a spitzel has hairs only at the front edges. She pointed at her own head; she wore a spitzel.

My mother wondered, "What does a wig have to do with the ability of bearing children?"

For the next few days my parents discussed the subject; they talked about it at breakfast, at dinner, and at every opportunity. My mother was desperate to have children, but she was also very fond of her wig. She did not want to take on the image of an old lady. The wig made her feel young and attractive.

My mother was deeply religious, but not a superstitious person; she wasn't completely convinced that removing the wig will change anything. Yet she did believe that there are holy people who have extraordinary insights into people's psyche. She also believed that a holy person, through prayers, could make things happen. It was her understanding from everything she learned and experienced, that a person who devotes an entire life in the service of God and is removed from the temptations of the materialistic world, such a person is nothing short of a saint. My mother had no doubt that her brother was such a person. However she continued to have this inner conflict for a few more days, and then she made up her mind. She decided to take her wig off and to never put it on again.

Within a few months after she stopped wearing her wig my mother became pregnant. The whole family was overjoyed and in disbelief. On the advice of her doctor, my mother was very careful; she rested a lot and followed the doctor's orders to the letter. Her mother, Rebetzin Chayah Sarah, came daily to be with her and sometimes she stayed overnight, especially in the ninth month. In the spring of 1922, my mother, Necha-ma Reizel[4] gave birth to a healthy boy. They named the child Moshe.[5] There was great joy and celebration in the family. Practically, all of Dés was taking part in the celebration, because everyone was aware of their yearning for a child and almost everyone knew that they waited for this for thirteen years. Then the second child came along, that was I; they named me Mordchai,[6] but everyone called me Mati. Then the third child came along, also a boy, whom they named Menachem Mendl.[7] The fourth child was a girl, whom they named Matel Leah. She was nicknamed Lulu.

Roize, the Devoted Nanny

In those days, most of the families with children had a helper in the house. They needed help because everything had to be done manually, from the washing of the laundry to the cooking of the meals. There were no vacuum cleaners, no washing machines, and no electric irons. No ready-made noodles; everything had to be prepared by hand. When my mother became pregnant with the third child, she was looking for a full-time nanny and housekeeper. Heretofore she had a part-time maid helping her with the first two children.

The Goldstein family lived in Dés for many years, but they had to move. They had a housekeeper/nanny by the name of Roize whom they wanted to take with them, but Roize's parents were unwilling to let her go. Roize was in every respect a normal Jewish girl, however she had a handicap; she was partially deaf and mute. She could read lips, and hear loud noises, like a clap of hands, but she couldn't partake in a conversation. She was able to utter some words, sort of speak, in a distorted manner, but it was hard to understand her unless one was used to her speech. Her parents were hard-working poor people from a nearby village. When Roize became eighteen, they reluctantly let her go

---

4. Photo of my mother, Nechama Reizel, is #1A in photo section of this book.

5. He was named after my mother's father, Rabbi Moshe Paneth, who died many years earlier.

6. I was named after my father's father.

7. My brother was named after my great-grandfather Rabbi Mendele, the first Dejer Rebbe.

to serve as a nanny at the Goldstein family. However, before they agreed to let her go they made careful inquiries about Roize's new master. They also asked their relatives, who lived in Dés to keep an eye on her all the time. When the Goldsteins informed Roize's parents that they are moving and wanted permission to take Roize with them, the parents were unwilling to let her go. Friends of the Goldsteins recommended Roize to the Judovits family. Roize's parents were very much in favor of her moving in with the Judovits family. The father expressed his approval by saying, "I taught my Roize to say all the Berochos and most of the prayers, it would be just right for her to live in the home of the Rabbi's daughter." However, my mother was reluctant to entrust the children in her care. She was afraid that Roize would not hear the children when they cry or when they are in trouble.

The Goldsteins assured my mother that Roize is excellent with children and she doesn't take her eyes off from the children when they are in her care. Soon afterward Roize moved in with the Judovits family and she lived with them for many years. She raised all four children and the children loved her like a mother. She was the happiest when the children complimented her for cooking a delicious dish or for doing something special for them. The children learned quickly to compliment her; they liked to see the big smile on her face. When they wanted her attention they clapped their hands. Early in the morning in the coldest winter days she used to take me to school. It was still dark outside when we left the house for the half-mile walk to the school. She would bundle me up in warm clothes, make sure I wore my gloves, which I usually forgot, and tie my shoes.

My favorite food was noodles sprinkled with nuts, sugar, and cinnamon. But noodles were not available ready-made in the stores; they had to be made from scratch. Roize was not lazy to prepare noodles in her free time, because she knew that Mati loved noodles. She loved the Judovits children as if they were her own, and they loved her. She was a noble person, an exceptional human being. She passed on to the children more valuable lessons than the best-trained teacher could ever teach.

CHAPTER TEN

The Town of Dej before the Holocaust

T HERE WERE THREE CHEDERS[1] IN DEJ; two for boys and one for girls. The newer Cheder was called The Talmud Torah, the older one was called The Machzikei Torah, and the school for girls was called *Beit Yaakov*. In the Cheders they taught Jewish religious subjects. In addition there was also a school where the curriculum comprised of both religious and secular subjects. My older brother Moishe and I went to the Machzikei Torah school, Mendi, my younger brother, went to the secular/religious school, and Lulu went to the Beit Yaakov school.

It was the custom in Chasidic circles to cut the long hair for all the boys when they became three years old; however they left some hair on the child's head next to his ears, which were called payos. When I became three years old my hair was already very long and plentiful. On that day my father took me to the barber, wrapped in a Tallis[2] to have my hair cut. No hair was left on top of my head, except the two side curls next to my ears. When my father brought me home from the barber and my mother saw me without my hair, she broke out in tears.

The next day I was taken to the Cheder, where an old man by the name of Reb Mendele was the teacher. The first day in school used to be a whole ceremony for a first timer; my father poured some honey[3] on

1. Jewish day schools
2. It was a custom to wrap the child in a Tallis to protect it from evil spirits.
3. When a new child was brought the first time to the classroom, they covered a new sheet of alphabet letters with honey, in order for the child to associate Torah with sweetness.

the alphabet, dipped his finger into the honey and then licked it. With an expression of delight he said to me I should lick the honey.

But I refused to lick it.

The teacher told my father not to worry, to just leave me there. My father tried, he gave me a kiss and started to leave, but I ran after him and began to cry. He picked me up and said to the teacher, "We will try again some other time."

Six months later I was taken to school again, but this time my mother arranged with another child's mother to be taken together with her child to Reb Mendele's school. This time I was so busy playing with my friend that I didn't even notice the new environment. A short while after we settled down, Reb Mendele called out to the children, "Repeat after me, Aleph, Beis."

I followed whatever the other children were doing and all went well for a few weeks. Reb Mendele was a very short person, no taller than some of his little students. He was also a very old man; one could tell that he had no more patience to teach his little students. He should have retired long ago, but he was well liked by the community, and because there was a shortage of good teachers, they let him continue to teach. Before I started going to school my father taught me many things at home; he used to put me on his lap and teach me useful things. He taught me how to say the blessings in the morning, how to make a blessing over fruit or water, and how to count to ten. Counting was a favorite pastime of mine; I had so much fun counting that when I was bored I counted everything in front of me. I also did fairly well in school, but I was a very restless child and very inquisitive. I could not sit passively; I had to do something all the time. On this day Reb Mendele was telling the children to repeat after him, "Aleph, Beis." I paid no attention to Reb Mendele, because I knew already the Aleph Beis. Instead, I was pointing at the children, counting off, "One, two, and three. . . ."

I was practicing on the students what my father had taught me at home. When Reb Mendele saw that I was counting the children he grabbed me by my hand, pulled me over to him, bent me over on his knees and spanked me a few times on my behind.[4] I started to cry. Reb Mendele yelled at me, "Go back to your seat, and don't do that anymore!" When Reb Mendele let loose of me I didn't return to my seat, but instead, I ran out of the classroom still crying, "I want my Mommy."

---

4. Direct counting of people is to be avoided.

I ran all the way until I reached the door of our home. I was calling out to my mother, who was in the middle of doing something when she heard my cry. When she opened the door she could not believe that it was I. She picked me up and examined me all over to see if I had been hurt. She tried to console me. She was alone at home with my younger brother Mendi; my father was away on a business trip.

After she had things under control she spoke to her brother-in-law, Reb Baruch Avruham Bindiger, who went over to Reb Mendele to find out what happened to Mati to cause him to run home. My uncle was a very well liked person in Dej and respected by everyone. Reb Mendele told him that Mati is not yet ready to be in a classroom with other children; he is restless and a distraction to the other children. My parents never sent me back to Reb Mendele's class again; instead, I was enrolled in a different classroom with a different teacher.

In those days it was standard practice for fathers to discipline their children with a spanking or even a belt, but my father never spanked us. Though, on occasion when a child was out of line he would point to his belt. On rear occasions my mother would spank my brothers, but somehow I was never spanked. I think I must have behaved like an obedient robot. My mother spoiled us a lot and she was very affectionate. She kissed each child before going to sleep, even when we were already teenagers, and my father also kissed us occasionally, especially when he came home from his frequent travels. We had a strict schedule. Every morning we had to get up hours before daylight to go to school and we stayed there until the late evening hours. When we came home from school we greeted our parents with a kiss on the hand and we never addressed them in the first person, but rather in the third person. No child ever sat in my father's chair.

After my experience with Reb Mendele, I was sent to the school of Reb Shmiel Elyeh. He was a kind and gentle person, about fifty years old. He always had a big smile on his face, even though I think he was in pain all the time.[5] His long beard was already partially gray with white hairs in between the black hairs. His students did not fear him, but related to him like to a loving father. When he taught the Bible the students always wanted more; they were spellbound by his stories.

The two Cheders in Dej were autonomous, built with Jewish Com-

---

5. Reb Shmiel Elyeh had a limp in his left leg, and he had to lean on a cane when he walked.

munity funds. The community owned the buildings, but tuitions were paid directly to the teachers. The teachers charged a set fee approved by the community board, but allowances were made for those who could not afford the full tuition. The teachers had to refund a portion of their tuition to the community for maintenance. The teachers had wide discretionary powers as to whom they accepted as students. Before I was taken to the new school my father had a talk with Reb Shmiel Elyeh, relating to him the incident in Reb Mendele's class. Most of Reb Shmiel Elyeh's students were a little older than I was, but it didn't matter, because I was very happy in his classroom.

I studied in Reb Shmiel Elyeh's school for three years. For some reason unknown to me Reb Shmiel Elyeh moved his classroom from Machzikei Torah to his own private dwelling, where he set up the school in his kitchen. It was a fairly large room with a huge table on one side of the room and a cooking stove on the other side. His wife did all the cooking on her side of the room and he did his teaching on the other side. About twenty children sat around the table on small chairs. I have fond memories of that classroom and I remember being very happy there. I preferred the kitchen environment to the austere classroom in the Machzikei Torah. Some of the children in the class knew already how to read Hebrew. The older children started classes two hours earlier; they began with the morning prayers. By the end of three years most of the children, including myself, knew how to read Hebrew fluently.

Lunchtime was a full hour, it was also called free time. Normally during study time each student was assigned a partner with whom to study, but during free time the children could associate with any student they wanted. I preferred to watch the activities of the older children, in particular Simon, a six-year-old child, who could draw faces. I tried to imitate him, but I lacked the talent. At the end of three years I was taken out from this school and sent to The Nasoder Melamed School, a new private school for advanced young students.

CHAPTER ELEVEN

The Rebbe's Piece of Wax

As a young child[1] I sometimes accompanied my father to the synagogue services. My father frequented a small synagogue in the yeshiva building, where his brother-in-law, the Déser Rabbi also attended services. The Rabbi had a habit of kneading wax between his fingers. He did it for medical reasons; he suffered from rheumatism in his hands. His doctor advised him to keep his fingers active as often as possible. Thus kneading wax with his fingers was the solution. When he finished his prayers in the synagogue he usually left some pieces of wax on his lectern. His Chasidim were always happy to get hold of his leftover piece of wax. They attached significance to it, because he kneaded the wax during his prayers. On one occasion during services I wandered off from the seat next to my father, towards the Rebbe. I was about five years old. The Rebbe picked me up and placed me on his lap. He was making nice to me and asked me to read for him from the prayer book. I started to read, but on this particular page the letters were small. I read very slowly. The Rabbi turned to another page with larger letters. This text was more familiar to me; it happened to be the morning blessings, which I did every day. I read the page quite fluently. The Rabbi was very pleased and he gave me a kiss on my forehead and a piece of fresh wax.

"Smell this wax, it has a good scent."

I smelled it and went away happy.

I wandered off between the congregants. One of the Rabbi's Chasidim

---

1. Photo of Martin as a young child of 11 years is #5B in the photo section of this book.

came over to me and wanted to exchange the wax for some candy, but I held on to the wax and wouldn't part from it.

Regretfully this is the last time I sat on his lap, because soon afterwards my uncle passed away. Rebbe Yechezkel Paneth died on Chanukah in 1930. I remember the funeral vividly; it was in the courtyard of the Great Synagogue. It had snowed all day without stop and the courtyard was full of people, all of them in black garments, carrying black umbrellas. A great many rabbis came from far and wide to be present at his funeral. Thousands of Chasidim from distant communities flocked to Dej to say goodbye to their Rebbe. The eulogies and speeches stretched on, lasting all day long without stop. One rabbi after another took the podium to extol the greatness of the Rebbe. The courtyard looked like one large black beehive. I also remember my mother crying and many people trying to comfort her. They buried the Rebbe inside the Ohel[2] next to his father and grandfather in the special building reserved for the Paneth family in the Déser cemetery. A wooden box the size of a coffin was placed on top of his grave, with a slit opening at the top. His followers would visit his grave and deposit notes in the slit of the box with personal petitions. On the day of his yahrzeit people would come from distant places; they would also come to his grave at all times when they were troubled.

Of all my grandparents I only knew my grandmother Chayah Sarah,[3] my mother's mother. The other grandparents of mine died before I was born. Grandmother Chayah Sarah came to visit at least once a week, however, when my mother gave birth to my sister Lulu, she lived with us in our house for a few days. During the time when she slept in our house I remember waking up one morning and she made me scrambled eggs for breakfast. I was four or five years old, and I recall feeling strange having my grandmother make me breakfast. She left a wonderful impression on me.

Regretfully, one year later she passed away. That day, when she died, was probably the worst day in my childhood; I didn't understand yet the concept of dying. My mother looked sad and she was crying, which upset me very much. In my mind, my world was turning upside down. I was concerned about my mother, but I also wondered why all of a

2. In Dej they called the cemetery enclosure "Ohel."

3. The photo of my grandmother, Chaya Sarah, is #3 in the photo section of this book.

sudden she was not paying attention to us children. I did not like the idea that she was crying, and I wondered what was happening to her. People were all around her trying to comfort her. Someone, a stranger I did not recognize, came to take us children away, but Moishe and I didn't want to leave; we were scared. They decided to let us stay. A woman came to perform the ritual of rending the garment. They made us children leave the room, but the door was open and I peeked into the room. I was horrified to see a woman approaching my mother with a knife in her hand and then proceeding to cut my mother's dress.[4] I began to cry, but fortunately my father had just returned and he took charge. My father explained to me everything, as best as he could to a five-year-old. He assured me that my mother is going to be better tomorrow. My father had no problems with my older brother Moishe, as he seemed to be calm and controlled.

From my window, which was facing the synagogue courtyard, I could see the large crowd at the funeral. Everyone was wearing black and most of them were crying. There were many eulogies. Speaker after speaker eulogized my grandmother, who was a humble person but a great lady. The eulogies lasted all day long.

---

4. It is a Jewish tradition to rent ones garments when a close relative dies.

CHAPTER TWELVE

My Schooling

My NEW SCHOOL, THE NASODER SCHOOL, was a private school and was located in the home of its teacher. The room was a long spacious area; it also served as a kitchen for the teacher's wife. The cooking section was on the other end of the room and it was separated from the school area by a folding screen. Many a morning the teacher would eat his breakfast in front of us while he was listening to us reciting from the books. I used to marvel at the way he sliced his corn meal with a yarn. His breakfast consisted of a Romanian dish called mamaliga; it was made of corn meal cooked in water to a dense consistency. He used a cotton thread in place of a knife to slice off a piece of mamaliga.

About twenty students, all boys ranged from ages seven to ten, sat around a long table. The Nasoder Melamed[1] was an excellent pedagogue; he knew the strength and the weaknesses of his students and taught them accordingly. He paid attention to each individual student and tried to make the students achieve their maximum potential. He also had a pleasant melodious voice and liked to chant traditional melodies. When he recognized special talents in a student, he encouraged him and taught him specialized biblical books. Many of these biblical books had their own traditional trop,[2] handed down through generations from time immemorial. When he noticed that I had a fairly good singing voice, he asked me if I would like to learn to chant "Oz Yoshir Moshe,"[3]

---

1. A teacher
2. Musical notes
3. "Oz Yoshir Moshe" is the song the Israelites sang when they crossed the parted sea (Exodus XV).

an ancient biblical composition with a melody. I answered in the affirmative. Within a short time I mastered the whole text very well. After that he taught me the trop to a composition titled "Shir Hashirim."[4]

As time went on I learned to read the Torah with the trop, which I practiced every Friday. Some years later when I was already in an advanced school, my teacher of that school, Reb Avruham Yosef Wurtzberger, had a chat with me. He asked me what I learned at the school of the Nasoder Melamed. I mentioned that I learned the melody to Shir Hashirim. He asked me to chant it for him. When I finished, he told me, "I want you to know that very few people know the trop to Shir Hashirim. Hold on to it, don't forget it, you have something very special in your possession. This very same melody was sung in the Holy Temple, in Jerusalem."

The Nasoder Melamed had two sons. One son was a yeshiva student, who was away studying in a yeshiva, and the other was a jeweler and watchmaker. One day, his son, the jeweler came home from work in midmorning; we were still doing our studies in the kitchen. During lunchtime he said to us,

"Listen boys! Who among you heard of the city of Jerusalem?"

All the students raised their hands. He then asked us, "Who among you saw the city of Jerusalem?"

No one raised a hand.

"Who would like to see Jerusalem?"

All the students raised their hands again. He took out a few fancy fountain pens and said,

"Look into the small magnifying glass in the middle of the pen and tell me what you see."

He handed the pen to one of the boys and the boy looked into the glass.

"I see a large stone wall."

"That wall is what remained of our Holy Temple in Jerusalem. What you see there is Jerusalem."

They passed the pen around and every child had a chance to see the remnant of the Temple in Jerusalem. Then he passed around the next pen, in which we saw the tower of David. Then we saw the Jaffa gate. When I saw the Western Wall I was very thrilled; I had heard and learned so much about the service in the Temple, and I didn't want to let go of the pen. I held on to it until I was made to give it up.

---

4. "Shir Hashirim" is the bible book called the "Song of Songs."

CHAPTER THIRTEEN

The School
of Reb Avruham Yosef Wurtzberger

AFTER THE HOLIDAY OF SUKKOS I was enrolled in a school of higher learning. This was a class where Talmud was the main subject, and Reb Avruham Yosef Wurtzberger, an expert in the Talmud, was the teacher. He was an imposing figure in his early forties, with a long red beard, huge muscular arms, bulging chest, attesting to his physical strength. Physically he looked more like a wrestler than a Talmudic scholar, but in reality he was a gentle soul, who handled his students with fatherly care, but with strong discipline. His students ranged from nine- to thirteen-year-olds. In addition to Talmud he also taught Chumash, the Prophets, Jewish Law, and the prayers. Reb Avruham Yosef's classroom was in the building of the Machzikei Torah School, of which he was the dean. He taught the same Talmud subject to all his students, but on different levels. To the younger students he taught the Talmud with the simple Yiddish translation, but to the more advanced students he added the more difficult commentators on the Talmud.

On Sunday mornings he would introduce a new subject in the Talmud and explain it in Yiddish. He would also add Rashi's commentaries. During this introduction, the entire class, the older and the younger students, would sit together and listen. After the first introduction of the new subject he would pair up an older boy and a younger boy to review what he taught. He would walk around the class to check how each pair was doing. If they had any questions, he was right there in the classroom to answer. The school was in session from the early hours in the morning until the evening hours, with time out for breakfast and lunch. Usually the students went home to eat breakfast and lunch. The older students also went to the daily prayer services. Twice a week, a part-time secular teacher would come to the school to teach secular studies, like reading, writing, and arithmetic. At this point in time, Dej was part of Romania, and the official language was Romanian. The secular sessions lasted one hour.

The Jews of Dej were a substantial minority in a community of three nationalities, consisting of Hungarians, Romanians, and Jews. Both the Hungarians and the Romanians claimed to be the rightful rulers of the area, and ownership shifted between the two countries, depending on who had more political influence with the major powers at that particular time. In the period between 1918 and 1940, the town was under Romanian control.

During the early years of that period, living conditions for Jews were tolerable, but in the later years there were many outbursts of anti-Semitic acts, especially during the Easter or Christmas holidays. In the later years it happened that when the Christian youth came out from the churches they attacked the Jews. They took extra pleasure in attacking Jewish school children.

One particular incident occurred during the Christmas season, when the children from the Machzikei Torah School were on their way home for lunch. They encountered a group of Christian youths, who were dressed in the traditional Christmas outfits, holding whips in their hands. They pounced upon the school children with their whips, while shouting at them derogatory anti-Semitic remarks. The Jewish boys tried to run away, but the attackers pursued them and beat them up. Two of the children received black eyes and bleeding noses.

On the other hand we also had our school hero. Yosi Fruchter was a strapping twelve-year-old, very muscular and strong. He was considered to be the strongest boy in our school; no one picked a fight with him. He was born in America and his family had lived in America for many years, but decided to move back to Dej. His family consisted of his parents and his two brothers. The father, who had a small business in Brooklyn, stayed in America. Yosi's grandparents, who lived in Dej, explained that the boy's parents wanted to bring up their children in a Jewish environment and a place where they can study. They planned to move back to America when the children were older. The father came to visit frequently. He had a nice income from his business in America, an income he could not duplicate in Dej. To them the Jewish upbringing was worth the sacrifice of separation.

Yosi Fruchter became very upset when he saw the sight of bloodied children; he was itching to teach the anti-Semitic boys a lesson. He spoke to the older boys in the school and suggested to form a defense group to fight off the attackers. About twelve of the stronger boys joined Yosi to form the group. The next time they sent out three of the boys just to take a walk on the street next to the school. The rest were hiding and waiting. About an hour later a group of Christian boys all dressed in their Christmas outfits, came marching towards the school carrying whips in their hands. Noticing the three Jewish boys walking, they followed them. One of them with a cracking whip approached the Jewish boys and began to taunt them with anti-Semitic slurs. The three Jewish boys hurried away in the direction towards the school. The intruders quickened their pace after them. Realizing that they were about to be overtaken, the Jewish boys started to run faster, past the school entrance. The intruders chasing after them reached the entrance of the school. Just then, Yosi and his friends jumped out from their hiding places. Yosi and his friends carried sticks and belts in their hands. A battle ensued which lasted a few minutes. Several of the Christian boys were beaten up and bloodied; one of them fell to the ground. Jewish women came out from their homes screaming and crying. They thought the Jewish boys were being beaten up.

"Call the police."

The leader of the Christian boys called out, "Let's get out of here."

The intruders picked up their fallen comrade and ran towards Main Street. Yosi and his group were behind them chasing after them, but once they were out of the Jewish neighborhood Yosi ordered the boys to stop. Some of the Jewish boys were also bloodied, but this time they didn't mind it; they were proud to show off their bruises. After this encounter Yosi became the school hero, and Kodor Street was quiet for several years, even during Christmas time. I guess the word got around.

Studying in Reb Avruham Yosef's classroom was difficult, because the subjects taught were difficult, but it was also rewarding and made me feel like a big boy. I was introduced to the tractate Baba Metzia, one of the complicated texts of the Talmud. It deals with disputes between two parties, which party has a stronger claim on properties. At first I just listened without asking any questions. My comprehension of the subject was so low that I didn't even know what question to ask. Several weeks into my studies I got used to the different Talmudic expressions, and it took me about a year to engage in questions and answers. When

I reached the point of asking questions, I was so much into it that I eagerly waited for the new weekly text to be introduced. There were tests in school, but that wasn't all. I also had to pass my father's weekly test. Every Saturday afternoon my father would give me a "Ferher."[1] This became a regular Saturday afternoon ritual, whereby my father would sit at one end of the table with a Talmud book in front of him, while I would stand at the other end of the table reciting the text by heart and translating the text in Yiddish. My brothers were also given the same Ferher.

Every morning, six days a week, I had to be in school very early in the morning. I studied two hours, and then I went to pray to the Beis Midrash; there were no prayer services in the classroom. It didn't matter what time I arrived in the Beis Midrash, as there was a new Minyan starting every so often. After prayer service I went home to eat breakfast and then back to school. We went home at one o'clock again to have lunch and then back to school at three. We stayed in school until the evening hours.

---

1. A home lesson test

CHAPTER FOURTEEN

My Friends in Dej before the Holocaust

THE EARLY FRIENDS I MADE while I attended junior schools did not last, they were just school friends for that period; I don't even remember their names. But when I attended school at Reb Avrum Yosef, I made several lasting friends. Those friends remained my friends until I moved from Dej to Naprad. One of them was Sholem Weinberger.

Sholem was a very unusual person; he was very bright and had a photographic memory. Even as a young boy of twelve he had more common sense than many grownups. He wore very heavy eyeglasses, about one-inch thick. They looked like binoculars and he needed them, because he was practically blind. At nighttime he could not walk without assistance. He had a wonderful disposition and never complained about anything or got angry with anyone in spite of many provocations. His poor vision was a family trait; his father also wore very heavy glasses. His brother Shimshon was also a very special person and was completely blind, but in spite of his blindness he was a genius. He remembered everything he ever learned. He knew the entire Torah by heart. The young boys in the synagogue used to enjoy testing him; they would quote a passage from the Torah and Shimshon would continue the passage and tell them the place, chapter, and verse where it could be found. Shimshon was just as familiar with the rest of the Bible – the Prophets, the Psalms, the Song of Songs, and the other books of the Bible.

Sholem and I paired up as study partners and we studied every day for about four hours. One evening I was walking him home from school. I was leading him; he had his hand under my arm. When we passed the great synagogue I said to Sholem:

"I see some figures on top of the synagogue roof, I believe they are dancing."

Sholem started to laugh. "Perhaps they are demons?"

I countered, "Why do they have to be demons? Perhaps, they are dead souls coming to pray?"

"Do you still see them?"

"No, I don't see them anymore, but I did see them earlier. There were about ten to twelve figures on top of the roof, holding hands and dancing in a circle."

"Perhaps they were shadows of the tall trees?"

After finishing our Talmud studies, Sholem and I played a game called mill. It was a board game, similar to checkers. Since Sholem could not be active in sport games, he played passive intellectual games.

Sholem also had a middle age friend; his name was Shmuel. Sholem used to have long conversations with him. No one knew Shmuel's background; he just showed up one day in the synagogue of Dej and stayed in town. He claimed that he was from Czechoslovakia. He spent most of his time in the anteroom of the Chasidic synagogue or in the courtyard, carving wooden boxes. He usually carved scenes from the holy land or just Jewish themes on very fine woods. They looked magnificent and he sold them to the congregants. He also carved boxes to order. The most popular theme was the city of Jerusalem. Shmuel was an intellectual and a philosopher; he liked to talk about world affairs, poetry, the cosmos, and philosophy. In Sholem he found an eager listener and a strong debater. Though Shmuel spoke incessantly, he did not stop carving even for a minute.

CHAPTER FIFTEEN

Chayim Tam

D<small>EJ HAD MANY EXTRAORDINARY PEOPLE</small> and some were colorful characters. One of those colorful people was Chayim Tam. No one knew where he came from; he was just there. His family name I do not know, but it was not Tam; they called him Tam because he was very pious. One could always find him in the synagogue, from the first Minyan early in the morning to the last Minyan around noontime. He responded with a loud voice to all the blessings with Amen, and his voice could be heard from one end of the synagogue to the other end.

I was still a child at that time and he was a man in his late thirties, but with his long black beard, his worn-out gray suit and rumpled hat, he looked older. His back was slightly bent and he walked with a shuffle. He earned a meager living from carrying water to the homes of several households. His main meal of the day was provided for him in different homes. He ate every day in a different home, and this was an established tradition for many years. In return he would carry the water to their homes.

He had his breakfast in the synagogue anteroom, consisting of schnapps and cake that he saved each day from the Tikuns[1] of the various yahrzeits.[2] It was a custom in Dej, as it is a custom in many communities, that when someone had a yahrzeit to observe, one would bring cake and a bottle of schnapps to the synagogue. The mourner

---

1. Tikun is a collation of schnapps and cake served in the synagogue by the person observing a yahrzeit.

2. Yahrzeit is the Jewish name for the observance of the anniversary date for a deceased person.

would recite the Kaddish during the prayer services and at the end of the service he would offer the cake and the schnapps to the congregants participating in the service. The congregants would then drink to the memory of the deceased. Since Reb Chayim Tam was always present at every service, he also took part in the collation. However, he did not eat or drink before he finished praying. Instead, he put the cake in a napkin and the schnapps he poured into a small flask, to be consumed later. It didn't matter to him that one congregant brought whiskey and another congregant brought rum and a third something else; he mixed all of the drinks together. By the time the last Minyan was finished he had enough cake and drinks for a hearty breakfast. He was known to drink moderately, but he never drank his flask all at once; he kept some of it for days when no drinks were brought to the synagogue.

There were rumors in town that Chayim Tam was getting married. Up to that time, in spite of his age he was still a bachelor, though he had numerous proposals from matchmakers. The date for the engagement party was set for the following week.

My father was invited to attend and he took me along to the party. To this day I don't understand why my father thought I should be present and I don't even know why my father was invited. To the best of my knowledge, my father was not a particularly close friend of Chayim Tam and certainly not as close to him as the families who fed him. Those families provided him with regular meals, but were not present at the affair. The engagement took place late in the evening in the home of Reb Wolf, the school custodian. From a chair next to my father I watched the whole ceremony with fascination. I think I was about nine years old and the only child there. I never saw Chayim dressed so nicely; he wore a brand new dark gray suit, a white shirt, and a tie (Chayim was never seen wearing a tie), and a new black hat. He looked tense, but his eyes sparkled and he had a big smile on his face. His bride-to-be was also dressed very nicely and she looked very pretty. Everyone was in a festive mood and they drank many Lechayims.[3]

Then came the formalities. They prepared a document and there were some negotiations. Several people spoke; some spoke on behalf of the bride and some on behalf of Chayim. At first Chayim didn't

---

3. In Hebrew, "Lechayim" means "to life" and is the expression used to make a toast.

say a word, but then there was a discussion about a job for Chayim, at which time he participated in the discussion. When everything was settled, they gave the bride and groom a handkerchief to lift[4] and they broke the customary porcelain plate.[5] At the sound of the shattering noise everyone called out in a loud voice, "Mazal tov!"[6]

---

4. Lifting a handkerchief is a halachic affirmation that a transaction took place.

5. Breaking a plate at an engagement is a reminder that the joy is not complete until the Temple is rebuilt in Jerusalem.

6. "Mazal Tov" is "good luck" in Hebrew.

CHAPTER SIXTEEN

Saved From the Flu Epidemic and Kuhl's Eidem[1]

T HERE WAS A YOUNG MAN in Dej by the name of Zelig. One fine day he arrived in Dés as a helper to a traveling-merchant, who traveled with his canvas stand to the markets of the small towns in the area. After the market was over the merchant left, but Zelig took a liking to Dej and decided to stay. He sustained himself in Dej by doing odd jobs for various people in town, but most of the time he hung around the rabbi's courtyard, doing work for the yeshiva.

There was a young lady by the name of Sarah who lived in Dej with her elderly parents. Her father was in poor health; he suffered from an ailment that caused his entire body, especially his hands, to tremble. Consequently he walked with a cane. He had to give up his tailoring job on account of his illness, but he did some tailoring at home from which he barely made enough money to buy food for the family. The father's only wish, which he expressed frequently, was to find a suitable husband for his daughter, but he could not afford to give a dowry to the young couple and without a dowry her chances were slim.

In 1918, the Spanish flu epidemic was spreading all over Europe. It went from country to country and from one town to the next community. Thousands of people became ill and many died. The epidemic did not strike Dej directly, but many communities close by, in particular Hungary, Romania, and Austria, were already affected. The people of Dej dreaded the disease; many kept their children away from school and they prayed a lot. The Jewish Community leaders were very concerned

---

1. "Kuhl's eidem" in Yiddish means "the community's son-in-law."

with the epidemic and they brought their worries to Rabbi Yechezkel Paneth, the rabbi of Dej.

They asked him if there was anything the community could do to avoid the plague. The rabbi told them that he would research the matter. After he had done his research, he told them that he found suggestions for similar situations in the Talmud and in some old manuscripts. He quoted the Talmud,

"In time of an epidemic a 'Segula'[2] is needed. The community has to perform a communal kind deed in order to merit redemption. It cannot be just any deed; it has to be a charitable deed, performed by the entire community in unison. My advice to you is that the community shall undertake a major charitable deed to ward off this epidemic. I have in mind a community sponsored wedding for a young man and a young girl, who can't afford to get married."

The rabbi also told them that according to the writings in some old manuscripts, the wedding has to take place in the cemetery. One of the community leaders suggested that perhaps Zelig and Sarah might be candidates for this charitable deed. The rest of the community leaders, who knew Zelig and Sarah, agreed that they would be a deserving couple to be taken care of. Rabbi Paneth urged the leaders of the congregation to speak to them and to make the necessary arrangements.

When he finished talking to them they immediately went into action. Two leaders of the community spoke to the parents of the bride, to the bride herself, and also to the groom; all of them were very receptive to the idea. It turned out that Zelig had his eyes on Sarah for some time. They had spoken to each other several times, but because they were very realistic, they never pursued it any further. They knew that they could not afford to maintain a household or to raise a family. Zelig barely made enough money to buy the clothes on his back. So when the community leaders made the proposal to them they were thrilled.

The community did not waste any time; they immediately formed a committee to implement the rabbi's request. They raised funds for a trousseau for the bride, new clothes for both of them, an apartment with furniture, and employment for the groom. The committee exerted itself to the utmost and the community responded very generously. The date was set for the wedding and the entire community was invited. On a Tuesday afternoon, the entire congregation turned out at the cemetery

---

2. "Segula" in this case means "a merit."

to watch and participate in this unusual wedding. The Chupah was erected near the entrance to the cemetery on a clearing, where no graves existed. The father of the bride and the president of the congregation escorted the groom under the Chupah, and they carried lit candles. The bride's mother escorted the bride under the Chupah with joyous tears in her eyes and a candle in her hand. The other escort was the rabbi's wife. The bride and her escorts circled around the groom seven times.[3] Rabbi Yechezkel Paneth performed the joyous and very solemn ceremony. In his speech to the new young couple, he wished them a happy future, blessed with children. He also made the following prayer: "In the merit of this holy wedding the Almighty should consider it a worthy undertaking to shield the entire community against all illness and misfortune."

He instructed the community that henceforth they should consider themselves the custodians of the bride and groom, and to welcome the groom as the son-in-law of the community and the bride as the daughter-in-law of the community. When the ceremony was over the groom broke the traditional glass and everyone wished them mazal tov. After the ceremony the congregation returned to the synagogue courtyard for the big party, which was prepared by many volunteers. There was enough food to feed an army, and most of the community stayed for the feast, as it was considered a Mitzvah to partake in the meal. The participants ate, drank, and danced till the early morning hours. There was also the traditional Mitzvah dancing,[4] and even the rabbi stayed and took part in the dancing.

After the festivities were over, the young couple went home for the first time to their own newly furnished apartment. Each day for the next seven days they celebrated the traditional Sheva Berochos[5] meals with invited guests, served in a different home each day. When the seven days were over, the community presented the young couple with a wedding gift. It was a little business, consisting of a canvas stand, which

---

3. This custom of circling around seven times is performed at every Jewish wedding.

4. Mitzvah dancing is a ritual dance with the bride. Male relatives and guests are called up by name to have one dance with the bride. The partners don't hold hands; the bride holds one end of a napkin and her partner holds the other end.

5. The Sheva Berochos meals are celebrated during the seven days after a wedding. Each day there is a festive meal in one of the homes, and after the meal they recite the seven blessings appropriate for the occasion.

was placed at the entrance to the Chasidic synagogue. The community provided the initial stock of merchandise, consisting of pretzels, rolls, kippels, candy, fruit, and drinks. From then on and for many years afterwards one could find the Shatra[6] every morning and evening in front of the Chasidic synagogue, fully loaded with merchandise. Behind the counter one could always find Zelig with a smile on his face, along his beaming wife Sarah and his father-in-law. His stand was known as "the Shatra," and eventually became a landmark in Dej. Zelig was known to everyone as the son-in-law of the community. I used to buy my candy there very often. The dreaded plague never arrived to Dej, not even to the surrounding area, and not one person died from it in Dej.

There was another Shatra in Dej, also a landmark. We called it "Moishe's Shatra." It was located in front of the Ashkenazi Great Synagogue. For business purposes it was even a better location, because it was on Kodor Street, the main street of the Jewish neighborhood. Moishe, the owner, was very popular with the children. He was a handicapped person, having only one arm. It was said that he made a very good living. I liked to buy candy from him, especially a specific bon-bon filled with a cherry and liqueur.

---

6. A "shatra" is an outdoor canvas stand.

CHAPTER SEVENTEEN

Life in Dej before the Holocaust

THE STORY OF DEJ would not be complete if I didn't mention several distinguised personalities, which were part of the landscape of Dej.

Zöldi

One of the well-known local celebrities in Dej was a guy by the name of Zöldi. That was his stage name. He was the son of Reb Chayim Grien, who had many sons and daughters. Most of Reb Chayim's children became rabbis or teachers, but Zöldi preferred to work as a comedian. He chose for himself the stage name Zöldi, because his family name was Grien, and "zöld" means "green" in Hungarian.

He had a great gift for comedy and was very popular not only in Dej, but also in all of Transylvania. There was hardly a wedding where he was not present, and usually he was the master of ceremonies. He called up the people by name to the Mitzvah dancing and poked fun at them by roasting them and bringing out the humorous side of that person's character. The performance was done in a special melody with rhymed verses. The people laughed and sang with him all night.

Once a year, a few days before Purim, he staged a Purim schpiel to a sold-out audience. If someone needed influence with the authorities he was the man to see; he was familiar with and a friend of all the politicians and officials.

Hoppalé

One of the steady characters in the landscape of Dej was Hoppalé. He had a residence in town, but stayed at home only the first days of every month; the rest of the time he traveled to the countryside to beg for money. When he was at home in Dej he would walk the streets and perform some acrobatics. He would stop whenever he saw a group of people and he would bow to them like to a theatre audience. People would throw him some coins and he would say, "Hoppalé." All the children knew him; they called him Mr. Hoppalé.

Yosele Kakas

Yosele Kakas must have been a cantor in the past, because he had a marvelous singing voice and he knew by heart many cantorial pieces. Something terrible must have happened to him to lose his mind. He was walking the streets of Dej and singing aloud as he stopped for handouts. On Thursdays he went from house to house begging. Many times he would give a rendition of a cantorial piece in front of the synagogue.

Hop-Lop-Marcilop

Another familiar beggar who lived in Dej was Hop-Lop-Marcilop. He traveled most of the time to other communities to collect handouts. When he came home from his travels he would stay for a few weeks. On those days he walked the streets from house to house and stopped here and there to perform magic tricks with his hat. He entered only those houses where he saw a mezuzah on the doorpost. While performing his magic he would say, "Hop, Lop, Marcilop."

Zsigi

There was a very interesting man in Dej by the name of Zsigi. He arrived in Dej sometime in 1940. He never spoke a word to anyone, because he claimed that he had no vocal chords, but he could communicate in writing in several languages. He was an educated person and played the violin like a professional and the piano like an accomplished pianist. People were saying that he was Russian and that he escaped from a

Communist prison camp where he was tortured and lost the ability to speak. He used to hang around the Chasidic synagogue, where he made friends with the yeshiva students. He understood Yiddish, and if spoken to, he would answer with gestures or with written notes.

Retyager Market

One fine afternoon when I was about eleven years old I was on my way to the synagogue. In front of the synagogue I met up with a group of boys talking among themselves. The boys were not my friends; they were a little older, but we were all acquainted with each other. They engaged me in conversation, and while they were talking, one of the boys pointed to a man pushing a cart and said,

"Mati, go over to that man and ask him this question: 'When is the next market day in Retyag?'"

I refused. "I don't want to know when the market is in Retyag."

The boy said to me, "I know you don't want to know, but you will get a very funny answer, ask him anyhow."

I hesitated, but the boys urged me on, so stupid me, I went over to the man and asked him, "When is the market day in Retyag?"

The man stared at me with furious eyes and said, "Why do you want to know?"

"I don't want to know, but my friends told me you have a funny answer."

Before I finished talking the man gave me a slap on my face. I was shocked and startled. The hurt was more to my pride than to my body. I was embarrassed to be such a fool; it bothered me terribly that those boys were able to perpetrate a practical joke on me. I walked away without even looking at those boys again. I went to the prayer services and then I went home for supper. During the meal I told the story to my family; my brother Moishe laughed.

"How stupid can you be? Every child in Dej knows the man with the cart is called 'The Retyager Market.' How could you let yourself being duped by those pranksters?"

I answered, "I didn't know."

My mother said to Moishe, "I also didn't know. Who is this man called 'The Retyager Market'?"

Moishe told us the story. The man's name is Nathan the schleifer. His trade is sharpening knives, scissors, and other tools. His place of business is on the street, consisting of a grinding stone mounted on a cart. He makes the grinding stone turn by pedaling the belt on his cart. To drum up business he calls out in a loud voice, "Knives and scissors to sharpen! Knives and scissors to sharpen!" Then he would leave the cart on the street and go from house to house to collect the cutlery. He also traveled around to the nearby communities to sell his craft.

Once on a market day he traveled to Retyag. After the market was over he went from street to street to sell his craft to the local residents. When he was away collecting the cutlery he left his cart unattended. During his absence a bunch of local boys – with nothing better to do – removed the belt from the grinding stone and replaced it with the guts of a cow, which they obtained from the slaughterhouse. When Nathan returned to his cart, unaware of what happened, he started to pedal the grindstone.[1] The guts burst and it sprayed the excrement from the guts on his face and clothing. The boys, who were hiding nearby and watching Nathan, broke out in a loud laughter and ran away. Nathan felt humiliated and embarrassed; he became so furious that he packed his gears and decided to leave town. However, before leaving he returned the unsharpened cutlery to their owners. He told them what happened and vowed never to return to Retyag again. The rumor of the story spread quickly in Retyag and in the nearby communities. The elders of Retyag felt very embarrassed; they summoned the parents and teenagers to a meeting. The teenagers apologized, but the elders felt that an apology was not enough. For punishment, they ordered the boys to clean the slaughterhouse and chicken coops for the next few weeks. Nathan never recovered from his embarrassment and would not tolerate the mention of the incident.

Reb Shimon Ragner

Reb Shimon Ragner was a very unusual person. One might call him a saint. He lived in Dej, but had no permanent residence in town. He spent most of his time in the Chasidic synagogue reciting Tehilim. Many nights he would sleep on the bare wooden floor of the synagogue. He fasted every Monday and Thursday, and on Saturdays he would speak only in the holy tongue of the Torah, which is Hebrew. If he wanted to address a person by his family name on Shabbat he would first translate

---

1. In those days there were no batteries to power the grinding machine.

the person's given family name into Hebrew. For instance if the family name was Goldwasser, he would call him Zahav-mayim. He always had a kind word for everybody and liked to tell humorous anecdotes. With his long white beard, black shiny caftan and penetrating friendly eyes, he had the look of a biblical prophet.

CHAPTER EIGHTEEN

Vacation in Dorna Vatra before the Holocaust

DORNA VATRA IS A RESORT PLACE in the mountains of Bucovina, a province of Romania. Thousands of tourists used to visit Dorna annually for summer vacations. The main attractions of this resort place are the mineral waters and the fresh air.

My mother's sister, Aunt Frieda,[1] was the widow of Rabbi Eliezer Nissan Margoshes; he was the Chief Rabbi of Dorna. In 1937, my Aunt Frieda and her daughter Fogerl, who was then still a young child, were on an extended visit to Dej. When they were returning home my parents decided to send me with them to spend the rest of the summer in Dorna.

My excitement was total, but also nerve-wracking. It was my first trip alone without my parents; I was happy, but I also had butterflies in my stomach. The day before our trip my mother ordered a fiacre to take us to the railroad station. It was the fiacre of Reb Meir Leib, whom the family and I knew very well. He always gave me a free ride on his fiacre when he was riding empty in my direction. Finally, that long awaited Tuesday arrived. I woke up on my own very early, while everyone else was still asleep. I tiptoed to the window to look out; it was still pitch dark. Shortly thereafter, my mother came into the kitchen.

"Mati, why are you up so early? You have a long trip ahead of you, you need to rest."

I answered, "I couldn't sleep."

At ten o'clock that morning the fiacre arrived with Reb Meir Leib

---

1. Photo of my Aunt Frieda in Dorna Vatra is #4 in the photo section of this book. In the same photo is my mother, Nechama Reizel, my brother Moishe, my sister Matel Leah, and my cousins Mendi and Fogerl Margoshes.

in the driver's seat. My whole family wanted to come to the railroad station to see me off, and there was room in the fiacre for six passengers, but Reb Meir Leib wouldn't permit more than five of us, plus the luggage. As he explained to us, "The load would be too heavy for my horse to carry."

We arrived a few hours before departure time, as we always did when we traveled, and we were just sitting around and waiting. Finally the train arrived and we boarded the train. A few minutes later the locomotive belched out a lot of smoke and it started to move. Hearing the sound of the train whistle made it even more exciting. I stuck my head out the window to look at the vanishing station and the smoke from the burning coals filled my nostrils, which I enjoyed, as strange as it may sound. I loved the smell of coals from the chimney of the locomotive.

We arrived at our first destination, which was at the edge of the Bucovina Mountains, where we transferred to another train. Aunt Frieda asked the conductor to call a porter, but no one came. She was looking out the train window and kept on calling for a porter, but there were many passengers and few porters. It was difficult for her to manage with two children; she had no other adult with her to help. I wanted to carry the suitcases, but she yelled at me, "Do not touch the baggage, they are much too heavy."

Finally the porter came and carried our luggage to the other train. The train we transferred to was not a regular train, but a much smaller miniaturized train. Everything on it was smaller – the cars, the wheels, and even the locomotive; it resembled a toy engine. This was a railroad system built for a mountain, because a normal size train wouldn't have been able to negotiate the sharp curves.

Most of the passengers were not happy with this mode of transportation, but there was no other choice. This was the only mode of transportation from Dej to Dorna Vatra. A normal size train brought the passengers to one side of the mountain, from which they had to transfer to the miniature train and then transfer again to a normal size train on the other side of the mountain. I stood at the window admiring the landscape of this magical mountain. The locomotive was moving very slowly, struggling to pull the train uphill and jerking at every twist and turn. At intervals it was possible to get a full view of the serpentine tracks ahead, which were precariously steep. At first I was so fascinated that I couldn't take my eyes off the scenery, but then I realized that I was gazing at the same scenery again and again.

I wondered, "If this train is really going anywhere, or is it just circling around the mountain?" After a while it became clear to me that the train did reach a higher plateau, and it was actually crossing over to the other mountain. All this jerking and twisting made me very uncomfortable; I suffered from motion sickness. My Aunt Frieda – I called her Tante Freide – asked me to sit down and to close my eyes. I did as she asked, but then all of a sudden I got up from my seat and ran to the washroom. My Aunt Frieda followed me.

"Mati, what happened? Where are you running?"

I did not answer her; I just held my hand over my mouth and kept on running.

She immediately perceived that I was about to throw up and handed me a bag. When I came out from the washroom, my aunt took me by my hand to my seat, washed my face with a wet towel, and told me to close my eyes to rest. I stopped looking out the window; the beautiful scenery was the last thing on my mind. I couldn't enjoy the trip any longer and neither could my aunt.

The train pulled into the Dorna Vatra railroad station late in the evening, and Rabbi Israel Margoshes was waiting for us at the station and greeted us. He gave me a big welcome, even though we did not know each other. I was only eleven and he was a man in his late twenties; I did not know how to relate to him. He was Aunt Frieda's stepson. His mother passed away when he was a small child and my aunt brought him up since he was eleven years old. I also felt awkward about calling him by his first name, because he was already the rabbi of the community. We took a fiacre to the house. The house they lived in was the rabbi's official residence and office. I went to sleep as soon as they showed me my room and bed.

The next morning I woke up to a bright sunny day. I tried to get acquainted with my new surroundings and walked around the house. I opened the doors from various rooms and looked inside. One of them was the rabbi's conference room. Rabbi Israel was inside with several guests. He asked me what I wanted and I just said to him, "Excuse me." I closed the door and stopped exploring the house.

Immediately after lunch my aunt took us to the park. I had never been to any other park besides the one in Dej. I was therefore completely surprised at the size of this park; it must have been ten times the size of the park in Dej. It had an iron fence around it and a tall iron gate. Many photographers were in front of the gate snapping pictures of the tourists coming in and out of the park. After the photographer took our picture he gave us a slip of paper with a number on it. The photographers had a system, whereby the finished pictures could be reviewed the following day at the photo stand and purchased for a small price. The festive atmosphere fascinated me; it was very different from what I was used to seeing in the park in Dej. In Dej I had never seen such a large crowd in the park, not even on the annual market day. Another striking difference was that in Dej they never snapped pictures of people on the streets.

The mineral waters of Dorna Vatra were famous all over Romania. When we arrived to the famous water fountains, we saw people lined up in rows in front of the fountains. They all had fancy cups in their hands, some with their names on the cups, others with souvenir pictures painted on them. I tasted the water and I didn't care for it at all.

"For this I had to stand in line? We have better water in Dej; it is much tastier. I can't drink this water, it is bitter, salty, and it has a metal taste. It is also rusty. Look at the color – it doesn't look like fresh water at all."

Rebetzin Frieda explained to me in a very patient tone, "This water may not taste so sweet, but it is good for your health. You lack sufficient iron and minerals in your system; this water will supplement the minerals you need."

Dorna is very high up in the mountains and the air is permeated with the aroma of the spruces and pine trees. I was also fascinated by the many walkways crisscrossing the park. There were benches everywhere along the way, occupied by people of all ages sitting on them leisurely. The areas between the walkways were densely overgrown with all kinds of trees; this park was formerly a wild forest. In the middle of the park stood an imposing wooden pavilion, where the military band played music several afternoons during the week. Not far from the pavilion was the road leading up to the famous Terente, the name by which the peak of the mountain was known.

Because I heard so much about it, I was anxious to get to the top of the mountain, so I ran ahead of the group. I was very excited and could hardly restrain myself. Aunt Frieda called after me, "Don't advance too far ahead of us! You will get lost."

After a half-hour climb we reached the first rest stop. It was built on a plateau carved out in the mountain and consisted of a gazebo-like building with a refreshment stand. Waiting for visitors was a photographer, who asked permission to snap a picture of us. We all sat down on the benches for the picture taking and also to catch our breath. My aunt declared,

"This was the easy part of the climb; it is only the first station. The difficult climb is still ahead of us. The higher we climb the thinner is the air, and it is harder to breathe. When you get to the third station, which is the top, then you have conquered the mountain. It dominates the entire area; it is called 'Terente.'"

Aunt Frieda went on to explain that there is a story associated with the mountaintop and with the name Terente.

"Folklore has it that there was a guy by the name of Terente who had trouble with the law. He spoke up against the authorities, claiming that they robbed the people of their livelihood with their exorbitant high taxes. He was sentenced to serve time in jail for nonpayment of taxes. But he ran away. Consequently, the authorities confiscated his property. He hid out in the area and in particular, in the Dorna Vatra Mountains. They say that he slept in a tent on top of this mountain from where he had a vantage view of the entire area and was able to watch his pursuers. At nighttime he used to come down and rob the rich barons. Some of the loot he distributed to the poor, which made him popular with the common people. To the authorities he was an outlaw, but to the common people he was a hero. In grateful appreciation, 'Terente' was chosen by the people as the name of the top of the mountain."

After a short rest, Aunt Frieda suggested that this is far enough for the first day. I was eager to continue, but my aunt told me that she is exhausted.

On the second day of our excursion to the park, a friend joined Aunt Frieda to keep her company. While the ladies were chatting away, my cousins, Fogerl and Mendi, and I went off to play in the open area near the bandstand. Two ladies stopped in front of us, asking in Yiddish, "Where are you from?"

I answered, "I am from Dej,"

My cousin Fogerl said to the ladies, "Excuse us! We have to leave."

We walked away from the ladies back to my aunt, but the inquiring ladies were not offended at all; they followed us to the bench where my aunt was seated. When the ladies approached the bench they introduced themselves; they spoke in perfect Yiddish.

"We are Americans from New York and we are touring this region. We are visiting Romania, Hungary, and Austria. We came to Dorna especially for the fresh air and the mineral water."

Apologetically one of the ladies explained, "The reason we stopped to talk to the children, because we noticed two nice looking Jewish boys with beautiful peyos. My father used to tell us that when he was a young boy, he also wore peyos, but he didn't wear a suit like you; let me show you his picture."

She reached into her pocketbook to look for a picture of her father, but she couldn't find it.

"Never mind, I can't find it, but I think he looked something like you."

I had long curly peyos, hanging loose on the side of my cheeks. I wore a double-breasted dark gray suit with my jacket reaching down to below my knees. On my head I wore a drum shaped black velour hat.

"How old are you?"

"I am eleven years old."

"For an eleven-year-old boy, you look very serious. You look like a rabbi."

I did not respond.

The ladies were talking with my aunt and her friend for a long while and then they shook hands. One of the ladies reached out to shake my hand. I turned red in my face and hid my hands behind my back. Aunt Frieda explained to the ladies that I didn't shake hands with ladies.

"But why?" she asked. "He is not yet a grown man, he is not even Bar-Mitzvah?"

Aunt Frieda explained that Chasidic boys are segregated from the opposite sex as early as nine years old. The ladies were very surprised.

"This is news to us; we have to tell this to our father. Maybe he did the same thing when he was a boy. Why does he wear that long jacket in a hot summer day? I can understand why adult rabbis wear it, but why do children have to wear it?"

My aunt answered, "The parents want their children to be shielded from assimilation. If they would dress like the non-religious children dress, they would blend in more easily and be more vulnerable to all kinds of influences."

"I am not completely convinced, but let's leave it at that. You clarified it for me somewhat."

After a while, the ladies left, saying to us, "This was a memorable afternoon; we can hardly wait to tell it to our father."

When we came home from the park, Rabbi Israel informed us that his young brother-in-law was arriving the next day. Rabbi Israel's wife,

Frieda,[2] had a twelve-year-old brother. I was delighted at the prospect of having a friend of my own age in Dorna.

The next day when we came home from the park, Susu Hazenfeld[3] was already waiting for us at my Aunt Frieda's house. As was mentioned earlier, Aunt Frieda's deceased husband was the rabbi of Dorna Vatra. Regretfully, Rabbi Elazar Nissan passed away some years ago at a very young age. After he died, Aunt Frieda continued to live in the house, even though the house continued to be the office of the rabbinate. Her stepson, Rabbi Yisroel Margoshes,[4] who became the rabbi of Dorna, conducted his official business in the offices of the house.

When Rabbi Yisroel Margoshes became rabbi of Dorna he was in his early twenties, still unmarried and studying for his ordination. The congregation did not even consider looking for someone else to replace Rabbi Elazar Nissan. They knew Yisroel since childhood; he grew up in front of their eyes in Dorna. They wanted Yisroel to be their next rabbi. It didn't matter that he wasn't ordained yet.

Susu and I became friends instantly. I showed him around the house, in particular the huge rabbinical library. Both of us liked this room. In the middle of the room it had a large rectangular conference table, with a dozen upholstered chairs around it. It was a very impressive, large room, with one side of the room covered from wall to wall with bookshelves, each shelf loaded with books to capacity. Susu and I had fun examining the large volumes of books. We removed one book after another and we were pleased to find the contents of the books familiar to us. They contained the same Talmudic texts we studied at school. It made us feel grown up and important. We found out that both of us had a very similar background, except Susu had a greater knowledge of the Talmud than I did. The next afternoon Rabbi Israel took Susu and me for a walk across the bridge over the river, which ran through the middle of the town. Looking down into the riverbed I noticed there was hardly any water in the river. I wondered how come in the morning when I crossed this bridge I saw a lot of water flowing in the river, but now there was none. Where did it all disappear to?

Rabbi Israel explained, "The reason there is no water is because

---

2. Rabbi Israel's wife's name was Frieda, the same as my aunt.

3. Susu Hazenfeld lives nowadays in Brooklyn, NY, USA.

4. In his later years, Rabbi Yisroel Margoshes lived in Manhattan, NY for many years. He passed away recently.

locks control the flow of the water. They open and close the water locks whenever there is a need for it. The riverbed in which the water is flowing down is not a natural river bed, but an artificial canal. It is used to transport the lumber from the top of the mountain to the lower level sawmill. The lumberjacks in the forest chop down the trees, join them together into large planks, and then place them into the river nearby. Usually one of the men is standing on top of the plank to navigate it to its destination. It is a cheap way of transporting the wood.

Terente Mountain Top

My vacation in Dorna was more delightful than I ever expected it to be, however, to my regret, the days went by too quickly. Every morning I looked forward with eager anticipation to the main event of the day, which was the walk in the park.

I said to Susu. "I would have never thought that walking in the park was something I would get excited about."

But both of us loved the walks; we never got bored with it. Each walk was a different experience and a new discovery. However, at this point in time, we still hadn't climbed to the top of the mountain. Ever since Susu arrived he also was looking forward, as I was, to explore the famous Terente peak, but my aunt kept putting us off. I think she thought that eventually we would forget about it; she didn't figure I would be so persistent. Not a day went by without me asking,

"Are we going to the top today?"

My aunt had her reason. She had already climbed the mountain several times, and for her, climbing the mountain was very difficult. Children usually don't realize how much energy one needs to climb the mountain.

To satisfy our curiosity, Aunt Frieda asked Shimon Rosenwasser, a friend of the family, to take us to the top of the mountain. He promised to take us the following week. The day arrived and to our luck it was a clear sky and a fairly cool day weather-wise. We started early in the afternoon and he instructed us to climb slowly. But Susu and I were in a hurry; we began to walk in great haste. We climbed as fast as we could, way ahead of Shimon. Shimon called after us to slow down. We slowed down for a minute, but then we picked up speed again. Shimon didn't bother anymore to slow us down. Soon we realized why he kept quiet. By the time we arrived to the first station we were already out of breath; we could hardly wait to sit down. Our climb to the next rest stop was considerably slower. I had a silver-handled cane. It was made of fine wood, with a curved handle on top covered with silver. I made good use of it, as I leaned on it all the way during my climbing up the mountain. Shimon picked up two solid tree branches and gave one to Susu and kept one for himself. Finally, after a lot of climbing, Shimon pointed to a clearing ahead higher up and said, "There is Terente."

When Susu and I heard that we are almost there we exerted a little extra effort to get there in a hurry. Planting our feet on the crown of this mountain was definitely an exciting moment. Susu and I embraced and we shook hands. When Shimon reached to the top we all embraced and congratulated each other; we were all smiles. Susu and I examined our new surroundings and we looked around in all directions to get a sense of this new environment. This was the last of the three rest stops on this mountain. In size, this rest stop was much smaller than the other two, but what it lacked in size it made up with its spectacular view. There was a clear view in all directions, a sight I had never experienced before. At this stop there was only one picnic table, two benches, and a small gazebo-like shelter. There were no photographers, no food stores, and not many tourists. As a matter of fact, there was only one other couple there and they were inside the gazebo. We entered the gazebo and looked longingly at the benches. The couple sitting at the table invited us to come in to sit.

At this high altitude the air was freezing cold, but until we did the climbing we didn't feel the cold. I was surprised to be freezing in the middle of the summer. Fortunately, Shimon told us in advance to dress warmly and to bring an extra sweater. We sat down at the table to eat the sandwiches we brought with us. By now the other couple had left. We were all hungry, but before we began to eat we had to clean the table and to spread some newspapers on it to avoid picking up remnants of non-kosher food, which might have been left on the table. We did the ritual hand washing from the bottle of water we had with us and made a blessing over the bread. Susu wanted to know if we needed to say the blessing of Shehechyanu[5] for this new experience of ours.

After we finished eating we stretched out on the grass and we were gazing at the sky above. We stayed at the top for about two hours.

5. "Shehechyanu" is a blessing one recites when experiencing something new and pleasant.

Even after Shimon told us that we had to leave, we were still lingering around for a while, leaning against the railing at the edge of the cliff. We didn't want to leave yet. We could see many distant places and villages, but with the naked eyes everything looked the size of a postage stamp. Shimon lent us his binoculars and the scenery jumped in front of our eyes full size. I looked in all directions with the binoculars and then we passed them back and forth.

Shimon said to us, "Look at your heart's content, because it is not likely that you will come soon again to this place."

He was right; I never climbed the mountain again.

CHAPTER NINETEEN

Rabbi Israel Margoshes
and his Rebetzin Frieda Hasenfeld

A FEW DAYS LATER I was invited to Rabbi Israel Margoshes and his new bride for a Shabbat meal. They were married only a few months and had just moved into their newly furnished apartment. Rabbi Israel Margoshes and his new wife Frieda made it their policy, after they were married, to invite their congregants to their house as guests for a Shabbat meal. It was a different group every Shabbat. This was their way to introduce the new bride/Rebetzin to the congregation. Frieda Hazenfeld was a gracious hostess and a very fine young lady from Satmar.

The most exciting event of the season for the congregants of Dorna Vatra was the Rabbi's recent wedding and the dinner parties for the congregation. Everyone looked forward eagerly to be invited to the young couple. As a young boy of eleven I went to the dinner reluctantly, as I anticipated to be surrounded by adults only. But when I got there I had a good time anyhow. I was very impressed with the newly furnished apartment; everything was new and very modern. I wrote a letter to my parents, describing the beautiful apartment to the last detail. Even as a young boy I loved beautiful furnishings, and in particular I liked fine woodcraft.

My newly found friend, Susu Hazenfeld amazed me; I was in awe at how advanced he was in Judaic studies. He had already studied several tractates of the Talmud and had memorized many of its pages. During the dinner I kept quiet, I was content to be quiet and just listen, because most of the conversation was above my understanding. However, Susu seemed to be familiar with the subjects; he was even able to contribute to the conversation. Needless to say I was envious of him.

Two days later when we went to the park, Susu challenged me to race him to the entrance of the park. I accepted, but I forgot to put my cane down. I hardly began to run when I tripped on the cane and fell. Susu could not restrain himself from laughing. I felt very embarrassed; I didn't mind as much the bleeding on my left knee, but I minded the tear in my pants and the hurt to my pride. My aunt assured me that she could mend my pants. In spite of this incident I was inseparable from my cane during my entire vacation in Dorna; I always walked with it to the park. It had a silver handle with my name engraved on it.

One day Susu asked me, "Did you ever meet Reb Yoilesh Teitelbaum, the Satmar Rebbe?"

I replied, "Yes, I had a brief encounter with him in Dej. I think it was last year, or maybe two years ago. He was in Dej for a short visit; I think he came for two days. I went to see him in the company of my older brother, Moishe. When we arrived to the place where he was staying, we saw a large crowd surrounding him, filling the room almost to capacity. I saw him sitting at the head of the table, greeting the throng of people who were standing in line to kiss his hand and say shalom. Moishe and I also stood in line and when our turn came, we also kissed his hand. I am sure he didn't notice us, because in that large crowd we were in, we were just another two boys among a thousand others who kissed his hand."

Susu wanted to know, "Would you like to see him again?"

"Yes, it would be nice. I would like to see him again. Is he coming to Dej again?"

"No," Susu replied, "he is here in Dorna Vatra. He just arrived yesterday. I hear that he is staying here for the rest of the summer."

I mused, "Is that so? Wonderful! Yes, I would like to see him. Can we go to his Tish? Is he conducting a regular Tish during his vacation?"

Susu replied, "I don't know, I would think so. Let me ask my father."

Reb Yoilesh Teitelbaum, the Satmar Rebbe, was well known in Jewish circles all over Europe, especially Romania, Hungary, and Czechoslovakia. He was the first and the original Satmar Rebbe. Before he became Satmar Rebbe he was the rabbi of K'rolle, which was a small community. In those days he was known as the K'roller Rebbe. I remember the song his Chasidim made while he was still the K'roller Rebbe. It went like this:

"Tzu dem Rebben of K'rolle, zein Kiddush und Havdoleh."[1]

He had thousands of followers and was well known even in the non-Jewish world. King Karol of Romania wanted to meet him, so a special meeting was arranged between him and the Rebbe. The scene was captured in a photo, showing the king and the Rebbe shaking hands. This picture was circulated in the Jewish communities, where almost every yeshiva student carried a copy of the photo.

King Karol was for the most part benevolent towards Jews; he even consorted with a Jewish woman for many years.[2] Later on in his reign, when the Nazis became dominant in Europe, the king had to fall in line with the Nazis and had to appoint an anti-Semitic prime minister. As the Nazis became stronger, he himself had to abdicate in favor of his son Michael. After that Romania became a different country, and to this day it did not recuperate.

Reb Yoilesh took on the name of the Satmar Rebbe when the Jewish community of Satmar invited him to become their rabbi. He moved to Satmar, established a yeshiva there and became one of the most respected and influential rabbis of that region.

---

1. The song was extolling the Satmar Rebbe.
2. Her name was Anna Pauker.

CHAPTER TWENTY

At the Tish with the Satmar Rabbi

On THE NEXT SHABBAT AFTERNOON Susu and I were off to the Satmar Rebbe's Tish.[1] Usually one did not go to the Rebbe's Tish to eat dinner, but to be present there, to observe the ceremony, and to watch him have dinner with his invited guests. While on vacation in Dorna Vatra, Rabbi Yoilesh resided in a spacious house, which his Chasidim rented for him. The largest room in this house was set up as a banquet hall, with a large U-shaped table in the middle of the room. The tables were covered with white tablecloths, dinner plates, and utensils. When Susu and I arrived, the students of his yeshiva occupied almost all the seats at the table; they were waiting for the Rebbe to enter the room. These students here were all from Satmar, and they came to Dorna with the Rebbe; he always traveled with a large entourage.

After waiting for a while the door opened and the Rebbe walked into the room. Everyone rose to their feet and waited until he sat down. During the course of the dinner many local residents dropped in to pay respects to the Rebbe. Whenever a guest entered the room one of the students got up and offered his seat to the guest. Earlier, when Susu and I walked into the room no one offered us a seat and neither did we expect any. After all we were only children. We looked around the room to find a place where we could park ourselves, or at least find a wall to lean against. We found a good standing spot right opposite the Rebbe's seat and next to a buffet table, which was stacked high with many prayer books. Being present at a Tish was nothing new to us; Susu

---

1. Rabbi Yoel Teitelbaum, the Satmar Rebbe, immigrated to the USA after WWII. He passed away some years ago.

had attended the Satmar Tish many times and I had already attended many a Tish at the Dejer Rebbe. However, for me this was the first time at the Satmar Rebbe.

The ceremonies of each Rebbe differed in many ways; each had his own peculiar way of conducting a Tish. Here at the Satmar Rebbe the first course of the meal was the Eier mit Zwiebel.[2] They put before him a dish consisting of several hard-boiled eggs, a raw onion, some chicken fat, and chicken livers. He started to chop the different ingredients, making them into a pâté. This was called the "Eier mit Zwiebel ceremony." During his preparation of the dish he was chanting a song and leading the students in one of the Zemirot songs,[3] of which the text reads, "I shall prepare a feast of perfect faith . . ."

The text was familiar to me because it was the same text they used in Dej, but the melody was different. I had never heard this melody before. As soon as the Rebbe started, all the students joined in and sang in unison with great devotion. At first I was silent, and I was just listening to them sing, but it was a very catchy song and soon enough I sang along with them as if I had known the song all along. Intermittently, the Rebbe stopped and closed his eyes, while the students continued to sing. He seemed to be in the clouds, concentrating on something intently, and then he returned to the chopping of the onions. This went on for about ten to fifteen minutes. When the Rebbe finished the preparation, he tasted it, but ate very little of it. He took a few spoonfuls of the dish and offered a spoonful to a selected few people at the table, and then he pushed the plate aside. As soon as he moved the dish away, a hundred hands reached towards the plate to grab a little of the Rebbe's concoction. The grabbing a little of the dish was called "Shirayim."

Gradually many more people arrived to join the Rebbe's Tish and the room was getting crowded. Not all the students offered their seats to the guests because some hadn't eaten yet. Consequently, many of the guests had to stand behind those seated, and the guests also reached out over the shoulders of the seated to get a morsel of the Rebbe's concoction. No one wanted to miss a little morsel, as the Rebbe's leftovers were considered imbued with spiritual blessings.

Between the courses, the guests and the yeshiva students took the

---

2. Translated from Yiddish, "Eier mit Zwiebel," meaning "eggs with onions." It used to be a traditional appetizer on Shabbat.

3. A "Zemer" ("Zemirot," in plural) is a song sung at every Shabbat meal.

opportunity to converse and socialize. The Rebbe was also having a conversation with two of the guests sitting next to him. He seemed to be favoring the one to his right, but occasionally he turned to the one on his left to speak to him. Susu and I didn't take our eyes off the Rebbe; we watched every move of his from our standing station.

To our great surprise, the Rebbe looked towards us and indicated to us with his finger to approach him. I got red in my face; I was overwhelmed and so was Susu. We couldn't believe the Rebbe meant us. We were hesitating and we didn't move, because we were sure he was pointing his finger to someone else. We were dressed in traditional Chasidic garb and we were the only young children in attendance. I had *peyos*, I wore a traditional Chasidic black velour hat, and my jacket was long, reaching below my knees. One of the students came over and said to us. "The Rebbe would like to say hello to you, would you come with me to greet the Rebbe?"

We followed the student to the Rebbe, and when we reached his chair he was still talking to the guests seated at the table next to him. We stopped behind his chair and waited to be addressed by him. When he finished talking he turned to us and asked for our names.

Susu answered first. "My name is Susu Hazenfeld."

"Do you live here in Dorna or are you here for vacation?"

"We are here for vacation."

"Where do you come from?"

"I am from Satmar."

"I thought you look familiar, does your father have a hardware business?"

"Yes," answered Susu.

He then turned to me and asked me. "What is your name?"

I answered, "My name is Mati Judovits"

"Are you also from Satmar?"

"No, I am from Dej."

"What is your father's name?"

"My father's name is Reb Shlomo Judovits."

The Rebbe was repeating. "Reb Shlomo Judovits, from Dej, I think, I know your father."

I became curious, "My father? The Rebbe knows my father?"

"Yes. Is he the son-in-law of Reb Moishele Paneth, the Dejer Rebbe?"

I nodded with a big grin on my face. "Yes, Reb Moishele was my Zeide."

The Rebbe spoke again. "Then you are 'an einikel' the grandson of the Dejer Rebbe."

I was nodding my head, still with a big grin on my face.

When the Rebbe finished talking to me, he turned to Susu and asked, "Are you related to Mati?"

"No," answered Susu, "we are just friends, but my family is related to him indirectly."

"How are they related?"

"His cousin, the rabbi of Dorna, is married to my sister."

The Rebbe told us, "Don't go away, I want you to sit next to me."

But there were no empty seats next to him. That didn't matter. He instructed one of the students to find chairs for the two of us. The student brought two chairs. But there was no room next to the Rebbe; some distinguished guests were sitting on the chairs next to the Rebbe. So he placed the chairs behind the Rebbe's chair. Susu and I were tickled pink to sit next to the Rebbe; we didn't care that the seats were behind the Rebbe. We sat down humbly.

The meal continued at the Tish with the main course being served on a large plate; it was placed in front of the Rebbe. He usually shared his food with all those present. He took a few spoonfuls from the Tsolent and then from each of the other dishes, but ate very little. Some guests had the honor of being acknowledged by him with receiving a spoonful of the dish from the Rebbe. They also served out platters of food to the students eating with the rabbi. The student who brought us the chairs asked us if we wanted to eat, but both of us declined. The Rebbe offered us a spoonful, which we accepted. When he finished handing out spoonfuls to the special guests, he pushed the plate aside. At that point all hands from all directions closed in on the leftover dish and they all grabbed a morsel. I ate the piece of meat the Rebbe gave me, but I ate it only because the Rebbe gave it to me; I didn't like the taste of it, it was very garlicky. At home I would have never eaten it, but I was embarrassed to spit it out, so I ate it anyhow.

There was a lot of singing during the meal. The Rebbe assigned the songs to different students, by calling on them by name. The leader started and all the students joined in and so did many of the guests, who were familiar with the songs. After everyone finished eating the main dish the room became quiet. The Rebbe started to deliver a D'var Torah in his usual thin high-pitched voice. Everyone was listening attentively to every word spoken. It was so quiet; one could hear a pin drop. The subject of his speech was a passage in the Torah that was read that very morning in the synagogue. The speech lasted about fifteen minutes and then the singing resumed. When the singing stopped, everyone started to talk again. There was a lot of chatter and laughter; people seemed to be having a great time. After desert was served, they recited the after-meal blessing in unison. He gave the honor to lead the after-meal blessing to one of the guests. Then the Rebbe stood up to leave. Just before he walked out of the room he turned to us and said, "I am going for a walk in the park. Would you like to join me?" We were taken by surprise; we didn't expect this great honor.

We waited for him in the great hall to come out. While waiting we overheard a guest asking a student, "Why did the Rebbe deliver a speech in the middle of the meal, I thought the sermons are delivered during prayer services in the synagogue?"

The student answered, "It is the Rebbe's custom to speak Torah words when he dines. He believes that a meal without Torah is a barren table. He encourages his followers to discuss the Torah at every meal."

When the Rebbe came out, we joined him for the walk in the small park behind his house. As we were walking towards the park, I was on his left side. He put his left arm on my shoulders, walking at a slow pace into the park. I was very pleased with myself, but not for long, because he began to question me about my schoolwork. Susu and several yeshiva students were walking behind us.

"What are you studying in the yeshiva?"

I answered, "I am studying Talmud, Baba Bathra."

The Rebbe began quoting certain passages from that Tractate. I chimed in and I quoted from the source. Together we were repeating several dictums and passages from the Talmud. Then he asked me a question that seemed to contradict a statement just quoted from the Talmud. I looked at the Rebbe with a puzzle on my face and I answered embarrassingly, "I do not know the answer."

"I would have been very surprised if you had an answer, all the great Talmudic scholars are struggling with this question."

I said embarrassingly, "I never came across this question and I certainly don't know the answer."

The Rebbe said to me, "Keep on studying, you will find a lot of answers and many more questions."

Then it was Susu's turn. We switched places. He was walking next to the Rebbe.

"What are you studying?"

He answered, "I study the Tractate Berachot."

"That is a very important and timely Tractate."

The Rebbe began to recite one of the Mishnayot from that Tractate. He did not ask him any questions. I think he just wanted to feel him out if he is familiar with the subject. We walked in the park and talked for about an hour. Then we walked back to the house. He went into the house, probably to take a nap, and we went home.

On the way home I was lamenting, "I sure flunked his test. I wish I had known more about the question he asked me. I was very embarrassed."

"Don't be so hard on yourself, he told you himself that great scholars are struggling with this question."

I said to Susu, "But I felt inadequate. I think he wanted to see how deep I dwelt in the Talmud. My consolation is that we had a good day – that we walked with him and he paid attention to us for a full hour. Can you believe it? That he had his arm around my shoulders, like I was his buddy?"

We saw the Rebbe again the next day. The yeshiva students told us that the Rebbe walks every afternoon to the great park called Terente, except on Saturdays. The next day on Sunday afternoon after lunch we walked over to the Rebbe's house. We purposely didn't meet up with him in the park, even though our house was nearer to the park. We wanted to walk together with the whole entourage. There was always a large entourage accompanying the Rebbe. After greeting the Rebbe with a kiss on his hand we joined his group. As soon as we approached the park, a bunch of photographers descended upon us to take a picture of the Rebbe. The Rebbe pulled down the rim of his hat to hide his face.

And five or six yeshiva students formed a human wall in front of him. The Rebbe would not permit, consciously, to have his picture taken. It was his religious belief not to do so. Nevertheless, the photographers persisted and sometimes they succeeded.

Susu and I became quite friendly with some of the yeshiva students. We weren't their equals, neither in age nor in knowledge. We were not as old or as learned, but they were on vacation and they sort of took us under their wings. It worked out very well for us and for Aunt Frieda. My aunt wouldn't have let us go to the park alone, nor did she have the time to come with us every day. This way we joined the Satmar entourage every afternoon.

I was very fascinated by some of the students who smoked cigarettes, especially one particular guy, who could blow dozens of smoke rings into the air. I was telling Susu,

"I would love to try a cigarette and I would love to learn how to blow rings, but I am afraid I will get sick, and if I go home sick, my mother will be very upset."

CHAPTER TWENTY-ONE

Accident in the Szamos River

It was already the end of August 1937 and my vacation was about to end. In spite of having a wonderful time in Dorna, I began to be restless. I missed my parents and I was homesick.

I told Susu, "Until now I did not gauge the intensity of my love for my parents. I guess this was because I was never away from home for such a long period, and because they were always there for me when I needed them, I must have taken them for granted. I guess today is the day I grew up; from now on I will never take my parents for granted."

"What made you say that today is the day you grew up?"

"Because, as I was daydreaming and thinking of my parents a thought flashed through my mind. It is something that happened to my father a year ago. I remember on a winter day my father traveled to Naprad to hire some sharecroppers for his farm. He took the train from Dej to Udvarhely.[1] Naprad had no railroad station; the railroad station was in the next village of Udvarhely, and the Szamos River separated the two villages. In normal weather a ferry was taking passengers across the river, but at this time of the year the river was frozen and the ferry did not function. He tried to hire a horse and wagon to take him across the Szamos River, but no one was willing to risk crossing the frozen river; they were concerned that the ice might brake under their load. My father decided to walk across the river. About half way across the river, he stepped on a thin layer of ice and the ice broke under his weight. His feet and most of his body fell into the water. He was quick enough to

---

1. Udvarhely was the village with a railroad station. It was across the river next to Naprad.

spread his arms, which saved him from going under. He pulled himself up and was able to climb out from the hole.

With difficulty he managed to walk to the nearest house; his clothes were soaked in water and frozen stiff. His beard was like a chunk of ice attached to his face and so was his hat. The owners of the house had known my father, but they didn't recognize him. After he told them who he was, they gave him a change of clothing to wear until his own dried out. He also accepted some food, which he considered permissible to eat, and stayed for a few hours. Then he continued to Naprad by a hired wagon and he attended to his business. Two days later he returned to Dej with a very bad cold, which kept him in bed for a few days. When my father related the story to my mother she became very upset; she implored him not to take chances in the future.

When I finished the story, Susu said to me, "That was a horrible experience. Your father is a very brave man."

CHAPTER TWENTY-TWO

My Mother's Visit to Dorna Vatra

MY MOTHER HAD NEVER VISITED Dorna Vatra before; she never had an occasion that would permit her to get away from her children. This time my brothers, Moishe and Mendi, and my sister Lulu didn't need to be taken care of; they were vacationing in Naprad. My mother decided to visit now, because someone had to take me home from Dorna, as I was only 11–12 years old, and because she always wanted to visit her sister there. My Aunt Frieda and I went to the railroad station to greet her. While waiting for her, I was pacing up and down nervously and every so often I took out my pocketwatch to check the time. The watch was still very new to me, my mother gave it to me as a going away present and I carried it proudly in my vest-pocket, where a gold chain was attached to it.

I was overcome with tears when I embraced my mother, and I felt like I was in heaven sitting next to her in the fiacre. It was so good to be so close to her again after being apart for so many weeks. The next day, after she had rested from her journey, I took her to the park. By this time I knew every nook and cranny of the park and I was able to show my mother all the sights. I could see on her face that she was having a good time and that she took pride in being guided by her eleven-year-old son. She needed this vacation even more than I did. In Dej she never had time for herself, she was always too busy with her daily chores. She stayed for one week and then we got ready for the journey home. I dreaded the return trip; I was worried that I will get sick on the train, as I did on my way coming to Dorna. Especially, I didn't want my mother to have a hard time with me.

As it turned out there was no need to worry. The trip was very smooth and I forgot about getting sick again. My aunt advised me beforehand to keep my eyes closed during the ride on the miniature train, and I listened and obeyed. The rest of the trip on the regular train was very enjoyable; I was looking out the window most of the time. After several hours on the train, I heard the conductor call out, "The next stop is Dej."

Hearing the conductor call out, "Dej," evoked a special sensation in me. I looked out the window and I saw the familiar building coming up on the horizon. Heretofore, I never gave the station a second look, but all of a sudden that dilapidated railroad station looked very beautiful. We disembarked into the welcome arms of my father, receiving hugs and kisses all around. I kept on kissing my father's hand repeatedly. I could not control myself from talking a mile a minute; I wanted to blurt out all the stories all at once.

In the past I never thought much about Dej, but this time I also noticed how interesting and charming the town of Dej was. Of course Reb Meir Leib was there, waiting for us with his fiacre.

CHAPTER TWENTY-THREE

My Father's Door to Door Collection for a Worthy Cause

SOME OF THE JEWISH INHABITANTS in Dej lived comfortably as merchants or professionals, but there were also many poor people. Some were at one time well to do, but became impoverished in the years just before World War II due to the new economic realities. On Thursdays there was a constant flow of men, and sometimes, even women, knocking on doors to ask for charity. The need for charitable donations was so great that the students of the yeshiva had to commit themselves once a month to go from door to door to collect money for the poor. On some occasions, when a member of the community or even someone from another community came upon hard times and needed help, the rabbi would assign a respected member of the community to solicit funds for this person.

Once, a person from another community came to Dej and asked the rabbi to help him with money for a special cause. He needed a certain amount of money for his daughter's wedding expenses. The rabbi asked my father to raise the necessary funds. My father took a day off from his business and went from door to door to raise the amount requested. It took him all day to cover the town. The people were very generous and the end result was that he raised a lot of money, in excess of the amount requested. My father told the rabbi that he raised more money than was requested and he wanted permission to give the balance to a needy family in Dej. The rabbi told my father he could do so.

"A blessing on your handiwork, you have accomplished two good deeds."

My father gave the extra funds to a local resident who fell on hard times. The father of the bride on whose behalf my father collected the donations received the money he requested. The recipient was very grateful, but the next day he found out that my father raised more money than he was given. He wanted the rest. The rabbi told him that it was not available anymore, that my father gave it away to another needy person.

He told the rabbi that he wants to take my father to a Din Torah[1] and he actually did. The rabbi himself could not be the judge, because my father was the rabbi's uncle. Therefore a panel of three heard the case, consisting of the Dayan, Rabbi Berl Schanzer, and two businessmen. They listened to the arguments. My father argued that he raised the amount the man requested and that he could have stopped, but he went on collecting, figuring that he could give the additional funds to another needy family.

The plaintiff argued that when my father left the house to collect funds it was on his behalf and no one else's, and that his request for a fixed sum was the minimum and was not all the funds he needed.

There were several counter arguments. My father argued that when he left his house he did indeed consider collecting more in order to give it to another needy person. When the arguments were over the Dayan asked them if they are willing to accept a compromise. He pointed out that if a decision is rendered then one of them is a sure loser, on the other hand, if a compromise is reached then both will lose a little and both will gain a little.

My father was ready to accept a compromise.

However, the plaintiff was hesitating. He thought he would win and get the entire amount. He asked for a little time, so he could talk it over with one of the lay judges who represented him. The lay judge advised him to accept the compromise. The man took his advice and accepted the Dayan's compromise. The compromise was that the man received some additional money. My father had to make up the difference from his own pocket.

Leib Gottlieb had a textile store on the main plaza in Dej. He was a respected resident in the community and was referred to as Mr. Discreet. He ran a one man charity organization, in which he was the fundraiser and the sole distributor of the funds. As more and more anti-Semitic laws were enacted in Hungary, more people lost their livelihood. Some

---

1. A Din Torah is a religious court.

respected people who were well off became charity cases. They lost their businesses and even their homes. Many were too proud to ask for help. Leib Gottlieb made it his business to find these families and to provide them weekly with their necessities. He was always on the lookout for people who lost their business, and as soon as it came to his attention of someone's misfortune, he would approach the person privately and offer them assistance with the assurance that it will be kept strictly confidential. He did the same when a breadwinner was drafted into the army or passed away. He immediately spoke to the wife or widow and offered help. He never told any of his major donors who the recipients were of their charity. After a while most of the people in Dej became aware of his monumental work, and donations were given to him weekly on a regular basis. His work was considered the highest form of charity, because it was anonymous and it was for the people in their own community.

CHAPTER TWENTY-FOUR

The Sepinker Wedding in Dej

My cousin, Rabbi Yoseph Paneth, was the rabbi of Ileanda, a small community near Dej. He and his wife Liftse had twelve children. Their oldest daughter, Chaya Rachel, became engaged to Naftali Horowitz, the grandson of the Sepinker Rebbe. The Sepinker Rebbe was a well-known Chasidic Rebbe, with thousands of followers in several countries. The wedding was set to take place in Dej because Ileanda was a very small community and could not accommodate all the guests. Almost all the relatives of the Ileanda rabbi lived in Dej and he himself was the younger brother of the Dejer Rabbi. Therefore it was very natural to hold the wedding in Dej. The whole town of Dej was very excited; they were looking forward with great anticipation to this great event. However, accommodations presented a huge problem even for Dej. There were only two small hotels in Dej, The Europa and The Hungaria, each having very few rooms. The parents of the bride expected many more guests than the hotels could accommodate. Two relatives were put in charge to handle the accommodation arrangements. All the relatives and friends of the family were asked to host a family or at least one guest.

Our house was assigned to host the family of the groom's uncle. My parents relinquished their master bedroom to the guests and moved in with us children in our bedroom. My brother and I had to sleep on heavy blankets spread on the floor. I was excited, but also perplexed; I had never seen my parents give up their bedroom. Our whole house was in turmoil. The Sepinker were Chasidic, but their attire and customs were different from the Chasidim of Dej. From my perspective, having been raised in the small Chasidic world of Dej, I knew only the Dejer brand of Chasidism and the Satmar brand, but the Sepinker were different and it was an eye opener. Instead of a streimel on their heads they wore a spodik.[1] There were other distinguishing differences between the Dejer and the Sepinker.

Strangers streamed into town a whole week before the wedding; they could be seen on the streets or in the synagogue. The wedding was set for Sunday, but by Friday all the Chasidim were already in town to celebrate the Shabbat with the Rebbe. In spite of his fame and popularity, the Sepinker Rebbe also had his detractors. There were some Chasidim, followers of other Chasidic rabbis, who vehemently opposed him. Many of these detractors lived in Dej. Friday evening just before sunset when all the preparations for Shabbat were finished and manual labor was already prohibited, the lights in the synagogue went out; the electricity was short-circuited. Electricity could not be restored anymore without violating the Shabbat. Everyone was anxiously looking forward to hear the Sepinker Rebbe lead the services, and all of a sudden there were no lights. A murmur of disappointment could be heard from the congregation. Fortunately there were many wax candles lit on all the walls, and the room was not in total darkness. After a minute of anxiety the Rebbe spoke,

"My friends, do not be concerned, we will have a wonderful Shabbat."

They were not disappointed; he prayed and sang with such fervor that hardly anyone noticed the missing lights. After Shabbat, fingers were pointed at the opposition, but no one could prove it. At Shabbat lunch I went with my father to the Rebbe's Tish, but we didn't stay. There was such a large crowd, and my father was afraid I might be trampled.

The next day on Sunday we all went to watch the Chupah and the Bedecken ceremony.[2] As is the custom, before the Chupah there is the Bedecken ceremony, at which time there is socializing in separate rooms – one room with the bride and one with the groom.[3] The Chupah ceremony took place outdoors and the crowd was huge. It was estimated

---

1. Both of these hats were fur hats, but while the spodik is a tall fur hat with one continuous fur piece all around, the streimel consists of a center cap made of velvet, surrounded with thirteen fur pieces, lined up one next to the other. Some say that the thirteen points of fur are symbolic of the thirteen attributes of G-d, a reminder to the wearer that he stands under the protection of G-d.

2. "Bedecken" is the ceremony of veiling the bride.

3. Men and women were separated during the entire wedding

that several thousand guests attended. My mother sent us children with Roize, our nanny, to watch the Chupah. Roize was holding us by our hands so we could watch the Chupah from a distance. The crowd was so dense that it was impossible to see what was going on. However, from where I was standing I could see the bridegroom being escorted to the Chupah; he was walking arm in arm between his father and the father of the bride. The two fathers carried lit torches in their hands. The groom was dressed in a white kittel and a spodik[4] on his head. After a while I could see the bride being escorted by the two mothers; they also carried lit torches in their hands. Four young girls carried the train of the bride's white dress. The ceremony took place outdoors and lasted about an hour, but from where I was standing I didn't hear anything. Nothing could be seen or heard. Afterwards the crowd scattered in all directions to be returned later to the wedding feast.

Normally at a Chasidic wedding feast, the boys are seated with their fathers, but most of the time young children do not attend the wedding, unless they are brothers or sisters of the bride and groom. I was not invited, but I desired to be there; I was talking about going to the wedding many weeks before the event. My parents decided to let me go, but not with my father, instead my mother took me with her in the ladies section. The two camps, men and women, were in the Csizmadia hall, separated by a large screen. The Csizmadia building was a huge rectangular hall, the largest public hall in Dej; it could hold several thousand people. I was not assigned a seat, so I was just standing next to my mother for a while until a young lady, a cousin of mine, took pity on me and found a folding chair, which they squeezed in next to my mother's chair. My brother Moishe was already of age and he was assigned a seat in the men's section next to my father.

There was no shortage of food, and even though I was not invited, they brought me whatever I wanted. The acoustics in the room were terrible and the noise was unbearable. The band was not far from where I was seated and I hated the loud music they were playing. After the main meal was served they started the Mitzvah dancing. I was looking forward to it, because to watch and listen to the Mitzvah dancing was always great fun. The custom was to call up the relatives and close friends of the bride and groom to have each one dance with the bride. This dance was for men only; the women had their separate dances

_____

4. See previous page.

with the bride. The men were also dancing separately with the groom in a circle. In the Mitzvah dance the bride did not hold hands with her partner; instead they used a kerchief or a napkin, each holding one end of it. They rolled away part of the screen, which separated the men from the women, and the bride was seated in the middle of the room.

Zoldi, whom I mentioned earlier, was the master of ceremonies. He stood on top of a table not far from the bride, so everyone could see and hear him. He began to call up the individuals by name, to come forward to dance with the bride. To me he sounded very humorous; I just loved it and could not stop laughing. He poked good-natured fun at the individuals he was addressing. The audience laughed – some of them so hard that tears were in their eyes. After about two hours of dancing my mother suggested that we should go home. But I wanted to stay to the end.

My mother seated me on her chair, which was upholstered, and she took my folding chair for herself. While seated, I fell asleep. I woke up late the next morning in my bed. The next day I compared notes with my brother Moishe who stayed until the end.

There were parties every day for Sheva Berochos, but after a few days of celebration the guests left town and life returned to normal. I was especially pleased with having a normal home again, but Moishe and I talked about the wedding for a long time.

CHAPTER TWENTY-FIVE

Uncle Rabbi Itzik Mechel

My uncle Rabbi Yitzchak Yechiel Paneth was a very revered figure in Dej. We children called him Feter Itzik Mechel. He was also the uncle of Rabbi Yaakov Meilach, the rabbi of Dej at that time. In the Chasidic Beis Midrash, he was the de facto senior rabbi and received all the honors usually given to the rabbi. For instance, the sixth Aliyah during the Torah reading on Shabbat, which was traditionally reserved and given to the official rabbi of Dej, was given to Rabbi Yitzchak Yechiel when the official rabbi was not present for the Aliyah. In his later years he was ill and homebound, and after a long illness, lasting several years, he passed away. As befitting a great personality, his funeral attracted a large crowd, which was held in the court of the great synagogue. Thousands of people attended and rabbis from many communities delivered eulogies lasting several hours. My mother sat Shiva with the rest of the family in her brother's house, and during her absence my Aunt Frieda,[1] my father's sister, took care of us.

When he was still alive and healthy my uncle Rabbi Itzik Mechel was the chief executive officer of the *Kollel Rabbi Meir Baal Hanes*. The job and title were bestowed upon him when his father, Rabbi Moshe Paneth, passed away. His grandfather, Rabbi Mendl, also the rabbi of Dej, established the organization, and the presidency continued to be held by the rabbis of Dej for several generations. As mentioned earlier, when Rabbi Moshe passed away, the second son, Rabbi Yechezkel became rabbi of Dej, while the older brother, Rabbi Yitzchak Yechiel,

---

1. Frieda was a popular name. My mother's sister was also called Frieda.

became president of the Kollel. There was a third brother, Rabbi Mendl, who was still a young boy when his father passed away; he didn't inherit any position.

Rabbi Yitzchak Yechiel had four sons and one daughter. When he passed away his oldest son, Rabbi Meilach, claimed the presidency of the Kollel as his rightful inheritance. However, Rabbi Mendl, the youngest son of Rabbi Moshe, also claimed the presidency of the Kollel for himself. His argument was that two of the three sons inherited the rabbinate and the Kollel presidency, while the third didn't inherit anything. He did not challenge the inheritance before, out of respect for his older brother, but now that his brother passed away, he felt he was entitled to some inheritance from his father. On the other hand, Reb Meilach, the son of the deceased brother, argued that the inheritance passes from father to son.

Friends of Rabbi Mendel made an additional claim. They argued that Reb Mendele is entitled to the honor of the sixth Aliyah, which was heretofore given to Rabbi Itzik Mechel. They felt that Rabbi Mendele, the youngest son of Rabbi Moshe, is entitled to that honor, since he is the last surviving son of Rabbi Moishe. Supporters of Rabbi Meilach were saying that even this honor passes on from father to son.

This argument between the opposing parties was a subject that kept Dej buzzing for many weeks. There were some rumors that another Kollel might be organized with Rabbi Mendel as its president. The community elders were fearful that if another Kollel were established, both organizations would suffer; they wanted to put an end to the argument. A delegation was appointed to talk to both sides and finally a settlement was hammered out. The presidency was given to Rabbi Meilach and a new position in the Kollel was created for Rabbi Mendel. The sixth Aliyah was given one week to Rabbi Mendel and one week to Rabbi Meilach.

Rabbi Mendel and his wife Soshe had two children, Leitsu and Yechezkel. Leitsu was a very attractive young lady and very intelligent. She married Rabbi Moishe Hager, the son of the Vizsnitzer Rebbe.[2] Yechezkel, the younger son of Rabbi Mendel, was my closest cousin and I was very fond of him; we spent a lot of time together. He was very studious and became a great Talmudic scholar. One semester we

---

2. Rabbi Moshe Hager became the Vizsnitzer Rebbe and lived in Israel.

formed a group, consisting of my cousin Yechezkel, my friend Moishe Moskowitz, and me. It was of great benefit to me.

My uncle, Rabbi Naftali Horowitz was a Dayan[3] in Dés. He was my aunt Tzipora's husband. Rabbi Naftali was a very punctilious and righteous person, and he observed the commandments above and beyond the requirements. He studied all day long, except the very few hours at night when he slept. By tradition there is one night in the year when Torah study is not permitted. It is called Nitel night. In order not to waste time Rabbi Naftali used the Nitel night as time to cut up newspapers to be used by his family as toilet papers during the rest of the year.[4]

My mother's sister, Aunt Matel, was married to Boruch Avraham Bindiger. They lived in Dés. His occupation was insurance salesman. He was a terrific salesman and a marvelous storyteller with a great sense of humor. On summer evenings, when the daylight hours were long, one could find him in the courtyard of the Chasidic synagogue, surrounded by a large crowd. He would be telling them the latest news or some humorous stories, but most of the time he would be telling just stories, a talent for which he had no equal. The crowd would listen to him attentively with admiration. He was a good-looking man with a charcoal black beard. He was always meticulously neat in his garb, which consisted of a black hat, black caftan, white or black socks, and black shoes. When he spoke, one could discern the manners and voice of an orator. His height was on the short side, but the magnetic force of his presence filled a room when he entered.

They had one son and two daughters, Lipe,[5] Mashi, and Sheindi. Their son Lipe became rabbi of the small community called Moldowitze, in Romania. Their daughter Mashi was married to Yidele Paneth, her first cousin. The couple lived with my uncle and aunt for many years.

---

3. A Dayan is a Halachic judge. There were several Dayanim in Dés, and any dispute between Jewish litigants was brought to these judges for adjudication. The Dayanim also supervised all the kosher establishments and gave rulings on all questions of a religious nature.

4. Toilet tissue paper on rolls was not yet available in Dej.

5. My cousin Lipe Bindiger, who was the rabbi of Moldowitze, survived the Holocaust. He died a month after the holocaust was over in Kolozsvar. He was on his way to Dej to visit and be reunited with his sister Sheindi. I had the merit of the great Mitzvah to attend and assist to his funeral needs before burial. His widow Chanele and his son Meir survived him. His son lives in the USA.

Mashi and Yidele had three daughters, Sarah and Rivka, who were twins, and Malchi.

Malchi died at a very young age, about eight years old, of a rare disease. My aunt and uncle's youngest daughter, Sheindi, married Mendi Friedlander. They had no children.

CHAPTER TWENTY-SIX

The Judovits Family, Uncle Peretz

Uncle Peretz was my father's younger brother. He was a businessman and lived in Lechnitz, a small community near Bistritza. He and Aunt Sheindi (Stieglitz) had four children, Puki, Maati, Etta, and Sarah Gitel. Uncle Peretz used to be a frequent visitor in our home in Dej and in Naprad and I remember him fondly, but my Aunt Sheindi I met only once. My uncle was a very pious and upright person, religious but not Chasidic. However, he wore dark suits, a black hat, and sported a small beard. His son Puki spent a few years in Dej and was a frequent guest in our house. Puki immigrated to Israel and lived in Holon,. He married Tzivia Mendl and they have two children, Nava and Peretz. Maati, uncle Peretz's daughter, married Yosef Trichter and they lived in Haifa, Israel. Etta, the other daughter, married Jeno Brattman and they lived in Haifa, Israel. Only Puki, Mati, and Etta survived; my uncle Peretz, my Aunt Sheindi and their daughter Sarah Gitel perished in Auschwitz.

My father's youngest brother, Uncle Shmelke and his wife Blanca (Dimantstein) lived in Naprad. I used to vacation in Naprad in their house a many summers. They were extraordinary wonderful relatives and I enjoyed my vacations in their home. He was a very jovial person and Aunt Blanca was also a wonderful caring aunt. They had no children. As I mention in another part of this book, I was in the same work camp with my Uncle Shmelke in Wustegiersdorf. He was transferred from Wustegiersdorf to another camp together with my brother Mendi, from where he never returned. My Aunt Blanca also didn't survive.

My father's sister, Aunt Bella, was born in 1891 and died in Auschwitz in 1944. She married Uncle Adolph Rosenbluth, who was born in Olaszliszka in 1884 and died in Auschwitz in 1944. Their last place of residence was in Zsibo, a small town sixteen kilometers from Naprad. They were wonderful people, very kind and outgoing. He was a scholarly person and had studied in the Yeshiva of Presburg. Aunt Bella was known for her goodness and generosity. I have fond memories of my Uncle Adolf from my childhood years. He used to tell us interesting stories and I loved to listen to him; he was a marvelous storyteller. They had two children, Bandy and Klari. They and the entire Jewish community of Zsibo were taken away to Auschwitz in 1944, from where they did not return. Their son Bandy survived, but Klari did not. Bandy married Klara Szenes and they have two sons, Avraham and Gabriel.

My Aunt Sidi lived in Kolozsvar. She was married to my uncle Maximilian Friedman, but he passed away at a very young age. My Aunt Sidi raised her only son Pali in Kolozsvar. When Pali was a young man of about eighteen, he lived for a while in Budapest; it was during the same time that I lived there. In Budapest he was very close with my brother Mendi. Aunt Sidi was deported to Auschwitz, from where she did not return. Pali survived and after the war settled in Israel. He married Gerda Vininger and they had one son, Meir.

My father's sister, Aunt Esther, was born in 1894 and died in Auschwitz in 1944. She was married to Nandor Berger, a businessman, and they lived in Dés. They had one daughter, Magda. My Uncle Nandor was a respected member of the community and was elected president of the Jewish community in Dés. Aunt Esther was a wonderful aunt; she visited our house frequently and always brought us little trinkets or candy. Uncle Nandor had other children from a previous marriage. Uncle Nandor and Aunt Esther were taken away to Auschwitz in 1944, from where they did not return. Their daughter Magda also perished in Auschwitz

My Aunt Frieda was single for many years. She married around 1940 to a gentleman from Dés by the name of Markovics. Regretfully he passed away two weeks after their wedding. Before she was married she resided in our house with my parents. She divided her residence between our house in Dés and her brother Shmelke in Naprad. She was a wonderful aunt and was very kind hearted. When I was a young child I remember her reading to me children's stories to put me to sleep, and she did the same when I was sick. She was taken away to Auschwitz in 1944 from where she did not return.

Aunt Blanka, the youngest of my grandfather's children, did not marry. She lived with us in Dés part of the year and with her brother Shmelke in Naprad the rest of the time. She was also a wonderful aunt and used to read stories to me when I was a child. She certainly had a hand in our upbringing. She died in Auschwitz in 1944.

Reb Moshe Judovits was my grandfather's brother. Reb Moshe and his wife had several children. Their oldest son was Yosef,[1] who we used to call Yoshka Batshi. He was married to Bertha Dimantstein and they had five sons, Moshe, Shimshi, Imre, Hugo, and Erno. They lived in Naprad and they owned the general store in the village. Uncle Yosef left the management of his store to his sons. All of his sons were active in the store, but Shimshi and Erno were running it. Moishe and Hugo were sent to a university to become professionals. Hugo, who became a lawyer, lived after the Holocaust in New York, in the United States, and Erno lived in California. Moishe, Shimshi, and Imre did not survive the Holocaust. Hugo married Erna and they have one daughter, Dalia. Erno married Eva Weisz, and they have two children, Edith and Tom.

Reb Moshe Judovits' second son, Sholem was married to Zseni Glick and they had two sons and one daughter, Moshe, Olga, and Yosef. They lived in Dej. I used to see them often in Dej. One year Yosi and I were on vacation in Naprad at the same time and we spent a lot of time together. Moshe and I became very close after the Holocaust in the United States. He was the most unusual person; everyone claimed to be his friend, because he was genuinely everyone's friend. Moshe was married to Isabel Knoll. Moshe and Isabel had two children, Sheila and Stanley, and a son Jimmy from Isabel's previous marriage. Olga and Yosi, Reb Sholem's other children, did not survive the Holocaust.

Reb Moshe Judovits, my grandfather's brother, had another son, Mendel Judovits. He married Luisa Glick and their children were Joseph and Susan. Susan married Ben Glance and they lived after the Holocaust in the USA. They have two children, Fanny and Sidney. Fannie married Peter Davidson.

---

1. My father's first cousin

CHAPTER TWENTY-SEVEN

Rabbi Paneth's Trip to Palestine

IN DEJ, AS IN EVERY JEWISH COMMUNITY of Transylvania, the Zionist organization was very active and was recruiting young people to join the movement. All shades of Judaism participated in the movement, from the religious to the non-religious. But the Chasidic rabbis in general were against the Zionist movement. They believed that Zionism and emigration to Palestine would lead to secularism and eventually to the abandonment of the faith.

After the rise of Nazism in Germany the Zionist movement took on new impetus. It attracted thousands of young people, even from the ranks of the very religious. The Zionist leaders pleaded with the rabbis to change their position and to encourage the people to return to Zion, but the rabbis were reluctant to sanction such an exodus. As time went by and conditions for Jews worsened, alas in some communities conditions became intolerable, and the rabbis could no longer ignore the Zionist movement. Eventually, the clamor of the average religious Jews became loud enough that it became a subject of discussion at the rabbinical assemblies.

Rabbi Yaakov Meilach Paneth[1] was the rabbi of Dej at that time and also one of the leaders of the Jewish assembly. He was under pressure to take a stand for or against the Zionist movement. He had private discussion with other rabbis and as a result of those discussions, he undertook a mission to travel to Palestine on a fact-finding tour.[2] The

---

1. Photo of Rabbi Yaakov Meilach Paneth is #7 in the photo section of this book.

2. Photo #15 is a copy of a poster that was printed and distributed in Jerusalem in 1935; it announces the arrival of Rabbi Paneth to the Holy land. It was given as

community of Dej was very much in favor of his tour and he was given a tremendous send off. He took the train from Dej to Constanza, the Romanian port on the Black Sea, and from there he took a boat to Palestine.

Dej had already a small colony of several families living in Palestine. Those families were informed in advance of the rabbi's trip and when he arrived there, they gave him an enthusiastic welcome at the Haifa seaport. Josef Singer, who was the leader of the Dej landsmanshaft, gave the welcoming speech. Singer was a major in the Palestinian police, appointed by the British mandate. Prior to immigrating to Palestine, Singer was a Talmudic student and Rabbi Paneth was his teacher.

The rabbi toured the land from the south to the north and visited Hebron, Jerusalem, Tzefat, Tiberias, and several Kibbutz communities. In Tiberias, he visited the Kollel of Rabbi Meir Baal Hanes, of which he was the titular head.[3] He also visited the Kibbutz communities of the left wing, as well as the religious. He and his Rebetzin spent several weeks in the land and then returned home. They returned again by boat to Constanza and from there they took the train to Dej.

On the day of his return, half of the Jewish community waited for him at the Dej railroad station. I also wanted to go to greet the rabbi, but at that time I had been bedridden with a blistered foot for two weeks. My foot was almost healed, but the doctor wanted me to stay in bed for another few days. I was nine years old and I was begging my mother to let me go to the railroad station. I didn't want to miss out on what was billed to be the event of the decade; I had to be there. Eventually, my mother gave in and let me go. She bandaged my foot in heavy rags and allowed me to go with my father. My father made arrangements with Reb Meir Leib to pick us up and drive us to the railroad station. Reb Meir Leib was driving to the station anyhow to pickup the rabbi in his fiacre. When we arrived to the station a large crowd was already there; they were dancing and singing. As soon as the train pulled into the station a huge roar went up from the crowd, accompanied by applause. The rabbi and his wife descended the steps of the train into the midst of a huge crowd. The train moved on, but the rabbi stayed there on the spot for at least half an hour until everyone had a chance to greet him

---

a present to the author by his friend Eli Genauer from Seattle. Mr. Genauer found it on the internet in 2014.

    3. Rabbi Paneth was Nasi of the Kollel, see chapter 3.

and kiss his hand. The non-Jews who happened to be at the station were watching in amazement at the outpouring of affection and respect given to this religious leader. When the greeting was over, the rabbi was led towards Reb Meir Leib's fiacre for his drive home. But his students and Chassidim were not content to let him ride in a horse-drawn carriage. They unhitched the horses from the carriage and the students took the place of the horses. They wanted the honor of pulling their Rebbe from the station to his home. Seated in the carriage were, in addition to the rabbi and his wife, the community president and the rabbi's son. My father was able to secure a ride for me on one of the steps of the carriage. I was euphoric, I never dreamed to have the privilege to be drawn in a carriage by the yeshiva students. Rabbi Yaakov Meilach[4] asked me why my foot was bandaged. I explained to him what happened. My father had already told him that I came from my sickbed to greet him, but he didn't explain any further. During the two-kilometer ride from the railroad station, the crowd followed the carriage by foot in a festive mood, singing and dancing. People were also lined up on the sidewalks, watching a sight they had never seen before. When I got home my foot was hurting. My mother took off the bandages and sure enough, many of the blisters burst open prematurely. The doctor came to visit and told my mother that for the next three days I cannot get out of bed.

The next day, Reb Avrum Yosef Wurtzberger, my teacher, came to visit. I had missed school for a long time. He wanted to know why I was able to go to the railroad station, but could not show up to school. My mother explained to the teacher that Mati did not want to miss such a great event. The teacher brought some homework for me and told me to study it and that otherwise I will never catch up with the class. I didn't mind the homework, because I was already bored being home doing nothing, and I was flattered that my teacher came to visit.

Everyone in Dej was waiting with great anticipation for the rabbi's speech, which he delivered on Shabbat. At that time I was still a child and I did not hear his speech. It was years later that I became aware of his speech, reading about it. In his speech, he spoke about the religious life in Palestine, which he found to be very disappointing. To his regret, he said, there were too many non-observant Jews in Palestine; they are not even observing the Shabbat. He was lamenting that a great many men and women go to the beaches on Shabbat, dressed scantily, prac-

---

4. We were first cousins.

tically naked. However, he put the blame on himself and the rabbis of his generation, for not encouraging young pious rabbis and observant teachers to join the immigration to Palestine. Had they gone to Palestine, they would have laid a foundation and they would have established religious institutions.

Rabbi Yaakov Elimelech Paneth was born in 1888 and died for Kiddush Hashem in Auschwitz in 1944. His Rebetzin Miriam Chevtsu Kanner was born in 1889 and died for Kiddush Hashem in Auschwitz in 1944.

CHAPTER TWENTY-EIGHT

The Rosh Beis Din Story[1]

Rabbi Chayim Baruch Paneth was the oldest son of Rabbi Yaakov Meilach. After he got married, he became the rabbi of Tekendorf,[2] but a few years later he, his wife, and children moved back to Dej. His wife was the daughter of Rabbi Chayim Halberstam, the grandson of the well-known and revered Sanzer Rebbe. Rabbi Yaakov Meilach Paneth requested the community to elect his son as the Rosh Beis Din of Dej.

The community was split, the rabbi's supporters wanted him elected, but there was a vocal opposition that was against him. Some felt, in their opinion, he didn't measure up to the job. Others felt that there was no need for another rabbi, that the community could not afford it. In his request to the Elders, Rabbi Yaakov Meilach pointed out that before he became chief rabbi, he was already junior rabbi in his father's lifetime. He also reminded the elders of the community that he was the fourth Paneth to occupy the position of rabbi in Dej. It started with his great-grandfather, Rabbi Mendel Paneth. He wanted to assure the continuity of the chain of succession with the election of his oldest son.

The opposition distributed pamphlets and for many weeks the community was buzzing with heated arguments. The election meeting was postponed on technicalities or a lack of a quorum. A meeting of the board was held and the decision by the board was against the Rosh Beis Din. Friends of the rabbi protested that the board meeting was held hastily and that some board members could not attend. They sent an

---

1. "Rosh Beis Din" is the title of the head of a religious court.
2. Tekendorf is a small community in Transylvania.

appeal to the Orthodox Central Bureau. The rabbi was very annoyed and upset at the rejection of his son. A few weeks later the Orthodox Central Bureau notified the community that they found the results of the last board meeting problematic. They ordered the community to hold a new general membership meeting to decide the issue. A new meeting was called to vote on two issues: to elect a new president of the community and to decide the issue of the Rosh Beis Din. The meeting elected Ferenc Ordentlich as president, who was pro Rosh Beis Din and Chayim Baruch Paneth was elected as Rosh Beis Din.

Rabbi Mendel Paneth

The second son of Rabbi Yaakov Meilach was a more popular figure than his older brother. He was a mild mannered person, very humble and very studious. Many people in Dej considered him a great scholar and a deserving heir to his father's position. After his marriage he continued to study and teach in his father's yeshiva, but this did not satisfy his needs. He wanted to lead a congregation. He was offered a position in the nearby village of Areshor, which he accepted.

Areshor, as was mentioned earlier, was the village where the Jews lived before they were granted permission to live in Dej. His great-great-grandfather, by the same name, Rabbi Mendel Paneth, was also rabbi of Areshor before he became the first rabbi of Dej.

The entire congregation of Dej was invited to come to Areshor to hear him speak; it was his inaugural speech in Areshor on the first Shabbat of his new position. Many of the residents of Dej and the yeshiva students were eager to walk the two kilometers to hear him speak, but the village was beyond the limit of the permissible walk on Shabbat. The solution was an Eiruv.[3] One person was appointed to place the Eiruv on a certain location outside the town of Dej, and about one hundred people walked the distance to Areshor, including myself. I was too young to be much of a maven on his speech, but by all accounts it was a brilliant speech on a complicated Talmudic exegesis.

---

3. An Eiruv is a device used to acquire a temporary dwelling, by placing food – before the Shabbat commences – at the limit of the permissible walking distance, and designating it as a temporary home for this Shabbat.

CHAPTER TWENTY-NINE

The Sulyedes

IN THE OUTSKIRTS OF DEJ was an abandoned salt mine, known by the name of "Sulyedes." It was a very dangerous open pit on a stretch of land without any fence around it, and it had a depth of many hundreds of feet. There were a few horrible incidents of people actually falling into the pit and dying. One of those tragic figures was the daughter of Reb Yidele and Mrs. Edelstein. When the last tragic incident happened, the whole town was outraged, and they demanded that something should be done to safeguard the community from such a tragedy. Everyone surmised that Reb Yidele's daughter fell into the mine and died there, because she was last seen heading in that direction. The parents were grief stricken; they lost a daughter and could not even give her a proper burial. No one in Dej ever ventured into the old salt mine to explore it, and nobody knew for sure that she actually fell in there. The parents were anxious to know what happened to her, and if possible, to find her body.

Reb Yidele was a very popular man in Dej; he was an accomplished violinist and playwright and directed the local choir. When Purim time came around, he organized and directed the annual Purim festivals. Those talents did not provide for his livelihood; he made a living from his barbershop, which was in the Jewish section of Dej. The barbershop was also a hangout and a source of the latest news for the locals.

Several years after the tragic incident a man by the name of Janos came to Dej; he was a daredevil person. By profession he was a tightrope walker. One evening he put on a show on the Corso.[1] He stretched

---

1. Corso was the main street in Dej.

a tightrope from one building to another building across the street. The distance between the two buildings was about fifty yards. He then walked across the tight rope with a wooden pole in his hands for balance. While walking across, he performed several tricks, pretending to be losing his balance. The show was a big hit in town; every young boy tried to imitate him. I also was enamored by this craze; I tried my skill of walking on top of every stone fence and holding a balancing pole in my hands. Naturally, a wood-balancing pole was very much in fashion. Prior to becoming a showman, this tightrope walker was a coalminer. Word got to him about the abandoned salt mine, and he was telling people that he would not be scared to go down deep into the abandoned salt mine. Janos let it be known that for a fee he would lower himself into the salt mine to bring up the corpses. He was introduced to Mr. Edelstein, who wanted desperately to have closure and a proper burial for his daughter. Janos came to an understanding with Mr. Edelstein and a date was set for the exploration of the mine.

The day before he lowered himself into the mine, he sunk two vertical wooden beams into the ground and tied two heavy ropes to them. He also placed a heavy and smooth round log horizontally next to the pit, which served as a smooth surface for the ropes to roll and slide down. Hundreds of people turned out to the site to watch Janos perform the stunt with great skill. He lowered three ropes, one for himself, one for the corpses, and one for a bell. With the bell he sent prearranged signals to the men above. There were two men waiting for his signal to pull up the ropes. The first signal came and the two men pulled the rope to the surface. They brought up the first corpse in a bag. Another signal came and they brought up another corpse and then a third one. After that, Janos sent a signal that he is finished; the men proceeded to pull him up.

One of the bodies brought out from the pit was Mr. Edelstein's daughter. It was amazing that none of the bodies were decomposed; people were saying that the salt kept them preserved. Mr. Edelstein was able to give his daughter a proper funeral and there were two more funerals for the other bodies recovered. Many people showed up to the funerals and to pay their respect. The next Sunday Janos was given a hero's parade on the main streets of Dej, with the military band playing and the school children marching.

CHAPTER THIRTY

My Brother Moishe

MY BROTHER MOISHE[1] was a very gifted person; even as a child he showed great abilities in many fields. He had great social skills and was able to converse even with adults with great ease. He could tell a story or a joke skillfully and spoke several languages fluently. He taught himself to read music, and people admired his beautiful singing voice. On Saturdays after lunch my father would take him to the Rebbe's Tish, where the Chasidim and the yeshiva students would sing Shabbat songs during the meal. Moishe, as a young child, would sing along and his voice could be heard above the chants of the crowd.

He also had tremendous organizational skills. When he was still a very young boy he decided to organize his friends into a military brigade. He called it the Torah Brigade. Many of the young school students were eager to join his army. He commissioned the older boys as officers and assigned to them ranks of colonel, major, captain, and lieutenant. He designed their insignias, which were made of dark blue cutout cardboards and gold stars on the blue. They were pinned on their jackets and caps. Whenever they had free time they practiced marching. They also did hand combat. I tried to join, but Moishe would not accept me; he said I was too young. Nevertheless, whenever they practiced I was always there just to watch. They had their own banner. The brigade lasted only a few months, until the rabbis found out about it. They summoned Moishe and his leading boys and ordered them to

---

1. Photo of my brother Moishe is #4 in the photo section of this book. He is in the black hat. He died in the labor camps; a copy of the death certificate is #16 in the photo section of this book.

stop it. They told them that "Jewish boys should be studying and not wasting their time with silly military games."

The Military Barracks in Dej

In the outskirts of Dej was a large military barrack, quartering a whole brigade of Romanian soldiers. Moishe, who was about sixteen years old at that time, befriended a Jewish soldier from the barracks. In his conversation with him, he found out that the soldier was an observant Jew. In further conversations he found out that due to his observing kashrus, his diet consisted only of bread and vegetables; there was no kosher food in the barracks. He informed Moishe that there were about thirty Jewish soldiers in the barracks who did not eat non-kosher food. Moishe got a list from the soldier and he went around town from house to house to find them places to eat.

Moishe spoke to the rabbi, who encouraged him to carry out the plan and to take time out from his studies. No household refused him; some even accepted two or three soldiers on the same day once a week. He was able to accommodate all the thirty soldiers for one meal a day. Later on more soldiers came forward and Moishe found more hosts for them. The program was so successful that other communities copied it and it became a fixed institution in Dej. When Moishe had to move from Dej, others continued the program.

Moishe was also interested in music and spent time practicing cantorial pieces. In this endeavor Reb Yidele the barber helped him a lot.

During the High Holidays he sang in the choir of the main synagogue, under the direction of the choirmaster, Reb Patye. The choirmaster was a mason contractor by profession, but he conducted the choir as a hobby with great skill. The cantor, whose name was Reb Yehoshua Wurtzberger, was leading the services on the High Holidays and the choir accompanied him. Reb Yehoshua Wurtzberger was a Chasidic person and he was also a Shochet.[2] Several weeks before the High Holidays the choirboys used to gather at the home of Reb Yehoshua Wurtzberger to practice the melodies for the High Holidays. I sometimes accompanied my brother Moishe to the practice session. I wanted badly to join the choir, but I was not accepted. However, I persisted in going along to the practice with the hope of being accepted someday.

_____

2. Kosher slaughterer

My brother Moishe befriended the conductor of the military band that played in the park. The Romanian military band used to play in the park a few times a week in the summer afternoon, from the spring until the fall. The conductor of the band was a non-Jewish military captain. In those days it was unheard of that a non-Jewish Romanian officer should befriend a Chasidic boy, but my brother Moishe managed somehow to befriend the Romanian army captain.

From personal experience I know for a fact that some of the soldiers who played in the band were anti-Semitic. One time, when I was walking on the street, passing the band, one of the soldiers stepped out from his ranks to trip me. As I was passing him he stuck his foot out under my feet and I tripped, but I managed to avoid falling. As I was staggering to keep my balance, the soldier was grinning and uttering an anti-Semitic remark, while the other soldiers burst out laughing. He knew for certain that I was Jewish on account of my garb.

The captain however was different; he was educated and liberal minded. He liked Moishe, probably for his familiarity with music and his good sense of humor. My brother always had a good joke for him. Moishe was frequently seen in the park talking to the captain during recess time. He consulted with Moishe regarding which pieces to play. One day they were comparing musical notes and Moishe showed him the Kol Nidrei melody. The captain became interested in the piece and he promised Moishe that his band will practice and play it in the near future. Moishe gave him some additional Jewish pieces and the captain set aside a date in September to play the Jewish music. Moishe spread the word in the synagogue and on that afternoon, just a few days before Rosh Hashana, the park was full of Jewish listeners who came to hear the melody of Kol Nidrei.

CHAPTER THIRTY-ONE

The Vizsnitzer Wedding

My cousin, Leitsu Paneth, was the daughter of Reb Mendele and Sosha Paneth, of whom I wrote earlier. She was an attractive young lady, very intelligent and spoke several languages, including English. Several matchmakers were competing to find her a match. But Reb Mendele and Sosha turned down many of the offers; they were very particular, because they knew they have a very special and outstanding daughter. One day a matchmaker told Reb Mendele that he has a very special young man in mind for his daughter. When he inquired whom he had in mind, he was told that he has in mind the son of the Vizsnitzer Rebbe. My uncle, Reb Mendele was very interested.

The matchmaker explained that he has contacts with several people in the Vizsnitzer Rebbe's court and he had proposed to them Leitsu as a bride for the Rebbe's son. They spoke to the Rebbe and he gave them the green light to explore it further.

Rabbi Chayim Meir Hager, whom they called The Vizsnitzer Rebbe, lived in Grossverdein.[1] The Vizsnitzer Rebbe had followers in many countries and towns, some also lived in Dej. The Rebbe's oldest son, Rabbi Moshe,[2] was the young man they proposed for Leitsu.[3]

The discussions advanced so well that a trip was arranged for Moshe to come to Dej, to meet his prospective bride. The young couple met and

---

1. Grossverdein was the name of the town in Yiddish and in German. The Hungarian name for the town was Nagyvarad and the Romanian name was Oradea Mare.

2. Rabbi Moshe Hager became the Vizsnitzer Rebbe when his father passed away. He was the Rebbe in B'nei Brak in Israel.

3. Leitsu Hager, my cousin, was the Vizsnitzer Rebetzin and lived in B'nei Brak with the Rebbe until she passed away a few years ago.

liked each other, and they gave their approval. Wedding plans were set in motion and they decided to have the wedding in Dej.

As soon as word got out that the wedding would take place in Dej, the whole town was abuzz with rumors and speculations. The community was making preparations to be ready for the festivities. People with larger homes were asked to host a guest. All the ladies were busy ordering custom-made dresses and shopping for dresses for their children.

The bride's dress was rumored to be something extraordinary; a seamstress was working on it for weeks. Some of the ladies were curious to have a peek at it, but it was kept under wraps.

A few days before the wedding, the guests started to arrive. A large delegation went to the railroad station to welcome the Vizsnitzer Rebbe and his family.

On the wedding day thousands of people, most of them uninvited, came to the synagogue courtyard to watch the ceremony. The ceremony started with the groom being escorted by the fathers of the bride and groom, Reb Mendele and the Vizsnitzer Rebbe. Both parents were carrying lit torches and were dressed in their Shabbat garb of streimel and caftan. The groom wore a white kittel over his black caftan. As they were approaching the Chupah canopy, which stood in the middle of the synagogue courtyard, the cantor started chanting the customary welcome blessings for the groom. After a short interval, the bride came out from the house adjacent to the synagogue; she and her escorts were walking towards the Chupah canopy.

"Ah, uh, ah," went up the sound from the crowd.

"She is beautiful," "She is stunning," were the comments. "Look at that gorgeous dress," "Look at that beautiful long train."

Six young girls, all relatives of the bride and groom, carried her train. The bride was escorted by the mothers of the bride and groom, the bride's mother, Shosha, and the Vizsnitzer Rebetzin. They walked slowly and deliberately, arm in arm, while the band played sweet melodies. When they reached the canopy they circled around the groom seven times.

Reb Mendele, the bride's father had a difficult task to handle the honors diplomatically. Who to honor with the recitation of the seven blessings had to be handled delicately, because there were so many prominent rabbis present and no one could be slighted. Each rabbi was called up by name and title for each blessing. Additional honors, like witnessing and reading the marriage document, were given to other guests. When all the rabbis had their turns and all the blessings were recited, the ceremony was finished with the traditional breaking of the glass. Afterwards the crowd dispersed.

The wedding feast was to be held in the largest hall in Dej, the Csizmadia hall. Men and women were in the same large hall, but separated by a large screen. One thousand guests were invited, but they prepared food for many more. Many uninvited guests also attended. They had no seats, but were standing against the wall. No one was turned away; the uninvited guests were also served food after the seated guests were served. The Mitzvah dancing[4] was lively and colorful; it lasted for many hours. The Vizsnitzer yeshiva students were a lively bunch; they were singing and dancing all night. There were about one hundred guest students who came along with the Rebbe.

The next few days there were the Sheva Berochos[5] meals. Many local people, who were not invited and were not present at the wedding, could attend the Sheva Berochos and also attend the Rebbe's Tish. The Dejer and the Vizsnitzer Rebbes conducted a joint Tish; it was held in the big hall of the Talmud Torah, where a larger crowd could be accommodated. No invitation was needed to attend; it was open to everyone. My brother Moishe and I were present at the wedding, but we still went to the Tish anyhow.

Saturday afternoon, right after our Shabbat meal was over, we rushed over to the Tish. When we arrived, it was still early enough with very few people present. There were plenty of empty seats, but we knew that we could not be seated. Children were not seated, so we positioned ourselves on the opposite side of the head table, just across from the two Rebbes. The two Rebbes were already seated in the center of a long dais, which formed a huge U-shaped table. Additional tables were in between, running parallel to the end tables. The Dejer Rebbe, as the host, yielded the chair on the right side to the Vizsnitzer Rebbe. In the center between the two rabbis was the groom, and next to the Dejer Rebbe sat Reb Mendele, the bride's father. All the other guest rabbis and the various local rabbis occupied the rest of the seats on the dais.

---

4. Mitzvah dancing is performed at a religious wedding. The bride dances with male relatives or friends, but they don't hold hands; instead a napkin or a kerchief is held by both, each holding one end of the kerchief.

5. Sheva Berochos are meals in honor of the bride and groom served for seven days after the wedding.

The students and the teenagers were all standing. Those who came early were lucky to find standing room next to the dais, but the rest were content to find any place close enough to watch.

After the food was served they started singing the zemirot for Shabbat. The Vizsnitzer Rebbe was leading his students like a symphony conductor, with his hands waving up and down and in all directions. He looked at them straight in their eyes, encouraging them and making each one feel his voice is important. The Dejer Rebbe tried to stay in the background; he wanted to yield the limelight to his guest. The usual zemirot singing went on while everyone was seated, but then the Vizsnitzer Rebbe whispered something to the Dejer Rebbe. Both of them stood up and began to dance. They beckoned the crowd to join them, and everyone did. They danced hand in hand for a long time, circling around the tables in the center. It seemed like hours, but in reality it was more like a half hour.

At one point, the screen separating the men from the women was slightly moved away; one could see the bride and the rest of the ladies were having a festive meal with similar arrangements as on this side of the screen. After the dancing was over, several rabbis delivered brief D'var Torahs[6] and then they did the blessing after the meal. For the after-meal blessing they brought in the bride to be seated next to the groom in the men's section. Several rabbis and guests, who did not have any honors before, were given the honor of reciting the seven blessings. This meal was the last public formal meal for the bride and groom. Dej was talking about this wedding for a long time. It was a wedding to be remembered.

---

6. A D'var Torah is a few words of wisdom from the Torah.

CHAPTER THIRTY-TWO

The Yeshiva of Rabbi Elisha Horowitz

Rabbi Elisha Horowitz[1] was the son of my Aunt Tzipora and Rabbi Naftali Horowitz. They lived in Dej where Rabbi Naftali was a Dayan. Their oldest son Elisha moved to Bistritza[2] after he got married, where he was a teacher in a yeshiva. Around 1935 or thereabouts, at the urging of many people, he moved back to Dej to establish a yeshiva for teenagers. At that time Dej had only one yeshiva, but it was for mature students of eighteen years and older. There was nothing for students between the age of thirteen and eighteen. Students who were between those ages had to attend small schools run by individuals, or they were sent to yeshivas in other towns. Rabbi Elisha agreed to open such a yeshiva on the condition that it had the approval of Rabbi Yaakov Meilach, the rabbi of Dej. There was no problem with that; the rabbi of Dej himself wanted such a yeshiva established.

Rabbi Elisha distinguished himself as a Talmudic scholar when he was still a young student. He was also an excellent speaker and a natural teacher. After he established his yeshiva and settled in Dej, he also became the unofficial Magid (lecturer) for adults of the town of Dej. His lecture series delivered every Saturday afternoon attracted large audiences; latecomers had to contend with standing room only. He was an eloquent speaker and the subject matter was always interesting. The yeshiva he founded became a great success and he had to move from

---

1. In 1944, Rabbi Elisha Horowitz was deported to Auschwitz. Only his two sons Mendel and Chezkel survived; they settled in the USA. The rest of his family perished in Auschwitz. See photo of Rabbi Elisha, #8 in the photo section of this book.
2. Bistritza was a small town 60 kilometers west of Dej.

the small loft he originally rented to a much larger facility near Kodor Street.

I became a student of his yeshiva. With great trepidation and anticipation, I was enrolled into this yeshiva against the advice of my teacher. Reb Avrum Yosef, my teacher, thought that I was not yet ready, but for some reason, my parents and my Aunt Tzipora decided that it would be good for me, because, as they were telling me, I was a serious student.

The yeshiva was located on the second floor in a commercial court, where the Basch bakery shop was located. To everyone's regret I lasted in the yeshiva for only one day. I joined a class of about thirty students. They were all older than I was, and some were about two or three years older. I was confused and full of anxiety. The other children in the room didn't make it any easier. None of them spoke to me. They were friends with each other from their previous school, a school I did not attend, as I was not of the same age. The teacher, though he was my first cousin, didn't pay any attention to me either. I didn't realize it then, but later on I was told that it was also his first day of teaching in this new yeshiva. He probably had his own anxieties, and was preoccupied with his own concerns.

That day, he began teaching a new tractate of the Talmud. My mind was not there, I was not able to concentrate, and consequently, I didn't understand much. When I came home that evening, my mother noticed that my face was flushed. She touched my forehead; it was burning hot. She measured my temperature and discovered that I had fever that was way above normal. She made me go to bed and gave me an aspirin. When my father came home they discussed the matter and decided to keep me home the next day. My father consulted with Rabbi Elisha and with Reb Avrum Yosef, and they were considering what would be the best course of action. All of them agreed that it would be best to send me back to Reb Avrum Yosef. When I was asked if I wanted to go back to Reb Avrum Yosef, I gave a sigh of relief and readily agreed. The next day, I went back to Reb Avrum Yosef's school and stayed there for another half a year. In this short period of six months I changed from a child to a grown student. I applied myself to the study of the Talmud, and Reb Avrum Yosef helped me a lot; he gave me special attention. By the end of the semester I was ready for the big time. Even Reb Avrum Yosef told my father that I was ready. They enrolled me again in Rabbi Elisha's yeshiva.

This time the school was no longer in the commercial court; it moved to Kodor Street, much nearer to where we lived. I was no longer nervous; I was eager to show off my knowledge of the Talmud to the other boys, who ignored me half a year ago. I was fascinated with the way my cousin Rabbi Elisha was teaching; he interpreted the text with clarity, and he cut through intricate questions like one cuts through butter with a hot knife. He made the complicated text seem simple. I had a complete transformation in this environment; I seemed to be thriving and gaining self-confidence. I began to master the intricacies of the Talmud.

Every Saturday afternoon, Rabbi Elisha conducted a Shalosh Seudos[3] Tish for his students, but many community adults also came to partake in the Tish. Light food was served and zemirot[4] were sung. I was given the honor every Shabbat to lead one of the main melodies at the meal, which I did with great pride. After the singing, Rabbi Elisha delivered a short commentary on the Torah.

Purim in Dej was a fun day, especially for children. Children used to dress up in costumes and go from house to house to visit the neighbors, who treated them with presents, candies, cookies, and small change. At least two weeks before Purim, my mother began the preparation for the day; she baked fancy cakes and cooked special dishes. When I was still a young child my parents sent me on Purim day on a mission to friends and relatives to deliver the Purim presents, which consisted mostly of cakes and fruits. Usually I would be met at the door with a token gift or small change.

Later in the afternoon of Purim there would be a lavish and festive meal in the house. The Challah for that day was always two or three times larger than the usual Shabbat Challah and the meal consisted of many courses; eight to ten courses were not unusual. After we finished the main meal at home, my father and brothers went to the rabbi's Tish. On Purim, hundreds of people attended the rabbi's Tish, where dancing and singing went on until the late hours of the night. At around midnight there was a Purim show, with Zoldi, the comedian, as the star attraction. In his usual style he was poking fun at everybody, especially at the rabbi and the prominent people of Dej. People in Dej liked a good laugh and Zoldi provided good humor for hearty laughs. The people were looking forward to this annual event and listened to him with rapt attention. One particular year, in addition to looking forward

---

3. The third Shabbat meal, which is eaten Saturday, late in the afternoon
4. Zemirot are songs for the Shabbat meal.

to the Purim fun I also had to combine fun with work, because Rabbi Elisha had an important mission for me. He gave me an assignment to go from house to house to collect charity for a very important cause.

On Purim day people were more generous than on other days. I began to walk the streets from house to house in the morning and it took me four hours to cover the route. When I completed the tour I went straight to my cousin Rabbi Elisha and gave him the money. I didn't even count it; I had no idea what was expected of me. Rabbi Elisha was very pleased; he told me that I did well, that it was a larger sum than he expected. I was tired but also very pleased. Came evening time and as tired as I was, nothing could keep me from attending the party at the rabbi's Tish. I stayed until Zoldi finished, which was in the early morning hours.

CHAPTER THIRTY-THREE

My Bar Mitzvah

As I reached my twelfth birthday[1] I began to feel a little nervous, because I hadn't yet begun to prepare for my bar mitzvah. In Chasidic circles, a bar mitzvah boy, who is a yeshiva student, is expected to deliver a major Talmudic discourse at the dinner celebration, and this is in addition to reading the Haftorah and leading the services. Rabbi Elisha, my teacher, asked me if I would be interested in delivering a major discourse on the Talmud.

I asked, "What will I have to do?"

He said. "You will have to memorize several pages of the Talmud, and then you will have to dissect the text, ask questions, and find answers. You will also have to do a lot of research."

He gave me my assignment and I went to work.

For the next six months I was busy studying, memorizing, and re-searching. This was in addition to my regular schoolwork. Whenever I was stuck Rabbi Elisha told me where to find the source for it. While I was studying, my parents were planning the party, which was to take place in our own home. When the day of my bar mitzvah arrived I was ready. They planned it for a Thursday, which was also my Jewish birthday. In the morning of my bar mitzvah, most of my family and friends came to the synagogue to hear me lead the services and to watch me put on my Tefillin for the first time. The Dejer rabbi, who was also my first cousin, also attended, and he placed the Tefillin on my arm and head for the first time. I was not called up for an Aliyah; that was to wait until Saturday, when I would be given the Maftir Aliyah. But my

---

1. A picture of the author at age 11 is #5B in the photo section of this book.

father was given an Aliyah and he recited the special blessing for this occasion. On Thursday evening the bar mitzvah feast was held in our home. At that time we lived on Deak Ferenc Street.

On the morning preceding the feast, they emptied the living room from all the furniture and set up long tables and chairs. Even with all the furniture removed, there was not enough room to seat everyone in the living room. More tables and chairs were set up in the veranda next to the living room. But the guests in the veranda seemed to have a party of their own; they could not hear the speeches, or see anything that went on in the other room. The Dejer rabbi was seated at the head of the dais; next to him were my uncles, Rabbi Itzik Mechel, Rabbi Mendele, and my cousin and teacher Rabbi Elisha. Zoldi the comedian was also present, entertaining the guests with his humor. Everyone seemed to have a good time; they were eating the delicacies, which my mother and her family prepared. The room was buzzing with chatter and pleasant conversation. Then the time came to deliver my speech; the rabbi asked everyone to pay attention. I walked over to a small podium behind the dais to face the crowd. I knew my discourse by heart. Just before I started speaking, my teacher Rabbi Elisha told me, "Do not hurry; you know your stuff, deliver it slowly in a measured way."

I was nervous, my face was flushed, but I was determined not to fumble it. As I was delivering my speech, several scholars in the room, including the Dejer rabbi, were indicating with their body language that they are familiar with the subject. They were quietly reciting the sources with me. I was very pleased, and as I perceived that the audience understood me and that they are on the same page with me, I gained more confidence and began to relax. I stopped being in a hurry and I was no longer anxious to get it over with. It took me twenty minutes to deliver my discourse. When it was over they started singing; they were all wishing me Mazal Tov. People wanted to dance, but there was no room for dancing; the room was packed like sardines in a can. The hour was getting late, but most of the people didn't feel like going home; they stayed long after they did the blessing after the meal. Zoldi was just warming up; he was telling jokes and stories. As long as he had an audience, he didn't stop. I was eager to open up my presents, but my mother told me not to, because she was concerned I might mix them up and that I will not know whom to thank for what.

CHAPTER THIRTY-FOUR

The Mareh Yechezkel's Yahrzeit

MY OLDER BROTHER MOISHE[1] was my role model; I always want-ed to emulate him and to keep up with him. When I found out that Moishe is traveling to Karlsburg during Chol Hamoed Pesach, I wanted to join him. The occasion was the yahrzeit of our great-great-grand-father, Rabbi Yechezkel Paneth, whose burial place was in Karlsburg. He was the author of the book *Mareh Yechezkel* and the chief rabbi of Transylvania. Every year the Jewish community of Dej chartered a bus to make the trip. Many residents of Dej made the trip, especially the grandchildren of the rabbi. Normally it was a full busload. I felt that I was old enough to make the trip, but my mother wouldn't let me. She promised to let me go the following year.

I was disappointed, but in a way I didn't mind; I had my doubts about going and I was pretty nervous about it. However, I was curious about the site of my grandfather's grave. When Moishe returned I was eager to find out everything about the trip. Moishe in his inimitable way was a terrific storyteller; he described the trip with gusto to the last detail.

As compensation, I was taken the next Chanukah to the Dejer cem-etery with my brother Moishe and family. I had been to the cemetery before, but I was too young to understand the meaning of it. On this occasion it was different; it was the yahrzeit of my grandfather, Rabbi Moshe, my mother's father. The yahrzeit is always on Chanukah and the whole family went to the cemetery to observe the yahrzeit. His grave

---

1. See photo of my brother Moishe in the black hat, photo #4 in the photo section of this book.

is inside the Ohel,[2] where the rest of the Paneth rabbis are interned. Everyone in the family lit a candle and they recited psalms and memorial prayers. There were about twelve graves in this room; three of them had wooden boxes on top of the graves; the boxes were the size of a coffin. The boxes served as receptacles for petition notes, which visitors deposited. I deposited my own personal notes into two of the boxes, of my grandfather and of my great-grandfather. My mother also visited her brother's grave, Rabbi Yechezkel, and she prayed there for a while. It was a very cold winter day, but surprisingly it was not too cold inside the unheated room.

---

2. The Ohel was a special room in the cemetery of Dej where all the rabbis of Dej were interned. "Ohel" in Hebrew means tent.

CHAPTER THIRTY-FIVE

I was Enrolled in the Yeshiva
of Advanced Learning

I STUDIED IN RABBI ELISHA'S YESHIVA for a few years, but when I became sixteen it was time to move on; my parents decided that I was ready for the great yeshiva of Rabbi Yaakov Meilach. I was anxiously looking forward to being considered one of the big boys, but when I got there, I wished I had stayed in Rabbi Elisha's yeshiva; it was an entirely new experience for me and I was completely unprepared for it. With hindsight, I am still perplexed at the lack of orientation given to the new students. Here I found myself in this new environment with no explanation of what is expected of me. Up until now I was used to learning in a structured curriculum; I knew exactly every hour of every day what I was supposed to do. Here in the great yeshiva, the curriculum was completely unstructured, everyone was treated like an adult, even sixteen-year-old boys. They were completely on their own. True the Rebbe was my cousin, but I had no personal relationship with him; he was much older than I was, and was even older than my mother, who was his aunt. I knew all the students by sight, but because I was the youngest, I had no personal friends in the yeshiva.

Every Sunday the rabbi introduced the text of the Talmud for the following week's study. The rest of the week the students were to study the text and to learn all the commentaries. Every Thursday afternoon the rabbi would sit at the head of the table, with the senior students sitting and the younger students standing. By Thursday the students had to be ready with answers. He would call at random a name of any student to explain one of the difficult questions. In the beginning of the semester I studied diligently and I was ready for the tests. But as many weeks went by without being asked to answer any questions, I became complacent. I was less studious and many times I didn't do my homework. The yeshiva structure was very loose; if you studied you became a scholar, but no one watched whether you studied or not. The only thing that kept students in line was the weekly test. My mind was not on my Talmud studies; I was already a young man worrying about the world situation, in particular anti-Semitism and Jewish survival. I also associated more and more with Gidi Rosenzweig, and I tried to acquire secular knowledge. I became so neglectful with the yeshiva studies that one Thursday afternoon during a test I caused my own embarrassment in front of the entire yeshiva. Unexpectedly, the rabbi called my name. He asked me to explain a difficult principle of the Talmud. I looked up from my daydream and I became red in my face; I repeated the question three times and then I said, "I don't know."

After this incident I started to concentrate more diligently on my studies, but I never gained back my original enthusiasm. However, it left me with a lasting impression and lesson – that it is necessary to be ready at all times. In the next semester there was some improvement in the organization of the yeshiva, each student was assigned a partner for study. I was assigned to study with Moishe Moskowitz. He was a few years older than I was and a very bright young man. He was already well versed in the Talmud. To this day I do not know nor understand why Moishe was willing to be my study partner. It is quite possible that my father arranged it; perhaps he even paid him to study with me. It might have been the result of the test I failed.

Moishe Moskowitz and I became very close friends. We studied six days a week in a neighbor's house nearby, which they made available to us. Later on I was thinking a lot about it and I wondered why these neighbors handed over to us their living room for study, unless perhaps my father made a rental arrangement with them. But I never asked and I was never told. The following semester we formed a threesome, my cousin Chezkele Paneth, Moishe Moskowitz, and I. I loved to study with Moishe and Chezkele; it was a very productive learning and it was also a lot of fun. Moishe Moskowitz was a good influence on me, and a good role model.

CHAPTER THIRTY-SIX

Gidi Rosenzweig

T HERE WAS ANOTHER GOOD FRIEND who had an influence on me; he was an entirely different type and not a yeshiva student. His name was Gidi (Gedalyeh) Rosenzweig,[1] who lived next door to us on Deak Ferenc Street. I knew Gidi for a long time, but he was not a close friend of mine and I had no interactions with him. We mingled in different circles; while I associated with yeshiva students, Gidi had his own friends from the gymnasium, from where he already graduated. Gidi and his family were religious and observant, but they were modern and he attended secular schools. On one occasion Gidi came to the rabbi's Tish, and there he struck up a conversation with me. He was about five years older than I was, but nevertheless he invited me to come over to his house the following afternoon. When I arrived to his house I found there two other guys, whom I knew slightly; they were Gidi's age, also about five years older than I was. The conversation centered on world events, in which I was able to participate, because it was a subject I was familiar with; I followed world events closely by reading the daily newspaper ever since I was twelve years old. But then the conversation turned to literature, music and science, algebra and mythology. I kept quiet, because I knew practically nothing about the subjects.

I whispered to Gidi that I wish to be excused, because I have no idea what they are talking about. Gidi apologized, but he wanted to know which subject I am uncomfortable with. I told him that it was almost everything. He asked me to stay and to just listen to the conversation. Gidi offered to teach me these subjects.

---

1. He survived the Holocaust and immigrated to Israel.

From then on Gidi taught me algebra, history, and grammar. I used to come to his house a few times a week for an hour or so and he would tutor me in these subjects. At first I felt a little guilty about spending my time on secular studies. In our circles it was a no-no, to spend so much time on secular studies, but I was thirsty for knowledge and I enjoyed learning things I didn't know. In the Cheders they taught only the minimum secular studies and even the few hours they taught us was only because the authorities mandated it. The time allotted was one hour, two times a week, and consisted of reading, writing, and arithmetic. I don't know why Gidi was willing to teach me without any remuneration. I don't even know why he wanted to be my friend; at that age, five years older makes a big difference. In any case I was grateful; he taught me a lot about the secular world. One time Gidi started to explain Greek mythology and the different gods the ancient people believed in. I objected to listen to such a conversation. I felt uncomfortable to talk about other gods, because I thought it was a sin.

I said to him, "I was brought up with the belief that there is only one God, any talk about other gods is improper. Why talk about something that doesn't exist? Besides, it is against my belief to talk or even think about other gods."

Gidi replied, "You are right; there is only one God and He is the God of Abraham, Isaac, and Jacob. I meant no harm; I just wanted to expose you to what the ancient world believed in. I am quite certain it will not influence you to believe in them. We will not discuss that subject anymore."

In general Gidi taught me a lot; he recommended to me certain books to read. He even gave me a small encyclopedia as a present; it was a condensed one-volume lexicon. He said to me, "If there is something you want to look up, you should be able to find it in this book."

One day I was walking home from my studies, and I was carrying the lexicon under my arm. On my way I encountered my uncle Reb Baruch Avruham Bindiger. I greeted my uncle warmly and we exchanged a few pleasantries.

My uncle asked me, "What are you carrying under your arm?"

"Nothing important, it is just a book."

"What kind of book?"

"It is a book of words, it is called a lexicon."

"What kind of words?"

"Words that explain different things in the world, like animals, new inventions, and other things."

"Let me look at this book."

I handed him the book. He looked at it from the outside, then he opened it and examined it from the inside. He studied it for a minute or so, and then he said to me, "A book like this is not for you, it will corrupt you. I will take it from you and I will discuss it with your father."

The next day my father told me, "Your uncle gave me this book, which he took away from you. He thinks it will have a corrupting influence on you. I looked at it and I think it is all right for you to read; I will return it to you, but I don't want you to parade around town with the book under your arms. Some people believe that a yeshiva student should study Torah and Talmud exclusively and not read these type of books."

"But father, how will a yeshiva student like me acquire knowledge and how will I be able to earn a living if I'm not allowed to study secular books?"

"Listen to me Mati. When a yeshiva student studies Talmud and understands its intricacies, then he has all the knowledge he needs to be able to make a living. The Talmud discusses all sorts of business transactions, especially in the tractates of Nezikin.[2] Therefore I can understand their point of view, but personally I think it is okay to augment your knowledge with some secular studies."

I took my book back and thanked my father. From then on I kept the book at home.

I liked my uncle Baruch Avruham Bindiger and so did almost everyone else in Dej. Reb Baruch Avruham did not know very much about lexicons, but he was a very smart person and very well informed about world affairs and politics. However, he was also devoutly religious and very protective of his family. He genuinely feared assimilation and corrupting influences. He was a fantastic storyteller and people loved to listen to him; he could tell a story with zest and humor. On summer afternoons he would hold court in the Chasidic synagogue courtyard. On those long summer-days people would come early to services and hang around in the courtyard until prayer time. During that period Reb

---

2. Nezikin is a series of Talmudic tractates on the subject of business and inter-personal relations. "Nezikin" in Hebrew means damages.

Baruch Avruham could be seen surrounded by a huge crowd, telling his stories, jokes, and the latest news.

Gidi invited me to go with him to watch the annual Romanian National parade, which I gladly accepted. Every year on the tenth of May there was a large military parade in Dej, celebrating the Romanian national holiday. There was a military regiment stationed in Dej; their headquarters were in the barracks outside of Dej. The main participants in the parade were the officers and the soldiers from the military regiment. The parade took place on the main street of Dej, which was called the Corso. The street had some other name, which I don't remember, but everyone called it the Corso. It was the focal point of Dej; everyone went to the Corso to meet everyone else. They set up a viewing stand in the center of the Corso from where the dignitaries would review the marching units. Gidi and I found a good viewing spot, right across from the viewing platform. We managed to plant ourselves right in the front, holding on to the rope, which separated the viewers from the marchers. As we were standing there, we saw the dignitaries arriving and taking their seats across from us. We recognized the Prefecture,[3] the Mayor, but there were many other dignitaries and we had no idea who they were. We saw the Greek Orthodox priest, whom I recognized, because he lived on Kodor Street and I used to see him often. Other priests took their seats; they wore their priestly robes. To our surprise we saw our own rabbi walk up the platform; it was Rabbi Paneth, who happened to be my cousin. An aide showed him to his seat next to the army general. The rabbi made a good impression, with his long gray beard, wide rimmed black hat, and black caftan. After a while we saw him chatting with the general. It was quite a contrast between the two, the general in his splendid uniform with red and gold braids and the rabbi in his somber attire. It was a beautiful sight to watch the soldiers march with precision in spectacular formations. All of the marchers wore their finest military uniforms. The orchestra played different marching tunes, which I enjoyed a lot. The military regiment in Dej had a very fine orchestra and a very gifted conductor. The band had stationed itself right next to us, opposite the reviewing stand, and remained there for the duration of the parade. There were also school children in their uniforms marching down Main Street.

---

3. A title similar to a governor

CHAPTER THIRTY-SEVEN

The Vienna Conference of 1940

FROM 1918 UNTIL 1940 Transylvania was a province of Romania. But on August 30, 1940, a conference was convened in Vienna by Hitler and Mussolini, and they awarded Transylvania to Hungary. After this decision the Romanians had to evacuate the territories and the Hungarians marched in. Some of the Transylvanian Jews were quite happy to welcome the Hungarians; they looked back with nostalgia to the old days of the Austro-Hungarian Empire. Especially the Jews of the older generations, who had attended Hungarian schools and spoke the language fluently; they were more accustomed to the Hungarian way of life. During the last twenty years of the Romanian rule, those older Jews didn't feel completely at home; they didn't even master the Romanian language. With regards to the treatment of Jews by the Romanian governments, it was spotty; some Romanian Prime Ministers were tolerant towards Jews, but others were outright anti-Semitic. The old-timers figured that the good old days are back, and the Hungarians will be friendly. However they soon found out that the new authorities in the new Hungary were even worse than the Romanian regime.

The new reality was that after the Hungarians marched into Transylvania, life for many Jews changed for the worse. People lost their livelihood, because the Hungarian laws prohibited Jews to be in many occupations. People became unemployed from one week to the next, either because they lost their business, or because they were not allowed to work in that profession. My father lost his insurance business, because the insurance company, Fonciera, was a Romanian insurance company, and they did not do business in Hungary; my father had difficulty providing a livelihood for his family in Dés. My father was considering several options; he talked about opening a textile business in Dej, but business conditions in general were not favorable and the plan was dropped. My family stayed in Dés for a while longer, but without an income they were consuming all their savings. They were compelled to consider moving the family to Naprad. In Naprad my father owned a farm, from which they would have an income there. My parents talked to us and they tried to explain that moving to Naprad was only a temporary solution until the economic conditions improve. We children wondered about our schooling, but my father had no answer and no real solution to our schooling. As he explained it to us, his first and foremost priority must be to provide food for the family and to make sure that our family survives.

He told us that our schooling will have to wait until our survival is not in question. He also had new plans for his farm. Three years earlier he had planted five hundred fruit trees. His new plan was to add a few thousand additional trees, like apple, cherry, apricot, peach, and prune trees. He also had plans to set aside a field for walnut trees. Walnuts were a lucrative business; the walnut trees produce nuts, which can be sold on the market, and also the wood of the walnut trees can be sold as lumber. As the walnut forest thickens and the trees get crowded, they need to be thinned out; those trees that are chopped down are then used as wood for furniture or parquet floors.

My parents were discussing my personal situation; they were trying to decide what to do about my schooling. When my uncle Reb Baruch Avruham found out that my father intended to move the family to Naprad, he suggested to him to leave me in Dés to study. He offered to keep me in his house. My father discussed it with us and it was decided that I should move with them for the time being, and later on in the fall when the new semester started I would be sent back to Dés. We got ready to move to Naprad. We took with us only the most essential belongings and some furniture. The rest of the furniture my parents stored with relatives. Their plan was to return to Dés as soon as possible.

In Naprad we moved into a house owned by our cousin Sanyi Goldstein. The house was spacious and comfortable; it had a huge kitchen, a large living room, and three bedrooms. My mother seemed to be happy with the house, especially with the kitchen, but she had a hard time getting used to the huge oven. My Aunt Blanca came over to show her how to bake the bread. In Dés there was no need to bake bread; one could buy it ready-made in the bakery. To bake bread in Naprad was a major task; it took many hours to heat the oven. The dough had to be prepared from the night before, to give it time to rise. Therefore bread was not baked every day, but once a week. A whole week's bread was baked at one time, usually on Friday morning. Friday was chosen, because one had to bake fresh Challah for Shabbat anyhow.

CHAPTER THIRTY-EIGHT

Our Family Moves to Naprad

Soon after we moved to Naprad, my brother Moishe found himself a job. It came about when he went to the office of the village administration in order to fill out forms necessary to receive food rations for the family. There was already a food shortage in Transylvania after the Hungarians marched in. Ration cards were issued in all of Hungary for basic food items. When the village notary noticed that Moishe filled out the forms efficiently in no time at all, he asked Moishe if he would mind staying for an hour to help the village people fill out their forms. Moishe obliged and stayed for an hour, helping fill out forms. They needed Moishe's help because when the Hungarians took over the village administration, it had a shortage of clerical help, as the local Romanian population of Naprad did not speak or write Hungarian. With the introduction of coupons for food rations, the workload in the notary's office became that much heavier.

The next day a messenger came to our house with a note from the assistant notary, requesting Moishe to come over. When Moishe arrived to the office, he found a long line of people, standing in line stretching out all the way from the office to the street outside. They were waiting to fill out the forms for food rations. It was so crowded that he could barely enter the office. The notary noticed him immediately; Moishe stood out conspicuously in his black velour hat,[1] and the notary motioned to Moishe to come forward. He asked Moishe to help with the clerical work and offered him a steady job to work in the office of the notary.

---

1. At that time, Moishe and I wore black velour hats and Chasidic garb. We were the only people wearing it in Naprad.

Moishe agreed to stay for the day, and with our father's permission he continued to work for the notary full time. Moishe had no office experience, but he had a lot of common sense and he was a quick study. He spoke, read, and wrote Hungarian fluently, though he never attended Hungarian schools; he acquired this knowledge on his own. We grew up during the Romanian regime, which ruled Transylvania until 1940, and they didn't teach Hungarian. As Moishe worked in the notary administration office, he quickly learned the system, the method, and the workings of the office.

A few weeks later on the first day of the new month, the entire village turned out to receive the food ration coupons. They lined up on the street by the hundreds and there was a lot of pushing and shoving. Arguments ensued and the more aggressive ones were the ones who received the coupons. It was a trying day for all, especially for the office staff. When the day was over, the notary told his staff that he is concerned that matters might get out of control and the people will cause a riot.

Moishe suggested a new idea: to designate a certain day for each resident based on the alphabet. People whose name starts with a letter between A and G will receive the coupons on the first day of the month, and those between H and M will receive them on the second day, and so on. The notary listened and looked at the assistant notary. They just looked at each other in wonderment, as if to say, "Why didn't we think of such a simple solution?"

Finally the notary said to Moishe, "I think your idea might work. We will try it next month."

A few days before the beginning of the next month they sent out the drummer to announce the new policy. He went around the village drumming and announcing the new policy. In the village of Naprad, as well as in other villages, it was the practice to inform the populace of any new policy via a drummer. They would send out the drummer, who would stop at every street corner. He would beat on his drum to bring the populace out to the street. When a large crowd surrounded him, he would make his announcement in a loud voice.

On the first of the following month they tried the new system and it worked quite well. There were but few villagers who were not aware of the new policy. The great majority knew about it and they were pleased.

Moishe was only eighteen years old at that time. There were occasions during the middle of the month, when the office was not so busy, that he was entrusted to take care of the entire office all by himself. On one occasion when Moishe was the only person attending to the office, a supervisor from Zilah arrived unexpectedly to look at the books.[2] The supervisor strode into the Naprad office and to his amazement, he saw a young Chasidic boy behind a desk. At that time Jews were already prohibited from occupying government jobs. Moishe asked the visitor, "Can I help you?"

The visitor answered with a question, "Are you in charge?"

"Yes."

The visitor introduced himself. "I am so-and-so, the supervisor from Zilah. I came to inspect the books."

Moishe responded, "At your service."

He then proceeded to show him the books, offered him a desk and tried to make him comfortable. The supervisor sat down and started examining the books. In the meantime, the assistant notary returned to the office. Upon seeing the supervisor, whom he instantly recognized, the assistant notary turned red in his face and apologized profusely. While the assistant notary was talking to the supervisor, villagers walked into the office and Moishe attended to them one after another. An hour later the notary arrived, and he also was embarrassed and apologized. When the supervisor finished inspecting the books he closeted himself in the inner office with the two notaries. When they came out, the supervisor said goodbye to Moishe, shook hands with him, and clapped him on his shoulder.

Later on the notary asked Moishe, "Aren't you curious to know what the supervisor had to say?"

"Yes, but I didn't think you would tell me."

"I can tell you part of what he said. At first he was furious with me for giving you a job and allowing you to handle the books, but after he examined the books and saw your handwriting, he changed his mind. He also liked the way you handled the villagers."

Moishe continued to work in the office, but after this surprise visit, they never left him alone in the office.

2. Zilah was the county seat for the supervisor of the whole county administration.

CHAPTER THIRTY-NINE

Life in Naprad for the Judovits Family

My time in Naprad was not very productive; I wasn't able to find anything to do. There wasn't much I could do on the farm, because I had no farm experience. I had my Talmud books, which I studied daily, but it was not the same as learning in a yeshiva. I had no interaction with other students, and I had no teacher to ask the questions I had.

Regretfully, the dislocation took its toll on all of us – our education was disrupted, our livelihood was robbed from us, and our mother suffered the most in silence. This dislocation was not unique to us; it affected almost every Jewish family in our region.

At this time, Naprad had no Hebrew teacher for the young children. The Shochet, who had taught the children for many years, stopped doing it on account of a dispute he had with the parents. The parents approached my father and asked him if I could be the teacher for their children. They wanted me to teach them five days a week, and they offered to pay me a token salary for my effort. The classroom was available in the synagogue. I agreed to try, but after one week the project collapsed. I had no teaching experience and I wasn't able to keep control in the classroom. The children were a mix of all ages, and I just could not handle it.

My brother Mendi felt right at home in Naprad; he liked to go out to the farm and spend time with the shepherds. He made himself useful in all kinds of farm chores. He milked the sheep and helped in the manufacture of the cheese. At that time we had three hundred sheep. Victor, the main shepherd, and several young assistants attended to the sheep. Mendi became so familiar with the sheep that he could tell one sheep from the other. This was very useful, because a few months later, some sheep were missing from the herd. Victor told my father that he thinks a wolf in the area carried them off.

One day Mendi happened to walk over to Alör,[1] a village next to Naprad, to pick up some extra sugar from a grocer.[2] On the way to the village he was passing a herd of sheep. He noticed that some of the sheep looked familiar. He went closer and he was sure he recognized the sheep as belonging to our herd. When he came home, he told our father what he saw. My father went over to the next village to look at the sheep. To his surprise, twelve of the sheep in the herd had the "J" brand on their legs.[3] The owner of the herd told my father that he bought them from Victor. My father confronted Victor with the discovery of the theft. Victor tried to make all kinds of excuses, but my father told him that he could only exonerate himself by bringing back the sheep, that way he will get another chance. Otherwise the theft will be reported to the police and he will be fired. Victor was happy to take the deal. Father was thinking of firing him, but Victor was an experienced shepherd and hard to replace. Also, my father figured, because Victor knows he is under suspicion, he would stop stealing, and now Mendi was also keeping an eye on him. Mendi was very happy on the farm, he felt useful and important.

Lulu, my sister, did attend public school in Naprad, and she seemed to fit in very well. She was a great help to my mother in every respect. My mother needed a lot of help; none of the conveniences of Dés were available in Naprad. There was no electricity, no indoor plumbing, no electric or gas stoves. The bread had to be homebaked and everything had to be made at home by hand.

Lulu had no friends in Naprad; there were no other Jewish girls of her age living in Naprad. She must have been very lonely, but I never heard her complain. Outwardly she seemed to be cheerful. In her free time she did a lot of embroidery.

1. Alör was a village two kilometers from Naprad.
2. Sugar was rationed and scarce; the grocer was a friend of the family.
3. Our sheep on the farm were branded with the letter "J."

CHAPTER FORTY

My Return to Dej to Live at the Bindigers

Aᴛᴇʀ ᴛʜᴇ ʜᴏʟɪᴅᴀʏ ᴏғ Sᴜᴋᴋᴏs, I was sent to live with my Uncle and Aunt, the Bindigers, in Dés. It must have been very difficult for my aunt and uncle, because my aunt Matel was very ill; she was bedridden all the time. The house had many rooms, but every room was occupied to full capacity. Their two daughters, Mashie and Sheindi, lived with them. Mashie was already married; she and her husband Yidele Paneth and their three children lived in one end of the house. Sheindi was about to be married and she was busy with making preparations for her wedding. In spite of the crowded house, my uncle and aunt cheerfully offered their home to be my home and for me to live with them. No, they actually insisted that I must stay with them. They didn't want me to stop learning. They had domestic help; Irina the maid prepared all the meals for the whole family and did the housework.

When I returned to Dés, the idea was that I would be a student in the upper yeshiva of Rabbi Yaakov Meilach. Soon I found out that in addition to being a student, I would also have to join the paramilitary organization named "Levente."[1] Noncompliance could have landed me in jail. I will describe my experiences in the Levente organization further on.

When I returned to the yeshiva of Rabbi Yaakov Meilach I was a different boy; life in Dés was not anymore the same for me. The move to Naprad, the splitting up of the family, and the rise of anti-Semitism changed me. In prior years I was very studious and a dedicated student.

---

1. The Levente was a paramilitary organization. Originally it was for all Hungarians, but a new law came out segregating the Jews from the Hungarians.

Now something changed in me, I could not focus, and consequently, I did not absorb what I studied. My uncle and cousins were very kind and indulgent with me, but I was not in my own home and I did not feel as relaxed as I would be in my own home. I did not relish the idea of being fed by relatives. This was my last semester in the yeshiva of Dés; after the Shevuot holiday, I joined the rest of the family in Naprad again.

When I reported to the Levente Organization at their office in Dej to register, I was asked, "Why didn't you come to register six months ago?"

I answered, "Six months ago I didn't live in Dés, I lived in Naprad."

"Do you have papers to prove it?"

"No, I don't have any papers with me. I will have to write to Naprad, to send me proof."

They told me to report to the office next morning at 8am.

When I showed up the next morning, many other Jewish boys were already waiting around. We were ordered to go out to the courtyard and wait. Within a short time, more Jewish boys arrived.

A Hungarian sergeant came out and told us to form a column and to line up two by two. Then he gave the order, "Follow me – march!"

Two other Hungarian soldiers marched in back of us to close the rear. We marched to the military barracks, which were just outside the city limits of Dés. When we arrived to the barracks the sergeant read to us a declaration.

"You are being punished for not reporting on time for duty and for other infractions."

All of us were herded into an empty room. We were about thirty boys crowded into this small room, with standing room only. The room was about 20 feet by 20 feet, with a very high ceiling, about 20 feet high. The sergeant opened the door and gave a new order.

"I want this room to be cleaned from wall to wall and from top to bottom. When you finish cleaning the room, it has to be spotless; I don't want to see a speck of dirt or dust. Do you see this white glove? I will examine the room with this glove, if it gets dirty, then you will be sorry you ever met me."

He left the room and locked the door. We looked at each other in wonderment of what to do. He had not given us any brooms, rags, brushes, or any instruments to clean with. There was no room to move around and we certainly had no ladders to climb to reach to the ceiling. The room must have been twenty feet high. Zelig, one of the boys, who seemed to be more mature than the rest of us, said,

"Listen guys, this is no laughing matter. He means business; I had already my share of military discipline. In the military we have to do what we are told. Now everybody, take off any clothes you can spare: a shirt, a jacket, or a sweater, anything at all. We will use them as rags. Let's start cleaning every part of this room. The short guys will climb up and stand on the shoulders of the tall guys to clean the upper part of the room. The rest of us will clean the walls, the floor, and the door. Let's not leave out any spot or corner. Okay, let's do it!"

Everyone listened and did what Zelig told us to do. We took off any extra clothes we could spare and started to clean. We climbed on top of each other and cleaned the upper part of the room. After about an hour the sergeant opened the door and asked, "Did you clean the room?"

We answered in unison, "Yes, sergeant."

He examined the room with his white glove and said, "You call this clean? Look at my glove – it is charcoal black. I ought to punish you for not obeying my order, but because you are new at this I will give you one more chance. I will be back in an hour."

He left the room and locked the door. As soon as he was out of the room, Zelig said to us,

"He is not too bad. I think if we try again he will pretend he is satisfied."

We started again to clean and scrub every inch of the room. We climbed again on top of each other and wiped the walls and the ceiling again and again. When the hour was over the sergeant returned. He examined again a few places with a clean white glove and then declared, "You still don't know how to make a room clean, but there is some improvement. I will have to teach you how to obey orders."

He ordered everyone out of the room into the courtyard and gave a command: "Form a line of two by two and follow me. Now start running in the same tempo as I am running."

"One; two; three; four . . ." He repeated the count a few times and then he stopped running but continued counting. He made us run around the grounds a few times until we were exhausted. He ordered a halt and dismissed us.

After this experience, I reported regularly every week for exercises to the Levente Organization until I moved back to Naprad. After a few sessions I got used to the exercises. At these exercises I had a chance to meet many Jewish boys I wouldn't have met otherwise. Most of the boys were not Chasidic, as I was; they had a secular education, which I did not have. But the group was an all-Jewish group, because the Hungarian government segregated the Jewish group from the rest of the Hungarian youth. Consequently, camaraderie and friendships developed among the boys in this group. We were made to sing Hungarian patriotic songs while we marched, and also familiar popular songs. Before this I had never been exposed to the popular songs of the time.

Later on when we moved back to Naprad, I dutifully reported to the local "Levente Youth Group," as I was ordered to do, and I attended one session. After the first session was over, the leader of the group told me that I was excused from attending any more sessions. He never gave me a reason, but my parents found out that I was dismissed because I was Jewish. The Hungarian policy was to segregate the Jewish boys from the Hungarians and I was the only Jewish boy in the group; they could not form a Jewish group with only one Jewish boy. The irony of the situation was that there were no Hungarian youths in this group, there were only Romanian boys present in the group, and furthermore the Hungarians did not like the Romanian. But it didn't matter. Since I was Jewish, I was out.

CHAPTER FORTY-ONE

My Life-Threatening Experience on the Train

As I mentioned earlier, my father lost his livelihood in Dej after the Hungarians occupied Transylvania, and therefore the family had to move to the village of Naprad, where my father owned a farm. My father had many sheep on the farm and he used the milk from the sheep to manufacture kosher cheese, which was a rare commodity in our area.

I was given the job of transporting the cheese to the customers to the nearby localities, which were a distance of a short train ride. Once a week I would take the train to Nagybanya[1] to deliver the cheese to our customers. But the delivery was not just a simple train ride to Nagybanya. Naprad had no railroad station; the nearest railroad station was two villages away. I had to walk to Udvarhely, a village eight kilometers from Naprad, where the railroad station was located. The Szamos River separated Naprad from Udvarhely and I had to take a ferry to cross the river. Though, we had horses and wagons, they were not available to me; they were needed on the farm.

The load of cheese was much too heavy for one person to carry; therefore my father hired Remus, the next-door neighbor's son, who was my age, fifteen years old, to help me carry the cheese to the railroad station. It was pitch dark, four o'clock in the morning, when Remus and I left Naprad to catch the seven o'clock train to Nagybanya. Together we walked in the dark, carrying the load of cheese on our backs. When we reached the station, Remus waited with me until the train arrived, he helped me put the cheese on the train, and then he returned to Naprad. I delivered the cheese to the customers alone; somehow I

---

1. Nagybanya was a town seventy kilometers away from Naprad.

managed with the double load all by myself. I also went to see other potential customers as my father instructed me. I booked new orders for my next trip and returned to Naprad satisfied. After a while my trips became routine. Every Tuesday morning I walked with Remus to the railroad station, took the train to Nagybanya, and returned home in the afternoon. The money I received from the customers I put in a kerchief and tied it around my waist.

✡ ⅃, I

DURING ONE OF MY RETURN TRIPS from Nagybanya something terrible happened. It was in the late summer just before the High Holidays. I was seated in the train next to the window, looking out at the scenery and minding my own business. The train was full of passengers, including Hungarian soldiers. I was returning home from a successful mission with the money I received for the cheese tied in a kerchief around my waist.

Six Hungarian soldiers were seated on the benches behind me. I was dressed in a dark gray suit and a black velour hat, and I had curly payos. Someone tapped me on the shoulder. I turned around to see who is tapping me. As I turned around, a Hungarian soldier reached over and grabbed my hat. I looked at him askance and he just stared back at me with a grin on his face and said, "This is a very nice hat. You want your hat? Come over here and I will return it to you. I just wanted to see what kind of a hat you are wearing."

I knew that it meant trouble, but I also knew that if I didn't go over I would have worse trouble. I got up and walked around the benches to get to him. The soldier, who took my hat, was laughing it up with the other Hungarian soldiers; they sized me up and down and then asked me, "What are those side curls on your face? Are you a boy or a girl?"

I answered them, "It is in my family's tradition to wear side curls."

They started to laugh and then one of the soldiers gave me a push; I found myself next to two other soldiers. One of them tossed me back to the first soldier and he in turn threw me to another soldier. This went on for about a minute or so, and then one of the soldiers took out a pocketknife. I looked around to see if there is a friendly face on the train or perhaps to make a run for it. But everyone seemed to avoid my gaze; nobody wanted to have eye contact with me. I couldn't run away either, because the soldiers surrounded me. I turned to one of them and asked, "Why are you doing this? What have I done to any of you?"

Instead of answering me, the soldier with the knife grabbed me and told his buddy, "Hold him!"

While one of them held me, the other put his knife next to my face. When I felt the cold metal touch my cheeks, I froze. I became motionless. The soldier proceeded to cut off my payos. By this time I was so scared that I didn't utter a sound; I must have been in shock. He then cut off my other payos.

One of the soldiers asked the others, "What should we do with him?"

The other answered, "I have an idea; let's throw him out the window."

The other soldier chimed in, "Yes, let's throw him out through the window."

The first soldier said to the one sitting next to the window, "Open the window wide, so we can throw him out."

The train was speeding at about forty or fifty miles per hour.

All of a sudden I felt an arm grab my arm. It was a middle age Hungarian woman who appeared in front of us and started yelling at the soldiers, "Shame on you guys! You call yourselves soldiers. I am the wife of a Hungarian colonel and I am embarrassed by your behavior. You are bringing shame to the uniforms you wear. Is this something a brave soldier would do? Attack a defenseless innocent child? This boy could not be more than fifteen years old. I will certainly report this to your commander."

The lady who came to my defense was not Jewish.

The soldiers were taken aback, they seemed to be embarrassed, but they did not respond. The woman grabbed me by the arm and pulled me away towards her. The soldiers stood by passively. She led me to a bench in a corner at the other end of the train next to the window, where she covered me with her shawl. She sat next to me until we arrived to Zsibo. Normally I would have stayed on the train until we arrived in Udvarhely, but under the circumstances and the good advice from the woman who saved me, I decided to get off in Zsibo.[2] The woman led me out to the station platform. She found what she was looking for, a large group of Jewish people, who were standing around waiting for passengers to arrive by train. She handed me over to them with an admonition. "Take care of this boy, he almost got killed."

Before I had a chance to thank her or to say anything she disappeared.

---

2. Zsibo was a small town, sixteen kilometers from Naprad. Udvarhely was only eight kilometers.

For many years after the incident and to this day I regret I didn't thank her or ask for her name, but I was so overwhelmed, so scared that I did not think clearly. I wonder who that woman might have been; it crossed my mind that she could have been Elijah the prophet in disguise.[3]

At the time of this incident I was fifteen years old. After I recovered from my shock, I hitched a ride from Zsibo with someone who was driving towards Naprad. When I arrived home my parents knew already what happened to me. I found out later that there were people on the train who witnessed the whole scene, including the cutting off my payos, and they heard the threat to throw me out of the train. They did not interfere or speak up, for the fear of being accused of threatening Hungarian soldiers. These people arrived to Naprad before I did, and they told my parents what they saw. Fortunately they assured my parents that I got off safely in Zsibo and that I was okay. When my mother caught sight of me getting off the wagon, she broke out in tears. She ran towards me, followed by my father, brothers, and sister. I jumped off the wagon, falling into my mother's arms. My poor mother was really shaken; she was trembling and could not speak. The whole family embraced me and they shed some tears of joy. I felt great to be in my family's arms. People were talking about the incident; they reported that the train was held up in Zsibo for an hour. There was some investigation, because the people on the train did complain and they called the police. As far as is known, nothing came of it. I did not go to the police and they did not come to me to question me.

After this incident my mother told me that she would not let me travel to Nagybanya anymore. But I was ready to continue. My position was that since my payos are already cut off, I look no different than any other boy on the train. However I decided not to wear a black velour hat, and I replaced it with a cap. I wanted to be useful, I didn't want to just sit around and do nothing. My father discussed the issue with my mother and they decided to let me continue to travel. I continued the deliveries without any incident.

---

3. Folklore has it that the prophet Eliyahu comes to save people in distress.

CHAPTER FORTY-TWO

My Life in Budapest before the Holocaust

My Brother Moishe and I Move to Budapest

After the Hungarian government occupied Transylvania, they began to draft young Jewish men of military age into a separate unit, they called it the Zsido Munkaszolgalat.[1] This was in line with their new policy of segregating the Jews from the non-Jewish Hungarians. Prior to this new law, Jewish men served with distinction in the Hungarian armed forces, where many became officers and achieved high ranks.

Many stories filtered back to the Jewish communities about the mistreatment and suffering of the draftees in the Zsido Munkaszolgalat. News came back from the front that the boys are being used to clear mines for the advancing German army on the Russian front. The commanders and officers of the Jewish brigade were notoriously sadistic and anti-Semitic. My brother Moishe was about to be drafted, because he was of that age. Everyone advised my father and Moishe to avoid the draft at all costs. After lengthy consultations with the family and relatives, Moishe moved to the big city of Budapest, where many Jewish boys settled. It was assumed that they would be lost in the big city.

Moishe found a job through a Jewish organization that specialized in finding jobs for Shabbat observers. In addition to his regular job, he also found a part-time job of reading the Torah on Shabbat. The Torah-reading job was in a small synagogue on the most famous boulevard

---

1. Jewish Work Brigade, or work service

in Budapest, called Andrassy út. There was only one large department store in all of Budapest; it was called *The Paris Aruhaz*, which was owned by an observant Jew. The owner established a small synagogue inside the store in one of the spare rooms on the second floor.

He found this job, because just about that time when Moishe arrived in Budapest, the regular Torah reader passed away and they were looking for a replacement. Moishe saw the ad in the Jewish paper and he applied for the job. Several guys were interviewed and Moishe landed the job. Moishe, in his correspondence with the family, urged me to get away from Naprad and to join him in Budapest. He felt that I should not wait until I became eligible for the draft, because it might be too late. At first my mother would not hear of it, but a few months later when it was certain that I would be drafted very soon, she relented. She also realized that I am just wasting away my life in Naprad. Economic conditions in Hungary, especially for Jews, became worse; my father's own livelihood was in jeopardy. None of my father's plans materialized; the political climate and economic conditions were not right to start a new business. The fruit trees, which he planted a few years earlier, were not yielding enough fruit for export.

I was only sixteen, but I was eager to join my brother in Budapest. My parents gave me their blessings and I took off for Budapest. The day I left Naprad, my mother was very nervous and so was I, but I tried not to show it. I had never been in such a large city before and I had never traveled alone for such a long distance. The incident on the train with the soldiers was still fresh in my memory. When I arrived in Budapest my brother Moishe was waiting for me at the Nyugati railroad station. He took me to his place, where I slept the first night. The next day I rented a room on Dob Street, which was the main street in the Jewish section.

My mother had given me the name of relatives who lived in Budapest, and after inquiring, I found their fish store on Dob Street. I dropped in to see them in their store and they were happy to meet me. The husband's name was Nissel Klein. I found them to be wonderful people, kind and generous. At first I didn't know how we were related, but after talking to them I found out that I had known Nissel's younger sister, Hindi, who immigrated a few years earlier to Palestine. When she was a young lady of seventeen she lived with my parents in Dés; I was a very young child at that time. The Kleins invited Moishe and me to dine with them every Friday evening. They had no children, but there were always other guests at their Shabbat table. They were always kind and attentive to Moishe and me.

Renting a room in Budapest was no picnic. I stayed in my first rented room one week only. I found out that my landlady was renting out my bed during daytime while I was away at work; someone was sleeping in my bed without my knowledge. I also found bedbugs in my bed, and in general it was not very clean. I became homesick and craved for the comforts and the protection of my parents. All of a sudden I realized that I had taken all the conveniences at home for granted. I was glad that my mother was not around to see my unhappy state of mind; she would have gotten sick from worry. I didn't even tell my brother Moishe about my problems. I found another room several blocks away. It was a more expensive room, but it was worth it; it was nicely furnished, clean, and it even had a good view. After a few weeks in Budapest, I began to feel a little surer of myself. An employment agency for Shabbat observers found a job for me in a tool supply company. The salary was modest, but enough for a single man to live on.

Accidentally, I found another source of income. The new apartment had another tenant, a gentleman about fifty years old, who was a journalist. When I moved in he befriended me, and he soon discovered that I was inexperienced with life in a big city. He tried to be helpful, instructing me in the intricacies of a large city. Part of his job as a journalist was to write critical reviews on the new plays being shown in the theatres. The journalist received many complimentary tickets to all the shows in the city. One day he knocked on my door and said to me, "Here are two theatre tickets for tonight's show; take your girlfriend to the show and have a good time."

I didn't have a girlfriend; in my world marriages were arranged through a matchmaker, and it was not proper to have a girlfriend. Nor did I know much about the theatre; I had never been to a theatre before. Dés had no theatres, and needless to say, there was no theatre in the small village of Naprad. Besides, in Chasidic circles they scoffed at going to the theatre. Hence I was never exposed to it.

But since I was no longer in a tight Chasidic circle I felt free to see a show, and I was curious about the theatre. But as curious as I was, it certainly was way down on my list of priorities. I had just arrived in Budapest, I could hardly support myself, and I certainly had no money for such luxuries. I accepted the tickets with thanks and rushed over to Moishe's place and asked him, "Would you like to see an Operetta[2] tonight?"

"Are you dreaming? What are you talking about? We can't afford to see an operetta, they are very expensive."

"I know they are expensive, but I have two free tickets."

I told him about the journalist and how I got the tickets. Moishe was thrilled. He loved music and we both went for the first time to see a musical. Moishe was somewhat familiar with modern music because he taught himself to read musical notes, but he had never seen or heard an actual live operetta. As for me, I was never exposed to modern music; I knew only Jewish and Chasidic songs. When the band started to play the overture I was so overwhelmed by its beauty that I declared to Moishe, "I never heard such beautiful music; I didn't know such beauty exists in this world."

We went home very happy. When Moishe told friends that he had seen the operetta, they all wondered how he was able to get tickets. Most of the theatre tickets were sold out, especially for the musicals; one had to buy tickets four weeks in advance. He told them that I have connections.

All our friends asked for tickets. I had a talk with my journalist friend. He was happy to supply me with tickets at a discount and Moishe and I sold them at a small profit.

The job I had at the tool supply company lasted only a few months. Bad economic conditions compelled the owner of the company to reduce his workforce. Another young boy by the name of Yosi also worked in the same warehouse. He was also from a small community in Transylvania. We were the last two employees to be hired by the company. To save some overhead, he had to let one of us go. The foreman in the shop recommended that Yosi should be retained. The owner of the company was a kind gentleman in his early fifties; he called me in to his office. I didn't see him too often in the business, because he was not a well person; he had to walk with a cane and was limping on one foot. He was kind, but also a businessman. He told me, "I have to reduce the staff in my company. One of you I have to let go. It was a choice between you and Yosi. My foreman tells me that Yosi is more diligent. He has more initiative and doesn't shy away from any kind of a job.

2. An Operetta is a musical show in a theatre.

He always volunteers to take the packages to the post office and cleans up the place in the evening without being asked."

At first I was hurt and angry, but after thinking about it for a while, I realized that he was right; he was telling me the facts as they were. In my thoughts I was grateful to him for being so frank and I never forgot his frank assessment of my shortcomings.

I was looking for a new job. The agency for Shabbat observers had no jobs. Someone told me that there were jobs available in Csepel, which was an industrial area outside of Budapest. It was a long trolley ride to the factory, but they had job openings. They offered me a night job, to work from 12 midnight to 8am. The pay was about 20% higher than my previous job. I started to work Sunday night, and worked until Thursday. It was a plastic company, producing molded forms from plastic powder. I hated the long trip to the place of work, and I hated even more the environment in the factory. Until then I had never been exposed to such vulgarity; every other word uttered was a four-letter expletive. But I needed the job. On Thursday night of the second week, the foreman told me that the company is running behind in its production schedule and that I have to come in tomorrow night for a sixth night this week.

"But tomorrow night is Friday and I don't work on Friday nights or Saturdays."

"Whatever you have planned for tomorrow, better cancel it. You have to come in tomorrow."

"I can't. I don't work on Saturdays, because I am a Sabbath observer."

"We can't make any exceptions. You will have to explain it to the office; maybe they can do something about it."

I walked over to the office and told the receptionist that the foreman directed me to the office. She showed me to the manager's office. I said to the manager, "I was asked by the foreman to come in to work tomorrow, but I can't."

The manager answered. "You have to come in tomorrow, there can be no excuses."

"I cannot come in; I do not work on Saturdays, because my religion forbids it."

"I am also Jewish and I work on Saturdays."

"I am glad to hear that you are Jewish. As a Jewish person you must know that an observant Jew does not violate the Shabbat."

"As you will get older you will learn that this is a luxury, and in the business world one cannot always afford luxuries."

"I am very sorry, but I can't come in."

"I am also very sorry, but under the circumstances, you can't work for us any longer. This is the company policy and if I would make an exception, I would also be fired."

"I am very sorry. Can I get my pay?"

"It is not ready. You will have to come in next week to get it, or we can mail it to you."

I found a new job in a mirror factory. During the interview for the job they gave me a description of my duties and I was told how much my wages will be. Then they asked me, "Do you have any questions?"

I said, "Yes, do I have to work on Saturdays?"

"No, but why do you ask?"

I explained that I am Jewish and that I do not work on Saturdays.

The owner of the factory said to me that she is also Jewish, but she is not observant. However she understood my request, because her grandfather was very observant. She complained to me that her husband was drafted into the Jewish work brigade and therefore she has to manage her husband's factory.

Mendi Also Joins Us in Budapest

My younger brother Mendi decided to join us in Budapest. He was only fifteen, but he was a daredevil, more so than any of the Judovits boys. He found a job as a delivery boy in a specialty store of expensive food delicacies. Mendi was riding all day long on a tricycle making deliveries.

My cousin Pali Friedman also moved to Budapest; he and my brother Mendi became good friends. Both of them were adventurous and daredevils, and they used to hang out together. Pali was from Kolozsvar.[3] He had lived there with his mother, Aunt Sidi, but Pali also moved to Budapest to avoid the draft.

In the meantime, I quit my job at the mirror company when a better job was offered to me in an office supply company. It was a very small company owned by a lady who operated the business out of her own apartment. It was a new business, which she started after her husband was drafted into the Jewish Work Brigade. Before he was drafted, her husband was an important executive in a well-established company with a very good income. Now she was left alone with a two-year-old

---

3. Kolozsvar is called "Cluj" in Romanian.

child and without any income. She lived in an elegant neighborhood, but after he was drafted everything changed. They lost their livelihood, and she couldn't go to work because she had to care for her infant. Similar tragedies happened all over Hungary in hundreds of Jewish homes. Some of her friends advised her to go to the Jewish welfare agencies, but she would not hear of it. Instead she established her own business with the help of her husband's business associates. It was a simple idea. Her husband dealt with many other companies; she contacted all of them and offered them office supplies at a lower cost. She did her business by telephone from her apartment. Her wholesale-supplier delivered the merchandise directly to the customer. My job was to be the troubleshooter. She could not leave the house to see the customers, and she needed someone to call on the customers when adjustments had to be made or when the wrong merchandise was delivered. Often I had to show the employees of the company how to use the merchandise. Of all the jobs in Budapest, I liked this one the best.

CHAPTER FORTY-THREE

The Lisker Rebbe

Rabbi Shlomo Friedlander,[1] also known as the Lisker Rebbe, lived in Budapest. He was a Chasidic Rebbe, but his followers were not the traditional Chasidic Jews with beards and black hats, but rather more modern Jews. They were attracted to the Lisker Rebbe because he welcomed everyone, and he made them feel comfortable with their Judaism. They all came to him with heavy hearts, unloading their problems; he listened and tried to solve their problems and gave them his blessings. He was very well known in Budapest, especially in modern circles. His wife Malka was my first cousin once removed; her grandmother was from the Paneth family.[2] They had two children, Leitsu and Chayim. Their residence in Budapest was on Eva Street, a very elegant and exclusive neighborhood. Before I left for Budapest my mother gave me their address, so shortly after I arrived in Budapest I went to see them. They were very gracious and warm people, and I felt comfortable in their home. Malka's two sisters, Leitsu and Reizi, lived with them in Budapest part of the year, whereas Bumi, Malka's brother, lived with them all the time. I dined in their home frequently and became a good friend with Bumi. Bumi was the Rebbe's assistant. The Rebbe had his own synagogue. It was a short walk from his house, and Bumi was in charge of it.

Malka's parents, Rabbi Mendele Friedlander[3] and his wife, were also

1. Rabbi Shlomo Friedlander, the Lisker Rebbe, survived the Holocaust. He settled in the US and lived on the Grand Concourse in the Bronx.
2. Malka Friedlander was my mother's great-niece.
3. Reb Mendele Friedlander was my mother's nephew.

in Budapest at this time. They were my cousins, but I got to know them for the first time during this visit. They resided in Nagyvarad,[4] a city in Transylvania. This was their first visit to Budapest and they wanted to see the sights of the city. I spent a lot of time with them, showing them the sights of Budapest.

---

4. Nagyvarad was called Oradea Mare in Romanian, and Grossverdein in German and Yiddish.

CHAPTER FORTY-FOUR

The Ileanda Rabbi

At ABOUT THIS TIME another cousin of mine, Rabbi Yosef Paneth, the rabbi of Ileanda, visited Budapest. One evening in 1942, my landlady knocked on my door, telling me there was a phone[1] call for me. When I answered the phone, the caller said, "This is your cousin, the Ileanda Rabbi. I have just arrived in Budapest and I would like to see you."

Rabbi Yosef[2] was my first cousin, but in age he was from a different generation. He was the same age as my mother, who was his aunt, and he had children much older than I was.

I answered him, "I am very happy to hear from you and I would also like to see you."

He asked me, "Can you come to see me today?"

I was very puzzled. I hardly knew him; I had met him only twice in Dej, and even during those meetings we only said hello to each other. I wondered, "Why this eagerness to meet me right away?" But I agreed to go over that evening. When we sat down to talk, my cousin said to me, "I have come to Budapest on a very important mission. My daughter Breindele is in Poland and she can't get out of there. She went to Krakow, Poland in 1939 to stay with her grandparents for a while, but in September of that year the Germans marched into Poland and she was trapped. They rounded up all the Jews and put them into a ghetto. I am determined to do everything within my powers to rescue

---

1. It was my landlady's phone; I did not have my own phone.

2. Rabbi Yosef Paneth immigrated to the USA with his wife and nine children, they lived in Brooklyn, NY. His children and grandchildren are rabbis in Israel and the USA.

her,[3] and with God's help I will be successful. But I need a lot of money to pay for the rescue, more than I can afford on my rabbinical salary. I will try to raise the money here in Budapest; that is the reason I came here. I need a favor from you. Can you help me?"

"That depends, if it is money, I regret to say that I don't have much to give you."

"No, no, I know that. It never entered my mind. What I need is your company. I am visiting a few well-to-do Jewish people here in Budapest and I would like you to come with me to be my companion. I cannot go alone, it doesn't look good."

"I will be glad to go with you, but it will have to be after four in the afternoon, that is when I finish work."

"That is fine. I am sure I can arrange the appointments for after four. I have already the names of three wealthy philanthropists, whom I want to visit, but I need some more. Do you have any ideas, or do you know of any wealthy individuals who could be of help?"

"Personally I do not know any such person, but I know someone who could be helpful. He could introduce you to some wealthy individuals here in Budapest."

"Who is that person?"

"It is our cousin, Rabbi Shlomo Friedlander, the Lisker Rabbi."

"I know of him and I know he is our cousin, but I never met him. How do you know that he can make the introductions?"

"He has a following of many wealthy individuals and he has great connections."

My cousin became very interested. "It is a wonderful idea, but I feel awkward to ask him for help the very first time I meet him."

"You shouldn't feel awkward, this is an extraordinary situation. Besides, they are very gracious and kind people, they will understand."

"Can you arrange a meeting?"

"Yes, but I think you should speak to them first on the phone. I will call them and tell them about you, then I will hand you the phone and you will speak to them."

I called the Lisker and a visit was arranged for the next day. We went together the next day to visit the Lisker Rabbi. The two rabbis had a

3. A book about his escape from the ghetto was written by Devorah Gliksman, under the title *A Sun and a Shield*.

very good meeting. His wife Malka[4] was also present. The Lisker rabbi was very helpful; he gave him a list of names and even called them in advance to make the introduction. Whenever I was free I accompanied Rabbi Yosef on these visits. After visiting all the individuals, Rabbi Yosef said to me, "I am still far too short from the amount I need. I must do more or the whole effort was in vain. Can you come with me to meet another distant cousin of ours? He is the head of the Orthodox Organization of Hungary and he has great influence here in Budapest. His name is Kahane."

I agreed to go with him to the main office of the organization, which was in the business section of Budapest. I remember I was very impressed with Rabbi Kahane's large imposing office; he had a very large elegant desk in the middle of the room and a heavy armchair. The doors to his office were tufted and padded heavily, to block any noise or eavesdropping. There were other small offices and in the anteroom were several secretaries. The two rabbis knew each other from before. In introducing me to Rabbi Kahane, Rabbi Yosef said, "This is your cousin, you probably never met before, and I thought it would be nice if you knew each other."

Rabbi Kahane provided Rabbi Yosef with introductions to a few individuals and we visited all those individuals. At the conclusion of his trip to Budapest, he reached his goal of raising the necessary funds. With bribery to many individuals, Breindele escaped from the ghetto,[5] and she was smuggled across the borders; first from Poland to Czechoslovakia and then to Hungary. There was a joyous reunion between Breindele[6] and her family. Breindele's first-hand knowledge and experiences with the atrocities the German Nazis committed saved the whole family. She warned her parents of the danger and persuaded them to flee the ghetto in Dej; her parents heeded her advice. All the Jews from Dés were transported to Auschwitz, but he and his family escaped from the Dejer ghetto and they hid in the woods for several months. The Rabbi, his wife, and nine children survived.

---

4. Malka Friedlander and Rabbi Yosef Paneth were cousins, but the two never met.

5. A book about the rescue was written by Devorah Gliksman, under the title *A Sun and a Shield*.

6. Breindele immigrated to the USA and lived in Chicago. She was married to the Weitzen Rabbi. Their children are rabbis.

CHAPTER FORTY-FIVE

Mendi's Injury

As was mentioned earlier, my brother Mendi was also in Budapest and worked as a delivery boy for a retail store. One day while he was making a delivery, a taxi hit his tricycle and injured his leg. He was taken to a hospital, given first aid, and sent home. The doctor told him, "Stay in bed and don't walk on that leg; it will heal by itself within a few days."

He did as the doctor told him, but it didn't heal. Just the opposite; it got worse and the wound became infected and swollen. Moishe and I decided that we couldn't keep this hidden from our parents any longer. But our parents had no telephone; no one in Naprad had a telephone except the notary. Moishe and I placed a call to the notary office in Naprad.[1] Moishe was very familiar with that office, since he worked there for a long time, but he didn't want to make the call himself, as he was worried the authorities will find out where he is residing. But Moishe told me which notary to talk to. I called and spoke to the notary; I asked him to contact my parents and to have them come to the notary office at a designated time. When I spoke to my parents, I informed them about Mendi's accident and his condition. My parents decided that Mendi should travel to Kolozsvar, where the family was familiar with all the doctors. It was also decided that all of us should go to Kolozsvar where our mother will meet us. Moishe and I asked our employers for a few weeks leave of absence, which were granted. I left most of my belongings in my rented room and I told them that I would be back in

---

1. There was only one telephone in all of Naprad, at the notary office.

a few weeks. The three of us, Moishe, Mendi, and I, traveled by train. Mendi was limping, but we managed to help him along.

When we arrived in Kolozsvar our mother was already waiting for us. She had already arranged for an appointment with the well-known surgeon Dr. Matyas. After Matyas examined Mendi, he advised my mother that Mendi needed surgery immediately. It was his opinion that the infection was so severe that it was beyond treatment with medication. Matyas was known as the best surgeon in Kolozsvar. People came to him from many cities, even from Budapest.

My mother was consulting with her family in Kolozsvar and with my father in Naprad; they were debating whether to get a second opinion. Everyone advised my mother not to wait, but to listen to Matyas. The consensus in the family was that Matyas does not recommend surgery unless it is absolutely necessary; he does not need patients, as there is a waiting list to get an appointment. The next day Mendi was operated on, and thank G-d, the operation was successful. Moishe and I stayed in Kolozsvar with our mother while Mendi was recuperating in the hospital. We spent every day from morning till evening in the hospital waiting room. Mendi was recuperating and beginning to feel better. After two weeks in the hospital he was sent home. Mendi was discharged from the hospital with his foot bandaged and was instructed to visit the hospital daily for the next two weeks. At the end of four weeks, Mendi and our mother returned to Naprad and Moishe and I returned to Budapest.

It was late in the evening when Moishe and I arrived in Budapest; Moishe went to his apartment and I went home to my place. I put my key into the lock, but it didn't fit. I checked my pockets to find another key, but I had no other key. I rang the bell. The landlady came to the door, looked through the glass and when she recognized me, she said to me, "Just a minute, I'll be back right away."

When she returned, she opened the door, and handed me a suitcase with my belongings.

I asked, "What is this?"

"Your room is already rented to someone else."

"But my rent is all paid to the end of the next month?"

"Sorry, take that up with Mr. Berger."

It was late in the night, I was tired from the long trip, and I had no place where to sleep. I arrived with a heavy suitcase, I was looking forward to unload, but instead, I now had to carry two heavy suitcases. I hesitated to call my brother Moishe, because he did not have his own phone. I would have had to call his landlady and perhaps wake her up. Moishe had told me his landlady is very critical and fussy, and I did not want to cause him problems. Instead, I called the Kleins and told Mrs. Klein what happened. She told me to come over. She put bedding on the living room couch where I slept the night. The next day I returned to my former apartment, where my friend the journalist lived. There was a vacancy and I moved in.

Mrs. Klein was a very upright and strong personality; she could not tolerate an injustice. That Friday evening, Berger came to the Kleins for dinner. She waited in silence during the entire meal, but later on after the meal was served she let him have it.

"How could you do such a thing to Mati? I remember here at this table that you discussed with him to find an apartment and he is the one who found the apartment and you benefited from his running around to find it. His rent was paid for a whole month."

He made excuses, but Mrs. Klein didn't accept them.

CHAPTER FORTY-SIX

Germany Invades Hungary in 1944

As I MENTIONED EARLIER, when the Hungarians marched into Transylvania in 1940, the Jewish suffering began and it became worse year by year. But in 1944 life became intolerable. Prior to 1944 there were rumors for several months that the Germans were unhappy with the policies of the Hungarian government. They wanted the Hungarians to be more active in the war effort and they wanted more anti-Jewish laws enacted. There were even rumors that Germany would invade Hungary. Then in the spring of 1944, it was no longer rumors; the German army actually marched into Hungary with full force. There was no resistance.

Hungary's Jewish Population was the first victim; within days after the occupation, the Germans issued many anti-Jewish edicts. They compelled the Jews to wear yellow stars on their chests. Anyone caught without wearing the star was subject to immediate arrest. As if they had nothing else to do, the Germans kept the Hungarian authorities busy with passing new anti-Semitic laws. Hardly a day passed by without inventing new anti-Jewish laws. Members of the Hungarian Nyilas[1] party were roaming the streets, looking for Jews to be beaten up. The mandatory yellow stars made it easy for them to spot Jews from a distance. They took their prey to the Nyilas party headquarters, where they were severely beaten; some were even thrown into the Danube River. Moishe and I met daily to assess the situation and to decide what to do. After a few days we came to the conclusion that at this time of

---

1. The Nyilas party was the Hungarian equivalent to the Nazi party; in some instances they were even cruder and harsher.

great danger it would be prudent for the whole family to be together. Mendi was already at home in Naprad; after his leg surgery he went home to Naprad and didn't return to Budapest. Our sister Lulu was at home, she never left Naprad. We decided to leave Budapest and go home. But Moishe could not return to Naprad; he could not take a chance to return to Naprad, as the police might arrest him for evading the draft of the Jewish Work Brigade. Instead he decided to continue to Dés. Moishe and I took the train from Budapest to Zsibo, where I got off, and Moishe continued on the train to Dés. We wore the yellow stars, as the law required us to do. There were several other Jewish men and women on the train who wore the yellow stars. At the Debrecen railroad station, new passengers came aboard. Moishe was observing the new passengers as they were boarding the train. All of a sudden he turned white. He said to me, "Can you believe it? Look who is boarding the train."

One of the passengers boarding the train was Mrs. Feher, the wife of the assistant notary from Naprad. She knew us very well, especially Moishe, because her husband and Moishe worked closely in the village administration office. The Fehers always pretended to be good friends of Moishe. After thinking for a few moments, Moishe said to me, "This might be trouble! I think we should pretend not to see her. If I acknowledge her and greet her, then she might feel compelled to tell the authorities that she saw me."

We turned our heads towards the window and at times we hid our faces in a newspaper pretending to read. I asked Moishe, "Do you think she will denounce you to the gendarmerie?"

"I hope not, but I wouldn't put it past her; she is a very two faced person. Maybe she didn't see us."

"How could she miss us? Everybody is staring at us. The yellow stars on our chests scream out loud – it is an exclamation mark."

"I am encouraged by the fact that she is not coming over to us. Perhaps she pretends not to see us for the same reason. Maybe she has the decency to pretend not to see us, in order not to be obligated to report us to the gendarmes."

"Yes, she pretends not to see us. She doesn't want to denounce you."

"As long as she doesn't call the gendarme to denounce me while I am still on the train, that alone is already a relief. Once I am in Dés it will be too late for her to denounce me."

We rode together in the train without any incident until we arrived to Zsibo, where I got off and so did Mrs. Feher. She still pretended not to see me and I played along. Moishe continued on the train to Dés. I got a ride to Naprad from a neighbor, and I was happy to be home. My mother, father, and sister were happy to see me, but I could detect the sadness in their faces. They didn't say much about the situation, but they looked scared and worried. The entire Jewish population of Naprad was scared and worried. There were all sorts of rumors of what was to happen to the Jewish people of Hungary, and none of them were good.

Two days after my arrival, I received a summons from the gendarmerie ordering me to appear at their offices the next morning. The gendarmerie was in Udvarhely, eight kilometers away from Naprad. The next morning I walked the eight kilometers to appear before the gendarmerie. When I arrived, I was taken into the office of the chief and I was made to stand for the interrogation.

"You haven't been in Naprad for a long time. Where did you come from?"

"I came from Budapest."

"Did you travel alone from Budapest?"

"No."

"Who was with you?"

"My brother Moishe was with me."

"Did he also come home to Naprad?"

"No, he traveled on to Kolozsvar."

"Why didn't he come home with you? Is he running from something?"

"There is nothing to do in Naprad, he needs a job."

"Do you have his address?"

"No, not yet. He has not written yet."

"You are lying. You know where he is."

I didn't answer.

"You are not answering, because you know where he is and you don't want to tell me."

"I told you, I don't know his address."

"You are lying."

I didn't answer. I was seventeen years old at that time.

"Why don't you answer?"

"I answered, but you don't believe me."

"You are right, I don't believe you. Show me your hand!"

I raised my hand to show it to the sergeant.

"Not like that, show me an open palm!"

I did what I was told to do. The sergeant had a ruler in his hand. He beat my open palm several times.

"Now, this is just a taste of what you will get if you don't tell me what I want to know. Go home and report back to me tomorrow morning at the same time. Be sure to bring me your brother's address."

The sergeant who interrogated me was also the chief of the gendarmerie. He was on friendly terms with the Judovits family for many years. He received gratuities from my father on many occasions. He also knew the children by name, but the climate has changed. I went home to my anxious parents and told them everything, except the beating. They were helpless to do anything. My father went over to Dr. Jacab, the village doctor, who had some influence with the sergeant. He was the only doctor for all the villages in this area. He was also the doctor for the gendarmerie. The doctor promised my father to talk to the sergeant. The next day early in the morning I walked again the eight kilometers to the gendarmerie and presented myself to the clerk at the desk. The clerk asked me, "What is your business here?"

I answered, "I am here to see the chief."

"He is away on business. Why do you want to see him?"

"I was here yesterday and he ordered me to come again today to see him."

"Well, you can't see him. He is not here."

"Shall I come tomorrow to see him?"

"No, he won't be here tomorrow either."

I went home and didn't report again. After that the gendarmerie did not bother me anymore.

A few days later I was walking on the street of Naprad where I encountered Mrs. Feher. I greeted her with a good day greeting and she nodded her head with a smile and walked on.

But then she turned around and asked.

"How was your trip home from Budapest?"

I replied with a thank you. "It was a very pleasant trip."

"How is your brother Moishe? Did he also come home to Naprad?"

"No, he continued the trip to Kolozsvar."

She repeated questioningly, "Kolozsvar? Do you have relatives in Kolozsvar?"

"No, but he wants to find a job and he figured he would have a better chance in Kolozsvar than here in Naprad."

"He could have gotten a job at the notary."

"I really have to go Mrs. Feher; my mother is waiting for me. Good day Mrs. Feher."

If there was any doubt in my mind whether Mrs. Feher reported us to the gendarmerie, it all vanished after this encounter with her.

After the war when I was liberated from the concentration camp, I returned to Zsibo. I heard rumors that she was worried that I would denounce her to the authorities. She sent intermediaries to me, asking me for a meeting. But I am getting ahead of myself.

CHAPTER FORTY-SEVEN

My Father's Suffering from the Cruelty and Greed of Cserefalvi and the Police Chief

THERE WERE TWO SISTERS IN NAPRAD by the names of Ilona and Edith Döri; they were descendants of Hungarian nobility. As befitting such a family, they lived in a tremendous mansion in the village, surrounded by acres of woodland. Edith Döri was married to a Hungarian military officer by the name of Farkas Arpad Cserefalvi. The two sisters' extensive estate was all around the fringes of the village, and one particular property of theirs was next to my father's estate. Being married to one of the sisters made Cserefalvi co-owner of the estates. Cserefalvi was never friendly towards Jews and he often used derogatory remarks and slurs against Jews.

After the Germans marched into Hungary, he became even more vocal with his anti-Semitic remarks. Through his connections with the new anti-Semitic government officials in Budapest, he found out that the Hungarian Jews would be deported to concentration camps. In his twisted mind he came up with a scheme to use this revelation to his advantage. He figured he could add more properties to his estate without risking any investment or effort. He sent a messenger to my father, asking my father to come over to his residence. When my father showed up to see him at his mansion, Cserefalvi told my father: "It has been revealed to me by government officials in Budapest that all Hungarian Jews will be deported, including the Jews from our village Naprad, to an unknown location. There is nothing I can do to stop the deportation and there isn't much time left to prepare for it. However, I can help you save your property. It is my understanding that the government will expropriate all properties. I am proposing to you to sign an agreement with me, whereby you will transfer all your properties to me. Then, after you return from your exile you can have your properties back."

My father answered him that his immediate concern would be to protect his family and that he is not worried about his property. Cserefalvi tried to convince my father that it would be a good idea to transfer his property. They argued, and Cserefalvi waved a prepared document, which he wanted my father to sign. My father refused. When my father left, Cserefalvi yelled after him. "Judovits! You will be sorry."

My father went home and told my mother the terrible news.

My parents discussed the situation and then my father spoke to Shmelke, his younger brother, and told him about the deportation news. Together they consulted with our cousins Shimshi, Hugo, and Erno Judovits.[1] They informed the rest of the community about the terrible news. Doom and gloom descended over the village, but nobody had any bright ideas what to do. There was some talk about hiding in the woods, but nobody knew how to go about it; nobody was prepared for it.

Early the next morning there was a knock at the door of our house. When my father opened the door he found a gendarme handing him a summons, which ordered him to come to the gendarmerie immediately. My father went with the gendarme to their headquarters in Udvarhely, a village eight kilometers from Naprad. Upon arriving to the gendarmerie, he was ushered in to the office of the chief, where Cserefalvi was already waiting. He and the chief were seated at a table, drinking alcoholic beverages from two tall glasses; a half-full bottle was nearby on the table. When my father saw Cserefalvi having drinks with the chief, he knew immediately it did not bode well for him. The chief asked my father to sit down and then brought up the subject of Cserefalvi's proposal.

My father tried to explain to the chief that this is a civil matter and it has nothing to do with the gendarmerie. The chief suggested that they should ride out to the fields to inspect the property. My father tried in vain to talk him out of it and suggested that he and the chief inspect the property at some future date without Cserefalvi, but the chief would not listen.

The chief got up and asked them to follow him. Waiting outside was a fancy carriage with two white horses, which belonged to Cserefalvi. The three of them mounted the carriage; Cserefalvi was the driver, my father

---

1. Shimshi did not survive the Holocaust, but Hugo and Erno survived, and they live in the USA.

and the chief sat in the back. They drove out of the village towards the Dumbrenitza.[2] During the ride to the fields, Cserefalvi kept on passing the bottle of whiskey to the chief. Both of them drank all the way until they reached the Dumbrenitza. They dismounted and Cserefalvi led the way into the fields. He was pointing out the boundaries of the two properties and claiming that his properties would be badly affected by being next to my father's abandoned properties due to my father's absence.

My father pointed out the opposite, arguing that fallow land is beneficial. He told Cserefalvi point blank that he is not fooled by his schemes to grab his property. Cserefalvi became furious and struck my father with the whip in his hand. He yelled at my father ordering him to sign the document. The chief of the gendarmerie also yelled at my father.

My father refused to sign.

The chief took off his riffle from his shoulder and beat my father with the butt of the rifle. My father fell to the ground. While he was still on the ground Cserefalvi lashed him with his whip, ordering him to get up and sign the document. My father could not get up; he was in pain all over his body. His rib cage felt like broken, his leg bones were aching. As he tried to get up he fell back to the ground and they whipped him and beat him more, again and again.

They told him they would keep on beating him until he got up.

My father, through sheer will power, managed to put all his strength into his legs and got up. They shouted at him, "Go home, run for your life!"

Painfully he walked slowly. They mounted the carriage and drove behind him. When they caught up with him, Cserefalvi whipped him and shouted, "Run in front of the carriage!"

My father moved away to the side of the road, but Cserefalvi followed him and whipped him again and again. "You have to run in front of the horses!"

At this point my father did not pay any attention anymore, he just ran on the side of the road. They kept on whipping him. Finally the chief picked up his rifle and hit my father real hard. He fell to the ground and they left him there. A few hours later a Romanian villager found him on the side of the road unconscious and bleeding; he rec-

---

2. Dumbrenitza was the name of my father's estate, located outside the village of Naprad.

ognized my father and put him in his wagon. When he brought him home to my mother he told us, "I found him unconscious on the side of the road."

My mother was beside herself; she was wringing her hands and crying. She thanked the villager and told him that she was very grateful.

My mother sent me to call Dr. Ferenc Jacab, the physician. I ran over to his office. I tried to tell the Doctor what happened, but I was not coherent, I could hardly talk; I was distraught and out of breath. The doctor came running, and I was running alongside him. He gave me an extra bag of medical supplies to carry. When we arrived at our house, he looked at my father who was still half unconscious. He examined him thoroughly and then he said to my mother, "Without an x-ray machine it is hard to tell, but I think he has several cracked ribs and some bone fractures. Under different circumstances, I would have recommended taking him to Kolozsvar, but due to the German presence in Kolozsvar and the whole Jewish situation in the country, that is not a good option. I will try to do the best I can here in Naprad."

He administered some injections and stayed with the family for a while. Before he left he told the family, "I'll be back the first thing in the morning, but if his condition gets worse then come to get me, even in the middle of the night."

Everyone in the family felt so helpless. We all walked in and out of the house in silence and in desperation. The backbone of the family was down; there was no one to give us advice or support, no one knew what to do. Heretofore, whenever there was a problem, my father always had an alternative plan ready; he was always prepared. But the rock of the family was half unconscious, just lying on his bed, groaning from his painful agony. All of us were very nervous, we could not sit still; we walked in and out of the room. The next day, in the presence of the doctor, my father told us every detail of the story.[3]

Before he was beaten up, my father had in mind to speak to Dragos[4]

---

3. I have sent a copy of this story to my cousin Hugo Judovits for verification as to its accuracy. Hugo was in Naprad at that time; he confirmed what I have written, and added that his brother Shimshi tried to intervene. He claims that Cserefalvi had a mental problem. After Shimshi found out about the beatings, he went over to speak to Cserefalvi's wife, but what he accomplished I don't know. Hugo does not remember the details.

4. Dragos was an educated Romanian gentleman. He was a close friend of my father and sometimes a business partner.

the following morning about the deportation order. My father had a plan in mind; to hide out in the Dumbrenitza farm. But after the beating he was in no condition to do anything, he could barely walk. It wouldn't have mattered anyhow, because everything happened so fast, there wouldn't have been enough time to implement any kind of a plan.

CHAPTER FORTY-EIGHT

The Hungarian Government Places All Jews into Ghettos

THE NEXT DAY AN ORDER CAME from the Hungarian capital of Budapest to the gendarmerie; that order affected all the Jews in the area. The order said, "Jews are forbidden to leave their place of residence until further notice."

There were all sorts of rumors going around. One of them was that informers are watching the Jewish homes, another was that the Jews would be taken to Zilah to be put into a ghetto and then would be deported. Germany and Poland were mentioned as places of deportation. Confusion reigned and no one knew for certain what was coming, not even those Jews who were supposed to be on friendly terms with the authorities. They tried to find out what was planned for them, but without success. One thing everyone knew, that something very terrible is being hatched. The non-Jewish villagers were also asking questions; they were concerned about their own welfare. They wanted to know what would happen to them if the Jewish doctor would be deported, what would happen to their children if they became ill. There was only one doctor in Naprad and the same doctor took care of the sick in the next three villages. They wanted to know what would happen to the general store and the pub. The general store and the pub were owned by the Judovits brothers, my cousins. The non-Jewish villagers wanted to know where they would buy groceries, hardware, and farming equipment and supplies. There was talk that the government would confiscate the store and run it. But there was no one in Naprad who knew how to run a store.

Notices came the next day to all the Jews to be ready to leave the village within three days. They were to pack only essential food, clothing, and bedding; everything else was to be left behind. The notices also directed all Jews to turn over their jewelry, gold, silver, and valuables to the authorities. On the third day, several horse-drawn wagons accompanied by many gendarmes entered the village and made stops at all the individual Jewish homes. They ordered the families to climb into the wagons, squeezing in as many as they could into each wagon. Only a few personal possessions, bedding, and some bags of food were permitted to be carried on the wagon. When the wagons were loaded, they took off with the Jewish captives. They paraded the wagons through the streets of Naprad with their captives. The villagers of Naprad were lined up on the sides of the streets watching the spectacle. Some villagers were visibly moved to tears, others had a wide grin on their faces. Some brave villagers dared to call out, "May G-d be with you." But others called out anti-Semitic clichés.

My mother was sobbing uncontrollably, holding on to my sister Lulu in embrace. My father, still in great pain from the beatings he received from Cserefalvi and the chief of the Gendarme a few days earlier, was not able to climb onto the wagon; he had to be assisted. He sat in the wagon silently, hiding his head in his hands. He probably didn't want to see his enemies and tormentors gloat. Mendi and I sat next to each other, scared, confused, and bewildered. We were talking silently to each other, making remarks about the villagers, whom we recognized in the crowd. I saw Remus, the boy next door who walked with me many times to the railroad station to help me carry the cheese. He was waving and yelling something, which I could not hear. Mendi was in pain, still limping a little on his left foot; his wounds from the leg surgery had not healed completely.

My sister Lulu, who was only fourteen years old, was holding on to our mother, looking sad, but she was not crying. The wagons stopped at another Jewish home and added another couple and their belongings onto the wagon. The wagon was loaded to capacity and there was no legroom. Nobody seemed to be concerned about the discomfort and no one complained. The caravan of wagons drove slowly to Zilah, a distance of about 50 to 60 kilometers, passing several villages on the way. The residents were lined up in each village on the sides of the road to watch the exile.

Could it be that Psalm number 44 had us in mind when it was crying out? "We have become an object of scorn and derision; we are regarded as sheep to be led to the slaughterhouse, to be killed, destroyed, beaten, and humiliated."

The caravan took several hours to reach its destination. The place we were brought to was an old brick factory on the outskirts of Zilah[1] that they designated as a ghetto. Here they gathered all the Jews from the entire county. I would estimate that they brought about five to ten thousand Jews to this ghetto. They converted the brick factory grounds into a camp, where hundreds of tents were already set up in rows. The wagons dropped us off at the entrance to the ghetto, and from there we had to carry our belongings to the assigned tent. My father was in no condition to carry any bundles and neither was my brother Mendi. A young yeshiva bocher came over and offered to help us. With his help, my sister and I carried the bundles to the tent. We were allowed to bring with us some pots and pans, other dishes, some bedding, and some clothes. We also brought with us some essential food items, like flour, potatoes, and oil. Each tent was assigned to several families.

The greatest burden fell on my mother; in addition to witnessing the fate that had befallen her family, she had to take care of all of us. She took out some food from one of the bundles and fed us. We were all starving, but no one said a word. Each one of us was absorbed in our own thoughts and despair. In the days that followed, my mother managed to cook and prepare whatever was available. Most families brought with them a little portable stove on which to cook; we didn't bring one, but our neighbors shared the stove with us. Food was scarce, whatever one brought from home had to last for the duration of our stay in this ghetto. Toilet facilities were nonexistent; however there was an open pit a few feet behind the tents, which was used by men and women as a toilet. Whenever my mother or Lulu needed to use the pit, Mendi and I went with them; we would stand there with our backs turned, holding a blanket to give them some privacy.

New decrees and restrictions were issued daily; they prohibited putting on a Tallis and Tefillin; anyone caught putting on a Tallis and Tefillin was hanged upside-down until he was unconscious. There were several hangings daily.

I don't know how my mother did it, but she managed to feed us from the little food we had. She cooked potatoes and fried pancakes daily under intolerable conditions.

---

1. Zilah was the seat of the county government.

The guards watching us were drawn from the Hungarian gendarmerie, but a young German soldier, who couldn't have been more than 20–22 years old, was seen strutting around the ghetto. This twenty-year-old seemed to be in charge of the ghetto and the whole operation. The gendarmerie set up an interrogation office near the entrance to the camp. From this office they summoned the head of each household to come in for interrogation. Every day they called in a different group of people for questioning and torture. They wanted the Jewish loot; to this end, they questioned the people where they hid their Jewelry and other valuables. Everyone received a beating. The people they interrogated were the respected elders of many communities, who were the rabbis and the businessmen. Some came out with bloody faces and broken legs, so badly beaten that they were unable to walk on their broken legs; they had to be assisted back to their tent.

My father, who had already received a severe beating from Cserefalvi and the chief of the gendarmes, was also called in for interrogation. His bruises were still raw and bleeding, but they showed no mercy; they beat him again and questioned him about the valuables he might have hidden. We were waiting for him anxiously outside the interrogation room. When he came out, we were aghast at the sight of his condition. He told us what happened, but minimized his pain and suffering; he probably wanted to spare us our suffering on account of him. He endured his suffering with courage and dignity. After this second beating he did not talk very much, he must have given up on life; he just kept to himself. Very often my thoughts flash back and think of his condition in those last days of his life; he must have been in unimaginable pain and agony.

With every day that passed, conditions became worse. There were no sanitary facilities, and no place for washing the laundry. The little food the people brought with them was almost completely gone. Even water was hard to come by; people were standing in line for an hour to fill up the buckets at the well. It was the end of springtime and there were some very hot and humid days. Without proper sanitary conditions the place began to reek from foul odors. Some days when it rained the tent floor became muddy and we had to sit with our feet in the mud. Luckily it didn't rain constantly, otherwise there would have been real floods. For four weeks we suffered in the Zilah ghetto the indignities and physical torture from the Hungarian police.

CHAPTER FORTY-NINE

The Train Ride to Auschwitz

Around the first of June 1944, we received an order from the authorities in charge to get ready to be transported to another unnamed place. The railroad tracks, which were formerly used to ship out the bricks from the brick factory, were now converted to roll in cattle wagons for our transportation. Every few hours they took a group of our people to be loaded onto the cattle wagons; this went on for two days in a row. My family was taken on the second day. We were told that we are permitted to take with us only the most personal items. The gendarmerie supervised the loading, but the German soldier was strutting up and down alongside the railroad cars, keeping an eye on the whole affair.

They loaded each car to capacity, with men, women, and children all together. There were no seats in the wagons. People wanted to know where they are being taken; they asked the gendarmes, but they didn't get an answer. They ordered the people to board the trains, but in the tumult family members became separated; there was a lot of crying and screaming. Families were still separated at boarding time; they were pleading with the guards to let them find their family. The gendarmerie lined up about eighty people alongside each railroad car. There were no stairs to walk up to the wagons; older people could not climb up. Some crates were placed at the door entrance and the young ones helped the older people. There was no resistance; everyone seemed to be resigned to his or her fate. The gendarme chose a captain for each wagon from the passengers; he just pointed at random to one of the group with a command, "You will be the captain of the car for this trip."

Two of the young guys I met in the ghetto approached me and suggested to escape. I told them without hesitation, "No."

They had warned us beforehand that if anyone escaped, the whole family would be shot. It could have been a scare tactic, but I had to take it seriously. Anyhow it didn't enter my mind to leave my family and run. Had I wanted to escape on my own I could have stayed in Budapest and tried to hide there, but I came home in order to be together with my family. I said to the guys, "Wherever they take us, I want to be there together with my family."

"Don't be a fool. There is nothing you can do for your family. You can't save them, but you might be able to save yourself. Join me and together we can escape and hide out until the danger is over."

"I would love to join you, but I can't. I wish you good luck."

I heard rumors that they escaped, but I don't know what happened to them.

The train ride was an awful experience. We were locked up in the wagon for three days. There were no sanitary facilities; they provided us with a bucket to be used as a toilet, which was placed in the middle of the wagon. Whenever a member of the family needed to use the toilet, the family formed a human wall to provide a little privacy. For air there was only one opening in the wagon, about 40 inches wide and 15 inches high, with barbed wire strung over it. This was in the month of June; the air was stuffy or practically nonexistent. Very little air also came in through the two-inch crack in the door. Some lucky young girls managed to grab the floor space next to the door crack. Another two buckets were provided for drinking water, which was used up very quickly.

Not only were there no seats in the wagon, but even sitting space on the floor was at a premium. We had to sit down on the floor in shifts. Each family yielded seating space on the floor, one to the other.

The train ride took three days; it was traveling at a low speed, stopping frequently and standing still for long periods. At one of the stops the doors were opened under heavy guard and two persons were ordered to empty the toilet bucket and refill the water buckets. This was repeated two more times during the entire journey.

CHAPTER FIFTY

Arrival in Auschwitz

O<small>N THE THIRD DAY OF OUR TORTURED JOURNEY,</small> we arrived at a remote place called Auschwitz. We didn't know the name of this location, we had never heard of a place called Auschwitz, and we didn't even know what country we were in. But upon disembarking, the orderlies that were waiting at this railroad station told us that we are in Poland and that the name of the town is Auschwitz. These orderlies were Jewish inmates in Auschwitz who were deported here from other Polish towns and already imprisoned in the camp for several years; the Germans called them capos. The scene in Auschwitz during the disembarkation was a nightmare, impossible to describe and even harder to believe. I never forgot it. As the people were getting off the train they were ordered to form a line and to march forward. Many didn't hear the orders or they didn't care to listen; some were crying, some were huddled together, whispering instructions to each other, and many of them were praying. One pious person had his Tefillin on. The orderlies were asking the people to quiet down to avoid beatings from the soldiers. There was a lot of yelling and screaming. The younger children were frightened and crying, while the older children tried to keep the younger ones occupied. Some of the people from our train were wandering around with empty looks in their faces. My father didn't say anything, he just held on to my brother Mendi and me. My mother was crying incessantly and holding on to Lulu's hand. It was like one large funeral.

The Jewish capos told us that if we were able to work we had a chance to be sent to work camps. These capos told the young mothers of small children not to hold their children in their arms if they wanted to survive. Many mothers didn't care; they held on to their crying children defiantly.

When all the people were out of the wagons, they made us march for a long distance until we arrived to a designated place. We were all standing there in a long line, and at the head of the line was a German officer who made selections. At this point they separated the men from the women. But we didn't know it; it came without warning. No one told us in advance that we would be separated, and I am sure the rest of my family wasn't aware that we would be. This was the last time I saw my mother and sister; there was no chance to give a hug, a kiss, or to say goodbye. The soldiers with guns just separated us and ordered the two groups to march their separate ways. Then, there was a second selection separating the able-bodied men from the older people, from the children, and from the disabled. At this point my brother Mendi and I were separated from our father. Again we had no chance to say goodbye. We were holding on to our father in order not to be separated, but someone yanked me away and made me march in a different direction. The same happened to my brother Mendi. At that time I didn't know who was making the selection, but the Jewish helpers told us later that the German officer was Dr. Mengele.

They led us to an open area in front of a building where they made us remove all our clothing. Several barbers were in the courtyard ready to shave us. We got undressed in the open court and then we stood in line to be shaved. They removed all our hair from top to bottom. All the barbers were inmates, most of them Jews from Poland. Another group of inmates poured some smelly disinfectant on our bodies. When they were finished with us, we were taken inside the building to be showered. Mendi and I kept close to each other. Sometimes during the day they made an announcement to line up for food. The food was served from a kibble,[1] and consisted of a soup. They didn't give us plates or receptacles in which to receive our soup, but directed us to a large pile of discarded dishes; it looked like a heap of garbage. Mendi and I decided that we were not hungry.

Mendi and I were kept in Auschwitz for three days, and during the entire three days Mendi and I ate only the piece of bread they handed us and nothing else. We didn't even stand in line to get the soup. Once

---

1. A metal container

we stood in line for food, but we decided not to eat it; we gave the soup to anyone who wanted it.

On the third day Mendi and I were shipped out from Auschwitz to an unknown destination. We were loaded into cattle wagons and shipped to a place called Wustegiersdorf; it was in Ober-Silesia. Outside of the town Wustegiersdorf was a newly constructed camp, surrounded by barbed wires. They led us into the enclosed camp where they lined us up on the campgrounds for appel. The commander, who was an elderly German officer, gave us a speech and told us the dos and the don'ts. The housing consisted of prefabricated, one-room units, lined up in rows on an open field. The inside furnishings consisted of double-deck bunkbeds. Mendi and I managed to get a joined upper and lower bunkbed. Our uncle Shmelke[2] Judovits happened to be in the same camp, but not in the same barrack. We didn't even know that he was in the same camp until a few days after we arrived, when we ran into him during the evening appel. Mati Goldstein,[3] our cousin from Zsibo, was also in the same camp. I didn't know him too well, but we got to know each other in the camp. He was a doctor and a very decent and wonderful human being; he saved many people in the camp. A man by the name of Steinmetz was appointed Lager Eltester.[4] He had several deputies, who were called capos. In many other camps the Lager Eltesters were notoriously mean characters, but Steinmetz was a fair and decent guy; he tried his best under difficult circumstances. He came from Bistritza, a small town not far from Dej, from a Chasidic family. He spoke German fluently.

At this camp I worked for a German industrial company, and later on I worked for several other companies; they were the industrial companies of Germany. One company name in particular stuck in my mind, it was called "Chemna."

Every morning before the crack of dawn, they marched us out under guard to the worksite, and in the evening they marched us back to the camp. They fed us three times a day. In the morning before going to work they gave us a slice of coarse bread with black ersatz coffee.[5] Lunchtime they gave us a soup made of vegetables, but it was all wa-

---

2. Shmelke was my father's younger brother.

3. Mati Goldstein was a medical doctor; he became the doctor of the camp.

4. Lager Eltester was the equivalent to the head of the camp. The Germans wanted a Jewish guy to deal with the internal affairs of the camp.

5. Ersatz coffee was a poor coffee substitute.

tery. In the evening we were given a heavier soup, which was made of potatoes, other vegetables, and some meat. We were always hungry, because we never had a satisfying meal. They also provided us with a few cigarettes per week. As soon as the cigarettes were introduced they became the currency of the camp. An exchange rate was established; nobody planned for it, it just happened naturally. The commodities were priced according to the scarcity of the item. There were smokers who offered their bread rations for cigarettes. Our uncle Shmelke was a heavy smoker. Mendi and I gave him some of our cigarettes, but it still wasn't enough for him; he sold some of his food for cigarettes.

The first Friday evening in the camp Mendi and I became very depressed. We sat down on the floor in front of our barrack and we spread out a used newspaper to serve as a tablecloth. We ate our Shabbat meal together and we talked about our parents and family. After that we decided to eat our meals together in a similar manner whenever we could. We managed to pick up old newspapers that were on the floor of the street when they marched us to or from work; we could do that only when the guards weren't watching. Though the newspapers were two weeks old and written for Germans, full of propaganda, it didn't matter. We could still read between the lines and got an inkling of how the war was progressing.

There was one guy in the camp who managed to smuggle in a pair of Tefillin. He confided his secret to a few guys whom he trusted, and they in turn told a few others. Consequently, every morning there was a long line of people in front of his barrack wanting to put on the Tefillin. They had to do it secretly and before the wake-up alarm was sounded, because if the Germans would have found out, there would have been severe punishment. Those who stood in line were given thirty seconds to recite the blessing, put on the Tefillin, remove them, and hand them over to the next person. Many had to be turned away every day because the wake up siren sounded.

During the time I was in this camp, two of our fellow prisoners escaped. Regretfully, their freedom didn't last very long; one of them was caught. The Germans made us suffer for it; they had the entire camp stand on appel for hours. A hanging gallow was prepared and we were made to watch the hanging. Poor Steinmetz, the Lager Eltester, was ordered by the commandant to hang the caught prisoner. At first he excused himself, claiming he does not know how it is done. The commandant ordered a soldier to put the rope around the prisoner's neck and then he ordered Steinmetz to kick the chair out from under him; Steinmetz had no choice.

Had I kept a diary, this book would have been several times its size, because the stories I mention here are only a selected few, which for some reason stuck in my mind and which I still remember. But even if I had kept a diary, it would have been confiscated and I would have been severely punished for it. Every day was a struggle for survival; life-threatening experiences were the norm of every day.

CHAPTER FIFTY-ONE

Being Blinded in the Labor Camp

✡ ♩, 2

MENDI AND I WERE WORKING on a construction site about two miles from our camp. We were digging holes in the ground for concrete pillars. One day while I was opening a cement bag, a strong wind blew the contents of the bag into my eyes. I became totally blinded. I thought my life was over; I was afraid that they would shoot me on the spot. My coworkers sat me down on a rock and I could hear a great commotion on the construction site. I could not see with my eyes, however I could hear the German guard speaking German and discussing with another guard what to do with me. It seemed to me that he decided not to do anything now, but to leave matters alone until I returned to the camp. He made me sit there on the rock, with the cement still in my eyes, until it was time to go back to camp. This was about eleven in the morning and we usually stopped working at 6pm, at which time we returned to the camp. My eyes were hurting and no one knew what to do. Someone suggested that I should wash my eyes with water, but others said that the water will cause the cement to harden and I would be blinded permanently. I decided to do nothing. Besides, the German guard was hollering at the prisoners in his German language, "Weiter machen."[1]

While I was sitting there on the rock, my whole life flashed through my mind. I was thinking about my parents, whom I did not see since our separation in Auschwitz. I was thinking about my age. I was eighteen, and what did I accomplish in the short years that I lived? Why was I sent to this world? Why was I born?

---

1. "Weiter machen" means, "continue to do" or "back to work."

My brother Mendi was working in the same unit, but not on the same site; he was working some distance away. We usually marched back together side by side. When his unit finished work he came over to me so we could fall in line together, but when he saw me sitting on the rock he said to me, "Why aren't you ready?"

When I heard his voice, I lifted my head, and he saw that I had my eyes closed. At first he became very upset and scared, but when I told him what happened he probably realized that he is making it worse for me. He quickly said to me, "Don't worry. I will take you back to the camp and our cousin Mati Goldstein will be able to help you."

He and another friend locked arms with me and they led me down the steep hill to the main road. Once we were down the hill it was much easier. We marched on the road until we arrived to the camp. At the camp Mendi took me immediately to our cousin. He examined me superficially.

Mendi asked him, "Will he be able to see again?"

"Let me examine him thoroughly and see how much damage was done. Open your eyes!"

I tried to open them, but they were glued together. He took some liquid solution and applied it to my eyes. It felt soothing, but I still could not open my eyes. He made me lie down and he applied more solution onto my eyes and told me, "Lie that way for a while."

After lying there for about half an hour I was able to open one of my eyes a little. A half an hour later I was able to open my other eye slightly, but not completely. He passed his hand in front of my eyes and asked, "What do you see?"

"I see your hand."

Then he tested me with his individual fingers. My first words to him were, "I can see."

Mati gave me the solution and told me to apply it hourly for a few days. He saw to it that I was taken off the work detail for a few days. After one week, Mati advised me that I should return to work, otherwise they may send me to another camp. I listened and went back to work.

CHAPTER FIFTY-TWO

Yom Kippur Service in the Labor Camp

While working in the labor camp of Wustegiersdorf, time was creeping very slowly. It seemed like we were in this place for years, but in fact we were in this camp only four months. It was September and getting closer to the High Holidays. The very observant guys and the more mature people were eager to arrange for prayer services. They spoke to Steinmetz and he was able to get permission from the German commander to have a short Kol Nidrei service. On Rosh Hashana we had no prayer services; we had to work like any other day, but while digging the ditches we did our prayers.

One of our fellow workers called out, "Let's pray! I will lead and you repeat after me. Repeat it loud, so the guy behind you will be able to repeat after you."

He started with Borchu, then he did the Shema and part of the silent Amida. The German guard came over to see what was going on.

He yelled out, "Mach Los."[1]

One of the guys, who spoke German fluently, explained to him that we are praying. When he saw that the work was not interrupted, he left us alone. The guy who was leading us had a pleasant voice; he might have been a cantor. He continued to chant "*Unesane Tokef.*" We all listened, but very few joined in; most of us did not know it by heart. Those who had a religious upbringing knew the daily prayers by heart, but few people could recite the High Holiday prayers from memory.

The Kol Nidrei service was a surprise. The day before Yom Kippur

---

1. "Mach los" is a German expression. It means, "hurry up and do what you are supposed to do."

rumors went around the camp that there will be a Kol Nidrei service in the evening, but people dismissed it as a false rumor. However the rumor was true. Steinmetz got permission from the commandant to have a one-hour service in the open field of the camp. Steinmetz, who was a Chasidic Jew, came from an area in Transylvania where many so-called folk Deutsche lived. German was one of the languages spoken in that area, and Steinmetz spoke German fluently. The commandant, who was in his mid-fifties, was interested only in running an orderly camp and Steinmetz was able to run it well. The commandant was a major in the regular wehrmacht. Like most German officers, he was very strict, but as strict as he was, his heart was not in his work. Anyhow, the rumor in the camp was that he had told Steinmetz that if it were up to him, he would let everyone go home.

A day before Erev Yom Kippur it was whispered that if we wanted to fast on Yom Kippur we should eat our meal before we came home from work, because the Kol Nidrei service would start early. The service started with a huge crowd in the open field. One of the rabbis was leading the services. Most of the people cried with tears running down their cheeks. The rabbi had a strong and pleasant voice. Mendi and I came back from work early so we were able to get a good spot; we were standing close to the rabbi and we could hear him very well. He was reciting the prayers slowly word for word, and the congregation was able to hear him and repeat after him. Since the service was to last no longer than one hour, he recited only the most important prayers. The next day we all had to go to work and there was no daytime prayer service in the camp. But in our trenches the group did chant several Yom Kippur prayers with its melodies. After this Yom Kippur prayer and chanting experience, we got the idea to chant zemirot in the trenches every Saturday.

CHAPTER FIFTY-THREE

Mendi's Leg is Injured Again

Mᴚ ʙʀᴏᴛʜᴇʀ Mᴇɴᴅɪ, who had leg surgery a few months before the deportation, was almost healed, but he was still limping a little. However, the lack of proper food and vitamins retarded his healing process, and consequently, his wounds did not mend completely. One day we were working on top of the mountain and something fell against his leg. His wound opened up and caused him so much pain that he could not even stand on his feet. The guard let him sit out the rest of the afternoon. When the workday was over, my friend and I locked arms with him and we tried to walk him down the hill. We hardly managed to walk a few steps when he said he could not go on. With the help of my friend he climbed on my back and I carried him downhill piggyback. Several other guys volunteered to help; each of us carried him for a stretch until we reached the camp. We took him to our cousin Dr. Mati Goldstein, who examined him and cleaned his wound with some antiseptic. After bandaging him, he advised Mendi not to get out of bed for a few days. He also arranged with the commandant to excuse Mendi from work detail. After a few days' rest, Mendi was assigned to work as an orderly in the guard's barracks. His wound never healed completely and he limped slightly when he walked, but he never complained. Our cousin kept an eye on him and cleaned his wound once a week. Mendi had such a wonderful disposition; when he saw me looking at his wound in a dejected mien, he made light of it and cheered me up. Instead of complaining, he gave me encouragement and started to talk about the good old days. He was always concerned about me and he brought back some extra food for me from the barracks where he was working, because there was always a lot of leftover food in the guardhouse where he worked.

In the camp, the simplest little incident became a major problem. For instance, a tear in my pants. When we arrived in the camp we all received prisoner uniforms. The outfit consisted of a striped jacket, striped trousers, and a cap. They were made of a flimsy material, without any substance to them; they looked like pajamas. On a windy day I could feel the draft going through my whole body. One day something unexpected happened. While I was at work, I got caught in something sharp and pointy, which tore my pants. Under normal circumstances I would have had a good laugh at it and I would have gone home to change my pants. The problem was that I had neither a home nor another pair of pants. Temporarily, I solved my problem by tying up the hole in my pants with a string. Back in the camp I went shopping to buy a needle. For cigarettes one was able to buy many items. After some inquiry, I found a guy who sold me a needle for two cigarettes. He also wanted to sell me the thread, for which he asked additional two cigarettes. I had no more cigarettes, but I had other ideas. Part of our bedding consisted of a blanket, which was bound at the edges with a thread, sewn in a zigzag pattern. I unraveled the thread and used the thread to sew up my pants. It was very easy to unravel the thread; I pulled on one thread at the end and the whole binding came apart. Once I got the idea for the thread, I also decided to cut off extra pieces from my blanket and used the pieces to line my pajamas. It was getting cold and I was freezing in my pajama outfit. I did the same for my brother Mendi. The blanket was too large anyhow; I didn't need such a large blanket.

The climate in Wustegiersdorf at this time of the year was very cold. Working in the trenches during the bitter cold days was almost unbearable. Before I had the idea of using the blanket pieces, we tried to shield our bodies from the cold by inserting old discarded newspapers inside our pajamas. We found old newspapers on the street when we marched to work and back to the camp. It helped a little, but we were still freezing. It was just as cold in the barracks during the night, because they were unheated barracks.

CHAPTER FIFTY-FOUR

Mendi and I are Separated

✡ ℶ, 3

SOMETIME AROUND DECEMBER OF 1944, the camp commandant announced that some prisoners would be transferred to another camp. The explanation was that in order to spare the old and the weak prisoners from working outdoors in the cold, they would be sent to work in a camp indoors. For this latest selection, the commandant ordered a general appel, and we all lined up in the open field to be selected. He inspected row after row and pulled out the prisoners he wanted removed. He told them to form a separate row on the other side of the field.

My brother Mendi was selected, but I was not. Mendi gave me a hug and went over to the other side. When it appeared that no one was watching, I snuck out from my place and ran over towards Mendi and stayed there next to him. I was standing there while the commandant continued to make his selections. All of a sudden the commandant came over to our unit to inspect us. When he saw me next to Mendi he asked, "Hey, you there, come here! What are you doing here? I didn't tell you to join them. Go back to the other side."

I was surprised that he knew my face. I did as he commanded me. He continued to make the selection; it lasted several hours. The group in which Mendi was standing grew in size; there must have been over one hundred prisoners in that group. I saw my opportunity and I ran over again. Mendi was happy to see me stand next to him. We watched the selection silently; talking was not permitted. Our unit consisted of people who were old or sick; they were either limping or bandaged. Finally the selection was finished. The commandant made a final inspection. He came over to our unit and looked at each one of us. When he saw me there he yelled at me, "You there, come here!" He slapped me in my face. "Didn't I tell you to go back to the other side?"

"Yes, but I wanted to be in the same camp with my brother."

He looked at me and seemed to be thinking and hesitating for a few seconds, then ordered me, "Go back to the other side!"

I did as he ordered me and I went back to the general assembly. From there I watched my brother being marched away. That was the last time I saw Mendi. My uncle Shmelke was also in that group. I found out later that the entire unit was taken to an extermination camp.

CHAPTER FIFTY-FIVE

Alone Without Any Family

AFTER MY BOTHER MENDI WAS TAKEN AWAY from me I found myself in this labor camp completely alone, without any family. When Mendi was still with me, we had each other and we clung to each other, but now after Mendi was gone I felt completely abandoned. I had no one. In my naiveté I believed that I would see Mendi again. One by one they tore away all close members of my family; Mendi was the last one, and now they tore him away also. As long as Mendi was with me in the camp, we didn't make any close friends with the other captives. We were friendly with many guys, but we kept to ourselves; whenever we had the time, we were with each other. Now that Mendi was gone I needed a friend. In the labor camp, it was a necessity and a matter of survival – everyone needed a friend. One needed a friend to look after him and make sure that no one would take advantage of him, and vice versa. Everyone needed someone with whom one could exchange a friendly word. After Mendi left I was looking for someone who had the same needs to form a survival partnership.

It was difficult for me to find a friend in this camp, to find someone I can trust, because I had no former friends here from my childhood. My childhood friends were all from Dej, and the entire transport from Dej was taken on a different day to Auschwitz and they were scattered to some other labor camps. Our transport came from Zilah, and in Zilah I had no friends at all.

Two days after Mendi was taken away I was standing in line for my evening food ration. Next to me in the line was a young guy about my age who started a conversation. He was bemoaning his fate by telling me that his father was taken away from him in the last selection. I listened to him with great empathy and lamented that I also lost my parents in Auschwitz six months ago and that my youngest brother, the last remnant of my immediate family, was taken away from me during that same selection. We kept on talking and we had our meal together. His name was Hershi Berkovits, from Nagyvarad, a large town west of Dej in Transylvania. We decided to try to form a survival partnership and to look out for each other.

Our daily routine continued as before. Four o'clock in the morning was wake up time; when the siren sounded everyone rushed to get ready for the zehl appel.[1] Everyone lined up for the breakfast, which consisted of hot ersatz coffee and a piece of bread. It was not real coffee, but it had a coffee flavor; they called it ersatz coffee. One day they suddenly decided to change the food rationing, and they no longer gave us the bread in the morning. The whole breakfast consisted of coffee only. We received one piece of bread in the evening, and that had to last until the next evening. Some guys managed to cut it in slices and make three meals of it. Others could not control themselves and ate it up all at once; they wanted to have a fuller stomach at least once a day, but they then had a hard time the rest of the day.

Our daily walk to work through the local streets was sometimes an opportunity to find some additional food. Whenever we had a chance we looked for some supplementary food items. Sometimes on a lucky day a potato or a carrot was dropped by a German on the street, but many days could go by without finding anything. Mendi and I used to share any additional food we were able to obtain on the side. Now that Mendi was gone, Hershi and I had the same arrangement.[2]

About two months after Mendi was taken away from me, we were transferred to another camp. Hershi and I were put in the same transport and we wound up in the same camp. The new camp was called Furstenstein. It was next to a scenic village with a castle by the same name. Our work assignment was to dig ditches in the ground for electric cables, to replace the cables that were formerly above ground. It was February of 1945, and the winter was very severe. Our clothes were very flimsy; they were not warm enough even for indoors, let alone for the freezing outdoors. When we were transported to this new camp

---

1. "Zehl appel" is "roll call" in German.

2. After the war I made inquiries to find out if Hershi survived, but I couldn't find him.

they exchanged our old striped suits for new ones. True, they were new and looked a lot better than the old worn suits, but my old suit had the blanket lining that I sewed into it. I would have preferred to keep the old suit. I was beginning to feel weaker from malnutrition and the cold weather. Every morning they marched us to the work area that was located a short distance from the castle. Each one of us was assigned to dig a trench of about ten feet long by two feet wide. It usually took a full day to dig the trench. The soil was rocky, and every time I hit a rock with my pick I felt the vibration in all my bones.

One day I had a sympathetic guard watch me dig the trench. I was working at some speed, because I thought if I move faster I won't feel the cold as much. The guard looked at me working in haste and said to me, "You don't have to work in such haste; it is okay to work at a slower speed, as long as you finish the trench today."

I answered him, "I am working in haste because I am cold and hungry."

He looked me straight in the eyes and asked me, "Are you Jewish?" I said, "Yes."

"But you have blue eyes and blonde hair. Are you certain you are Jewish?"

"I am very certain."

He walked away, but a few minutes later he returned with a brown bag and gave it to me. He said to me, "Here is some extra food for you."

I thanked him and put it away in my pocket. Later in the day when I opened it, I found in the bag a sandwich of good fresh bread with butter and jam spread on it. I shared it with Hershi. We had not eaten fresh white bread since we left home.

A few days later I was still at the same worksite digging trenches. That day I thought I was lucky, because the digging was easy; the earth was soft without any rocks. By mid-afternoon I finished digging the trench assigned to me. When the supervisor came by and saw me standing next to my finished trench, he said to me, "Follow me."

He led me past all the trenches being dug and took me to the head of the work area. He pointed to the spot and said, "Start a new trench."

I began to dig a new trench, but this time it wasn't so easy; this trench was rocky. I worked for about an hour and minding my business, when one of the guards came over to me and said, "You lazy so-and-so! Why don't you do your work? Is that all you produced in a whole day?"

He didn't wait for my answer; he just hit me across the face with an open palm.

I answered him. "This is my second trench of the day. I finished one trench a while ago, it is way back there. You can ask the supervisor."

"Is that so? I didn't know."

He walked away without saying anything more. It so happens I had seen this guard before. He was one of the folks-Deutsche from Hungary who spoke Hungarian fluently. He hated Jews with a vengeance, but in particular he hated Jewish lawyers and educated Jews. I saw him once beat up a Jewish lawyer, screaming at him at the top of his lungs, "You think you are somebody because you have a law degree? I'll show you that you are nobody and I can do with you anything I want; you are going to shine my shoes."

The lawyer who was from Bistritza told me that he received several beatings from him. He explained that the guard comes from a village near Bistritza and he had worked for the lawyer's family as a laborer.

I continued working in the trenches while Hershi was assigned some other work.

One day while at work I became very ill, I was coughing and felt hot in the head. On the way back to the camp I could hardly walk. I went to see the camp doctor, who was a Jewish guy from Nagyvarad.[3] The doctor checked my temperature, and it was very high. He told me to stay in camp for a day or two, but advised me, "Go back to work as soon as you can, otherwise the Germans will send you to a camp from where you will never come out alive."[4]

I heeded his advice and tried to go to work no matter how sick I felt. After seeing the doctor I went to my barrack and fell asleep on my bunk. I had wanted to get my supper first, but I couldn't stand on my feet, especially outside in the cold weather. The doctor didn't give me any medicine, not even an aspirin. He didn't have any.

---

3. My cousin Dr. Mati Goldstein was not in this camp; I left him behind in Wustegiersdorf, when they shipped me out from there. After the war I found out that my cousin died in another camp.

4. I began to wonder if that is what happened to Mendi.

CHAPTER FIFTY-SIX

Collapsing Unconscious at Work

T HE NEXT MORNING I FELT A LITTLE BETTER. The doctor came ✡ ☽, 4
to see me and told me that he can arrange for me to work inside the camp doing kitchen work. I was grateful and reported to the kitchen chef. In the kitchen they put me to work peeling potatoes, carrots, and other vegetables.

The work was easy, but for a person in my weak condition it was difficult to lift those heavy kettles. However, compared to digging ditches, it was child's play. I worked in the kitchen for about a week and I was beginning to feel stronger. While at work in the kitchen I was able to eat some extra food, like raw carrots and other vegetables.

One day I decided to bring some vegetables for Hershi. I stuffed some carrots and potatoes in the bottom of my pants, which I had tied at the bottom to keep the vegetables from falling out. The kitchen was not inside the camp, but in a fenced-in area outside the prisoner's camp and next to the guardhouses. One had to pass through a checkpoint to enter or exit the camp. During the entire past week I had entered and exited without being searched. But this time when I left the kitchen and was about to enter the camp, I was given a thorough search. They found the vegetables on me. The guard sent me to report to the commandant, whose office was next to the guardhouses.

When I entered, he was having a friendly chat with the Jewish Lager Eltester. I had heard rumors that his bark was worse than his bite. Unlike the commandant in Wustegiersdorf, who was in his mid-fifties, this one was very young, perhaps thirty. I wondered why he was not assigned to the front somewhere in Russia. Perhaps he was wounded. My impression of him was that he didn't like what he was doing, that he was bored with it all. He asked me why I was sent to come to his office and I told him. He yelled at me and started hitting me with a strap on my behind. It hurt, but I didn't let out a sound. I guess he wasn't pleased with himself, because he remarked to the Lager Eltester, in German, "This guy doesn't make a sound; I am probably not hitting him hard enough."

I realized then that he wants me to cry out, so when he hit me again, I let out a big scream and he stopped beating me. The next day I was sent out again to dig trenches.

For about two weeks I continued working in the trenches, but then one day I got sick again. After work I marched back to the camp with a fever and a terrible cough. I decided to stand in line to get my supper anyhow; I figured it would give me some strength. I took my food to the barracks, but I didn't eat my food. I had no appetite for food; I just wanted to go to sleep. I gave my soup to Hershi, put the bread away, and went to sleep.

The next morning I felt a little better and I went to work. It was still very cold, with snow on the ground, but the sun was out and I thought I was getting better. In mid-afternoon as I was working, I lifted my pick to hit the ground and I collapsed. I became unconscious, but it must have lasted only for a very short time, because I remember lying on the cold ground and being conscious. They took me to the side of the worksite and let me just lie there. When the workday was over, two guys asked me in Yiddish if I could walk. I said to them that I would try. They were kind enough to assist me and we walked back to the camp. The doctor examined me and didn't say anything to me. There weren't any x-ray machines or any other instruments in the camp. But Hershi told me that the doctor was voicing an opinion that I might have pneumonia. He arranged to keep me from going to work for the time being. A few days later, I was told that I would be shipped out to another camp. I asked the doctor, "Is this the place from where no one comes out alive?"

"No, it is a camp where you will have a chance to recuperate. I have been there in that camp. It is called Dörnhau."

Several days later, I and several other guys who were sick were transferred to Dörnhau. Dörnhau was in the same general area as Fürstenstein, maybe thirty kilometers away, in any case, not very far. When we arrived to the new camp it looked entirely different from the other camps that I had been in before. Unlike Fürstenstein and Wustegiersdorf, which were newly constructed on an empty field, this camp was converted from some old factory building to serve as our camp. It was a huge three-story building and some additional smaller buildings.

CHAPTER FIFTY-SEVEN

Camp Dornhau

Conditions in the Dörnhau labor camp were in some respect worse than the other labor camps, and in some manner, not as bad. Sanitary conditions were certainly worse. There were not enough toilets or showers for the multitude of captives. Rows and rows of bunks were set up in one huge room. I never counted them, but there must have been a few hundred double bunks in this one room alone. There were always long lines to use the toilet and most of the people suffered from diarrhea. However, in some aspects it was not as bad, because the building was heated, and if someone was sick, he wasn't sent out to work or to an extermination camp.

The first day I arrived to Dörnhau, a man, who was also a captive in the camp, came over to me. He was tall and still fairly young. He stared at me and then asked me, "Do you know who I am?"

I said to him, "You look familiar, but I don't feel so great and my memory is not functioning. I can't think clearly."

He seemed to be in charge, because he was ordering people around. He said to me, "I am Moshe Shlomo Hyman from Dej."

My memory returned quickly and I knew immediately who he was. His younger brother Hershi was one of my close friends in Dej. His parents owned a restaurant in Dej. Moshe Shlomo was about six to eight years older than I am, and of course he looked different; everyone looked different in this labor camp.

He secured for himself an important position in the camp; he was the capo and captain of the largest dormitory. There was an overall Jewish chief, who was called the Lager Eltester, and the rest were capos. I was assigned a bunk in Hyman's ward. There were two kinds of prisoners, those who had to work and those who could not work. Most of the work consisted of taking care of the camp, but there were also several battalions that worked outside the camp. During the first two weeks I was not required to work; they allowed me to stay in camp. About two weeks later Hyman asked me if I want to work for him as an orderly. I thanked him for the offer, but I declined with an excuse that I am not cut out to order people around.

He didn't persist. I was given a job to clean up the barracks, and load and unload the trucks when deliveries were made. In addition to loading merchandise, my coworker and I had to load several corpses a week on a truck to be taken out from the camp. At first we loaded about six to eight a week, but a few weeks later it increased to about twenty a week. Some of the corpses I recognized, I had seen them in my barrack when they were still well and walking. On my first loading job I was terrified from handling the dead corpses, but after a few weeks I became so desensitized that it became routine.

Soon after I arrived to Dörnhau, I developed blisters on my body. There was nothing one could do about it; the doctor said that a lack of vitamins is causing the blisters. There was a medical room where they treated the sick prisoners, but blisters were not considered serious enough to warrant medical help. My blisters took a long time to heal, in particular one blister on my back, which became a large open abscess. I went to the medical room for help. The doctor told me that he has no medication for it, but he proceeded to clean it with disinfectants and then he took a brown paper bag, cut off a piece from it and covered my abscess with it. To this day I still have a mark on my back from that abscess.

From time to time I saw my landsman, Moshe Shlomo Hyman. He was always friendly and liked to chat with me about old times. On one of those occasions he handed me a tiny bundle with some object inside it, he said to me, "I want you to hold this for me for safe keeping."

"What is it?"

"It is gold. Can you keep it for me?"

I took it. After he was gone I looked inside the bundle and lo and behold, I found a few golden teeth in it. I was filled with disgust and anger. I knew he was trying to buy my silence. He probably thought that I might talk about him when we go back to Dej. The truth is that I didn't see or hear any bad stories about him, except that he was a capo, but he must have thought so. I was afraid to give the teeth back to him, because he had the power to do me harm. I kept the teeth with me for a while.

The food rations given to us in this camp were the bare minimum. We were given every morning a hot ersatz coffee and at lunchtime a soup consisting of hot water with a few vegetables floating in it. In the evening we fared a little better; the soup was a heavier concoction with more vegetables in it and a slice of bread. The food was never enough, and we were always hungry. The capos and the runners were the only ones who had access to more food; they were able to eat better. The evening meal had to be redeemed with a ration ticket, which was issued every morning during zehl appel. There was also an underground market, and cigarettes were the currency.

One day as I was doing my cleaning job on the upper floor I came across a bunch of blank cardboards; they looked just like the ration cards, but without any markings on them. Our regular ration tickets looked like a theatre ticket, with the word "Dörnhau" stamped on them. The bunch of cardboards I found had about a hundred blank tickets in it. I showed them to Hilu and Shimon, two guys with whom I had struck up a friendship. They became excited and Hilu said, "We won't have to go around hungry anymore."

But I said to them, "This is only a blank card. How will you make this into a ticket?"

Hilu answered, "Give me a razor blade, a piece of rubber, and a black pen, and we are in business."

Shimon offered two items: the razor blades and the rubber. He saw razor blades and old shoes with rubber heels discarded in the camp.

I said to them. "Wait a minute, what will happen to us if we are caught?"

Shimon answered without hesitation, "They will probably shoot us, but there is not much to lose; we will die anyhow from starvation."

Shimon brought the rubber heels and the razor blade, but we couldn't find any black ink. In the meantime, Hilu started carving out the rubber heel. Fortunately, Shimon brought two shoes with heels, because the first try to carve the stamp was not good enough to fool anyone. I found a black coloring pencil; Hilu moistened the card and the writing looked almost like ink. We decided to take a chance and we stamped three tickets. They were not perfect, but they looked good enough. We crushed the new tickets to make them look old and worn and then we stood in line to exchange them for a meal. It was my lot to go first, and I received my meal without any incident. Hilu and Shimon followed and they also succeeded. A few minutes later we went to exchange our regular ration tickets. Hilu and I received our food without any incident, but the food distributor asked Shimon, "Didn't you get your meal already?"

He answered him with a smile, "Yes, I am very hungry."

He took it as a joke and laughed, and Shimon just walked away. We were happiest for receiving the double portion of bread, as that was something we could put away and eat later. We were now confident that if we are careful we could get away with it. We decided to do it only every other day in order to avoid detection. Regretfully, they detected us anyhow. A few days later Shimon stood in line with the fake ticket. The food distributor looked at the ticket and asked Shimon, "What is this?"

They took him to the Lager Eltester for questioning. They asked him to reveal his accomplices. He tried to conceal our identity, but after he was beaten up, he gave them our names. We were taken to the Lager Eltester. During questioning we also received a beating, and then the Lager Eltester told an orderly, "Lock them up in the cellar."[1]

---

1. After the camp was liberated, the former prisoners killed this Lager Eltester. I didn't see it personally, because at liberation time I was very ill with typhus fever and was unconscious for a few days. It was rumored that this Lager Eltester – whose name I forgot – was a German collaborator.

CHAPTER FIFTY-EIGHT

Locked in the Cellar

T HE CELLAR WHERE THEY LOCKED US UP was also used to keep the corpses who died during the week until they were shipped out. The cellar was also the location for the furnace that was heating the building. The orderly who took us to the cellar opened the door with the key and told us to enter. After we were inside we heard him turn the key to lock us in. As soon as he closed the door we found ourselves in a pitch-dark room, and it was especially so because we came in from a bright sunny outdoors. Shimon, Hilu, and I couldn't see a thing. We were standing motionless, keeping our eyes closed. Then we heard a voice speak in Yiddish, saying, "Walk straight ahead this way."

We walked towards the voice and gradually we were able to see somewhat. Actually, after a short while we were able to see much better, because our eyes got used to the darkness. It was not completely dark; the furnace was burning and giving off a glow. The voice we heard was another prisoner, who was in the cellar alone for the last two days. He was pointing to the corpses and told us, "Stay away from the corpses. Do not touch them, because they died from some disease."

Not so long ago, when I was a child at home, I used to be scared of corpses. I would not walk into a home with a corpse inside; it gave me the creeps. But here I became immune to those fears. I did worry that they might forget about us and leave us in this cellar. My mind was quickly distracted after I discovered that as bad as conditions were in the cellar, there were some positive aspects to our situation. The place was warm and there was plenty of food. There were sacks of potatoes and other vegetables piled up in one corner of the cellar.

The next morning we heard the key turn in the doorlock. I thought to myself, "Good, they didn't forget about us." They ordered us out and we were told to line up in formation with a company of prisoners ready to go to work. As my two friends, Shimon and Hilu, and I were standing in line with about forty other prisoners, the German commandant came over and singled us out; he told us to step forward and then he addressed us, "It has come to my attention that you made counterfeit food coupons. You will be punished severely."

Then he told us to step back into formation with the other prisoners.

They marched us off to a quarry, a distance of three kilometers, where we were put to work. They gave us picks and other tools to dig for stones in a mountain of solid rocks. Then we were to shape them into rectangular or square blocks. The tools were heavy and the stones were even heavier. Some rocks weighed as much as my total weight.

I was in a rundown condition and so were most of the prisoners. The first day I managed to get through the day and walk back to the camp on my own power, but the second day I did not have the strength to walk back on my own and had to be assisted by two other prisoners. I made up my mind that I will not return to the stone quarry. I didn't care about the consequences; I knew that I wouldn't survive another workday. I had no more muscles in my arms to keep lifting the heavy sledgehammer and no more strength to bang my tools against those hard surfaces. The next morning I didn't report to work. I anticipated the capos to come to get me, but no one came. I don't know why, perhaps the Germans didn't care anymore; by then they knew already that they lost the war. I didn't do any work for a few days; I was just hanging around in the camp. One day a capo saw me walking in the courtyard and ordered me to help unload a truck of supplies. From that day on, I was put in a work detail on a standby basis to unload supplies delivered by trucks.

CHAPTER FIFTY-NINE

Experiments with Fleas Carrying Typhus

✡ ℶ, 6

DURING MY IMPRISONMENT in one of the camps, I was subjected to an experiment with lice and fleas. They were testing a new chemical spray, which was supposed to be a flea and lice repellent. They put a group of twenty of us in one room; ten of us received long new nightgowns sprayed with a chemical. The other ten kept their old clothing. I received one of the new long nightgowns. The fleas and lice carried the typhus disease. When I found out about the experiment, I thought I was among the lucky ones to have received the new nightgown. But I wasn't so lucky after all, because later on I became very ill with high fever. I was diagnosed to have typhus. I wasn't the only one who became sick; there were several other cases of typhus in the camp. The others became ill a few weeks before me, and they were isolated in an upstairs dormitory in the Dörnhau labor camp. When I was diagnosed with the typhus fever, the doctor told me to get ready to be taken upstairs to be isolated. The first thing I did was to go over to Moshe Shlomo Hyman and tell him about my condition. I gave him back the bundle of golden teeth and told him, "I don't think this will be safe with me."

The upstairs dormitory had other patients; they all had typhus. One of them told me that he had been there for the past ten days and during this period twelve patients died. He said, "I don't know why I am still alive. Many patients were brought here after me and they died."

I became so sick that I couldn't swallow my food; I wasn't even hungry. But I was constantly thirsty. One of the German officers, a chubby guy who was the friendliest of the whole bunch, brought us a pale of crystal sugar. The doctor told us to drink a lot of sugar water or ersatz coffee. I listened to him, and whenever I was awake I drank the hot fluid. I don't know how long I was in this condition, because most of the time I was asleep or unconscious.

Waking Up in a Hospital Room

Then one day I woke up and I was no longer in the isolated dormitory, but in a nice spacious room lying on a bed with white sheets and pillows. I must have been unconscious for a long time, because when I awoke I didn't remember anything.

Upon opening my eyes, a nurse in a white uniform was standing at the side of my bed. She asked me in German, "How do you feel?"

I looked at her in complete confusion.

She spoke to me further, "Can I get you something for breakfast?"

By now I was even more confused. I haven't been addressed like this or heard such polite language since I left home. I didn't know where I was; it crossed my mind that I died, and that I am no longer in this world. But then I discarded that thought, because it didn't sound plausible. After all, if I died then I must be in heaven; and if this is the Gan Eden, then why do they speak German?

After keeping silent for a minute or so, I asked her, "Where am I?"

She responded, "You are in a hospital. How do you feel? Do you have any pain?"

"No, I don't have any pain. But where am I? Am I still in Germany?"

"You are still in the same camp, but you have been liberated. This was the officer's quarters; it was converted into a temporary hospital. You have been asleep for a long time."

"Who is in charge?"

"I don't know. I am just a civilian volunteer from the nearby town. Can I get you something to eat?"

"What do you have?"

"Would you like to have bacon and eggs? We also have cereal or marmalade and toast."

After great disbelief, I tried to absorb this new reality; it was difficult for me to believe that my most cherished dream has come true. I just kept quiet for a while. I asked her to repeat the menu and then I ordered eggs, toast, and marmalade. I stayed in this temporary hospital for a few days, slowly regaining some of my strength. But after a few days, I foolishly walked out of the hospital. There was no one there to consult, no one to ask what to do or where to go. This part of the country was liberated by the Soviet Union, but I didn't see a Russian soldier until many weeks later. My camp was liberated while I was still unconscious, and most of my fellow prisoners left as soon as they were liberated. They were gone and scattered while I was left completely to my own devices.

There was another guy in a similar situation, and his name was Cohen. I didn't know him too well, but I had seen him around in the camp among the other prisoners. He was a few years older than I am. We struck up a conversation, and it turned out that he was also from Transylvania. He suggested that we team up to return home. Though I didn't know him too well, I agreed to join him; I needed a travel companion. I had no money, not even a penny, but Cohen had some German money on him. We started out on our journey by going to the Dörnhau railroad station. At the station we were told that a train would be leaving in a few hours, but it will travel only to the end of the line.

"Where is the end of the line?"

The answer was that it was a distance of about 50 kilometers. The bombs destroyed the railroad tracks in that area. We were told that we must find some other mode of transportation from the end of the line to the nearest railroad station. We took the train, but I had no money to pay for the fare; fortunately they didn't ask us to pay for the fare.

I think most of the passengers were refugees and without any money; the railroad personnel must have been aware of it.

CHAPTER SIXTY

My Travel Back to Dej

✡ ♩, 7

WHEN WE ARRIVED AT THE END of this part of our journey we could see the bombed out railroad tracks. We got off the train and we started looking for other modes of transportation in order to travel to the nearest railroad connection, which was thirty kilometers away. A horse and wagon came along traveling in our direction, and the wagon stopped alongside us. The passengers on the wagon were three Jewish girls; they had hired the wagon for a fixed fee. We found out later that the girls were also liberated prisoners from labor camps. The driver was willing to take us, but the girls insisted that each one of us share in paying for the fare. It was a reasonable request, but I had no money. They told us how much the total fare was and they wanted to split the fare into five shares. Cohen consented to pay his share, but I told them I have no money. They agreed to take Cohen with them, but without paying for the fare, I could not join them. Cohen boarded the wagon and they drove off, while I was left standing there gazing after them. The wagon was already gone about fifty meters, when it suddenly stopped. I hadn't taken off my eyes from the wagon, but I suddenly saw Cohen waving to me and calling my name to join them. I ran towards them and boarded the wagon.

We were off to the nearest train station, and to my great relief, I was not abandoned. Cohen told me later that the girls agreed to split the fare into four shares and I was allowed to travel for free. At the next station we boarded a train, which took us to the end of the line, for the second time. The interruption was again on account of bombed-out railroad tracks. This time it was only an interruption of two kilometers without tracks. We walked the distance and we boarded another train. After this interruption we had one more disconnect and then we traveled uninterrupted. We arrived to a small German community (I already forgot the name of that community), we disembarked and decided to go into town. As we were walking towards the town to find some food, we were told that a liberated girl's camp is nearby. I was anxious to find my sister Lulu, or any of my relatives. I therefore decided to visit the camp. Cohen agreed to join me.

In the camp I made inquiries from all the girls I encountered, about my family and about survivors from Dej. I kept on asking everyone I met the same question: "Is there anyone here from Dej?" Finally one girl told me that a woman by the name of Friedlander from Dej was in the camp. At first I didn't remember anyone by the name of Friedlander, but I was eager to talk to her anyhow in case she has any information about my family. I was directed to go to the barrack where she was staying. When we saw each other we both had tears in our eyes. She was my first cousin Sheindi Bindiger. I had forgotten that her name changed to Friedlander when she got married. During most of my life I had known her as Sheindi Bindiger; she had married only one year before she was deported. We talked for a long time and inquired from each other about the rest of the family. Regretfully we had no encouraging news; neither she nor I saw any one from our family who survived. We made plans to travel together to Dej.

While I was looking for my relatives, Cohen went looking for his family. He didn't find any relatives in this camp, but there were many women who came from his hometown. We were able to get some decent food for the first time, and we stayed two days in the nearby men's camp. Here Cohen and I parted company; Sheindi and I took the train towards Hungary. There were no passenger trains in operation; we had to travel in open freight wagons. Sheindi brought along a girl companion whom she had met in the camp. She was from a village near Dej.

We crossed several borders, and luckily no one asked for any papers; I didn't have any identity papers and neither did Sheindi. When we reached Miskolc,[1] we were told that the train wouldn't leave for a few hours. I thought it would be a good time to find some food, because our food supply was down almost to the last piece of bread. Sheindi and her friend stayed on the train, and I walked towards the town. I

---

1. Miskolc is a nice-size town in Hungary.

didn't have money, but I figured that if I tell my story to someone, they would surely provide me with some food. On my way to town I saw the rich magnificent estate of the archdiocese of Miskolc. I thought to myself, this might be a good place to ask for assistance. It is a religious institution; they surely would help.

I walked through the long tree-lined driveway to the front door and rang the bell. A woman answered the bell and I told her I need help.

She said, "Just a minute."

She went inside and a priest came to the door. I told him that I was on my way home from a German labor camp and that I am in need of food until I reach my hometown. He told me in a stern voice, "We don't have any food to give away."

I walked away disappointed and dejected. I knew that I couldn't go back to the train empty handed, but I didn't know where I could get some food for the three of us. I was sure there were no Jews to turn to, because they must have been deported, just as we were deported. I was still walking towards the town of Miskolc figuring that I will try a bakery in town. Then all of a sudden I remembered that in one of the camps where I was detained I had a bunkmate from Miskolc. He was my partner in the experiment of repellent garments against lice and flees when the Germans used us as guinea pigs to test chemical repellent garments.

My bunkmate told me that he was a lawyer and a former officer in the Hungarian army. I remembered his name and I decided to inquire. It was a long shot, because I didn't even know if he survived. And even if he survived, he could still be somewhere in a camp. But I decided to make an inquiry. To my surprise I was told that he was at home in Miskolc and I went to see him. He received me very warmly and he wanted me to stay for a few days, but I told him about my cousin on the train and that I was anxious to travel home to find my family.

He told me that most of his clients are farmers from the nearby villages and that they are bartering food for his services. Fortunately he had a variety of provisions, from which he offered me to take as much as I needed. He accompanied me to the railroad station, where I introduced him to my cousin Sheindi and her friend.

From Miskolc, Sheindi, her friend, and I took the train to Budapest. Prior to my deportation I had lived in Budapest for two years, so I felt very much at home. I tried to find friends and relatives, but the only relative I found was Rabbi Shlomo Friedlander, the Lisker Rabbi. He and his family managed to hide during the deportation, but they lost most of their material possessions. I also visited my former boss, who was my last employer before deportation. She told me sadly that her husband never returned from the war; he perished in the Jewish labor brigade. She and her child were not deported, because she converted to Christianity a few days before the deportation. Many Jews used this device to avoid deportation; they converted in the weeks before deportation as an expediency to save themselves. But she assured me that she is reconverting back to Judaism.

From Budapest we tried to take a train to travel to Dej. But this was not a simple matter. The last time I traveled from Budapest to Transylvania there was a direct train to Dej and Kolozsvar, but not this time. The borders have changed. Dej was no longer in Hungary; it was in Romania. Dej was in Transylvania, and when the war was over, Transylvania was given back to Romania, because Hungary sided with Germany.

The trains in Hungary were not bombed out as they were in Germany, and consequently they were better than the trains in Germany and Austria. We traveled in regular passenger cars. We still didn't have any money or identity papers. The conductor asked us for tickets, but after Sheindi explained to him our situation he just nodded and walked away. We arrived to the Hungarian/Romanian border, where we had to walk across the border and board another train, but not before many hours of waiting. To us these delays were minor inconveniences compared to what we had to endure this past year in the concentration camps.

CHAPTER SIXTY-ONE

My Arrival at Dej

W E ARRIVED IN DEJ late in the afternoon; it was springtime of 1945. At the railroad station we were welcomed by several young Jewish people. We recognized most of the familiar faces; they were part of a delegation that came every day to the railroad station for the sole purpose of welcoming the returnees and to direct them to Jewish organizations ready to help. We were told to go to the old day school, which was converted into a refugee center. They had set up a cafeteria in the school building and some temporary bedrooms. Most of the returnees could not move into their own homes immediately or not at all, because the homes were vandalized and left without furniture. Some were even occupied by squatters.

I was offered sleeping quarters in the old school, but I stayed there for only one night. The next day, Muci Berger[1] invited me to stay in his house. Muci inherited and reclaimed my aunt and uncle's house and moved into it with his friend Rothenberg and his niece Martha; it was a large house with many bedrooms. He also reclaimed his father's businesses, which consisted of a grocery store, a liquor store, a bodega, and a postal stamps and candy store. The stores were located adjacent to the house; the stores were lined up at the front on Main Street, and the residence was on the same property in the back of the stores. There was also a huge garden in the back of the house.

---

1. Muci Berger was a stepson of my aunt, Esthi Berger. My Aunt Esther, her husband Nandor Berger, and their ten-year-old daughter, Magda, were deported to Auschwitz. They did not survive. From the whole Berger family, only one son, Muci Berger, and his niece Martha survived.

Muci put me to work as a clerk in the grocery store. I had no experience, but I learned quickly. There was one senior gentleman already working in the store and he taught me everything there was to know. The two of us took care of the whole store. Muci wanted me in the store so that he could attend to other business matters.

My cousin Sheindi Bindiger (Friedlander), who returned with me after liberation from the labor camps, found her uncle's house unoccupied and in good condition. She moved into the house with her uncle's grandchildren. This house belonged to our uncle, Rabbi Yitzchak Yechiel; none of his children returned from Auschwitz. While his grandchildren were only teenagers, Sheindi, their older cousin, was already a woman in her thirties. Consequently, Sheindi became their surrogate mother. Of the four cousins living with her, three of them had the same name: Leitsu. There was Leitsu[2] and her sister Yenti,[3] who were the children of Yechezkel Mendel Paneth. Then there was Leitsu,[4] the daughter of Shmiel Paneth; they called her Keshanever Leitsu. Then there was Leitsu, the daughter of Malka and Chayim Yudah Braun, who was the rabbi of Iklad. She was called Iklader Leitsu. All these cousins came back to Dej with the hope of being reunited with their parents. Sadly, none of the parents returned home; they were all murdered in the camps. Sheindi, who was married only a year before deportation, became a widow; her husband didn't come home either.[5]

During the few months that I stayed in Dej, I was miserable, but I didn't know what was wrong with me. At that time I was too young to understand my problem. But with hindsight I know now that I suffered from depression. I worked for a few months in Muci Berger's store, but I didn't feel alive. I had no interest in anything. I stayed around with the hope that by some miracle my parents will come home or that my brothers and sister will appear one day. As the days and weeks went by without any news from my family, I became very restless. One day I heard from some girls, who just arrived from a camp in Poland, that they were in the same camp with my sister Lulu. For a few days I was exuberant. They also told me that she was very weak and could not

---

2. Leitsu is married to Rabbi Hersh Meier Paneth, the Dejer Rabbi of Brooklyn.

3. Yenti is married to Rabbi Yidele Paneth, the Dejer Rabbi of Miami Beach.

4. Leitsu is married to Rabbi Feivel Halberstam, the Keshanever Rebbe from Brooklyn.

5. Sheindi remarried a few years later.

travel. They encouraged me to be patient for a while, that she would come home when she recuperates. I was making inquiries to find out more about her. I wanted to travel to see her. After more inquiries I found out that she was not alive any longer.

In the meantime more people returned to Dej, but none of them were my close relatives; those returning were all under forty. One of the young returnees brought news to me that my good friend Frank Friedman survived and that he lives in Munich, Germany. This bit of good news cheered me up, but in general I was not very cheerful.

In addition to feeling depressed over the loss of my family, I was also very unhappy with conditions in Dej under the Russian occupation. There were no employment opportunities and life just didn't seem normal. In the morning I wished I did not have to get up and in the evening I dreaded the sleepless night.

After Yom Kippur I told Muci Berger that I plan to leave after Succoth. Rothenberg, who also lived in the Berger home, became a close friend of mine. He was old enough to be my father, but he liked to talk to me and I often confided in him with my problems. I had already made up my mind to travel to Germany. I spoke to Rothenberg and told him that I will leave after Succoth.

Rabbi Yosef Paneth, who survived the Holocaust, became the temporary rabbi of Dej. Rabbi Yosef survived because he, his wife, and nine of his children escaped from the Dejer ghetto and hid in the woods, thus avoiding to be deported to Auschwitz. His escape happened because he listened to his daughter Breindele, who urged the family to escape. Breindele was visiting her grandparents in Krakow in 1939, and while she was there, Germany invaded Poland and Breindele was trapped. She was placed in the Krakow ghetto. Her parents tried everything to bring her back home. After three years and after spending a large sum of money they were able to rescue her. Breindele urged her parents to escape if they want to avoid the gas chambers. They listened and survived. A book was written about their escape, titled *A Sun and a Shield*, by Devora Gliksman.

However, his older brother Rabbi Yaakov Meilach and his family did not survive Auschwitz. Rabbi Yaakov Meilach was the last rabbi of Dej. In a book written by Singer Zoltan in the Hungarian language titled *There was Once a Town Dej*, he writes that while Rabbi Yaakov Meilach was in the ghetto, he visited every tent in the ghetto, urging his congregants to escape. He also writes that Zoldi, a well-known person in Dej, came to Dej with two German SS officers; they were ready to take the rabbi and his family out of the ghetto and place them on the transport train to Switzerland. He chose to remain with his congregants.

Since his brother did not return from Auschwitz, Rabbi Yosef took upon himself the tremendous burden of bringing some spiritual life into the community of Dej. He and his Rebetzin tried very hard to lift up the spirits of the few lifeless survivors. Their house was open to many hungry survivors, who ate there frequently. I had the pleasure of being their guest for Rosh Hashana.

CHAPTER SIXTY-TWO

My Trip from Dej to Munich

AFTER SUKKOTH, I SAID MY GOODBYES to my friends and relatives, and on a Sunday morning I left Dej on my journey to an unknown world.

I had a companion on my trip to Germany. Muci had a brother-in-law by the name of Blau. I didn't know him too well, as we were from a different generation; he was about fifteen years older. I had some conversations with him earlier with regards to my trip to Germany; he had told me that he would also be interested in leaving Dej to travel to Germany.

When the time came for my departure, I told him that I would be leaving within the next few days and asked him if he is still interested in joining me. Without hesitation he told me that he is ready to join me. On a Sunday morning in October of 1945, Blau and I left Dej on our journey to West Germany. I was nineteen years old, but in some ways I was no longer a teenager, I became hardened from the experiences I endured in the camps. But in other ways I was still an inexperienced teenager, who had no sophistication and no knowledge of the civilized world. I would have left Dej by myself; it was just incidental that Blau decided to join me, nevertheless I was very happy to travel in the company of an older more experienced person. We traveled towards the Romanian/Hungarian border, which was near Oradea Mare, a town the Hungarians called Nagyvarad. Dej and Nagyvárad and all of Transylvania were under Romanian rule at this time.

The Romanian border guards allowed anyone with proper papers to leave, but they searched every person for currency. There was a set amount of currency permitted to carry abroad. There was also a strict prohibition against smuggling gold coins out of the country. Blau and I were searched. They found on Blau Napoleon gold coins and American dollars; for that he was detained. I also had on me some Romanian and German currency, but it was insignificant and they permitted me to cross the border. I also carried with me German Marks, that did not belong to me; I carried them as a favor from a father to his son who lived in Germany. I was not familiar with the law; had I known about the prohibition against foreign currency, I wouldn't have accepted to carry the currency. I could have wound up in jail or shipped to Siberia. After a good search I was permitted to cross the border, but Blau was detained. Blau was not the only one detained; other refugees were also detained for one reason or another. Before we crossed the border, I met up with many refugees who were leaving Romania in similar circumstances. Those of us who were permitted to cross decided we would wait for those still detained. The next day they released some of the detainees, but Blau was not released. I was told that he was taken back to a Romanian jail. I was already across the border in Hungary and there was nothing I could do for him. I sent a letter to Muci informing him of what happened. Later on I found out that Blau was released, but they confiscated his gold coins.

All the refugees that crossed the border joined together to travel as a group to Budapest. I had no set plan how to get to my destination, which was Germany, and no idea what needs to be done to travel to Munich; I just improvised as I went along. I didn't know that the borders were closed, because a few months earlier when I traveled from Germany to Dej there were open borders.

In Budapest I found out that there was an organized group that smuggles Jewish refugees across the Hungarian/Austrian border. I made contact with the group and they told me to join them late in the evening the next day. I wondered why anyone would be willing to risk smuggling strangers across the border without a fee for the service. I found out later that they were Jews belonging to a Jewish army in Palestine. Their mission was to ingather the remnants of the Jewish people and bring them to Palestine.

The group of refugees I joined to cross the border consisted of about 80 people; some were single guys or single girls, and some were whole families with little children. They took us from Budapest by trucks to a village near the Hungarian/Austrian border. There were two checkpoints to cross, the Russian and the Austrian. One of the leaders of our group met with the border-crossing guide to discuss the plan for crossing. The guide might have been Hungarian, or Austrian. After their talk, the guide took over and led us up a hill, bypassing both checkpoints. It was dark, but not pitch-dark; the stars provided enough light for us to see our next step, but it was dark enough to hide us from the border guards. It was a long distance trek lasting four hours until we reached our destination. We had to be completely quiet while crossing the border; any sound would have alerted the border guards. However, we had children with us and they became tired and restless. Some of them began to cry and the parents had difficulty keeping them quiet. Fortunately we made the journey without being caught.

When we arrived in Austria, Jewish relief workers waited for us and took us to a DP camp in Salzburg. Each one of us received a relief package with a variety of delicacies. It was a complete surprise to me; whoever organized this agency did a marvelous job. They served us a very fine meal and gave us sleeping quarters. I was amazed at the variety of food items available in Austria; it was such a contrast to what was available in Romania. This part of Austria was in the American zone. Since I didn't know anyone in Salzburg, there was no point for me to stay, so I stayed only one night. The next day I took a train to Munich in the company of a whole group of refugees. The trip was arranged and paid for by the Jewish Agency. In Munich they took us to the Jewish relief agency, which was set up temporarily in the Deutsche Museum. Everyone registered and we were given choices to select a DP camp. I telephoned Frank Friedman,[1] who told me not to sign up for a DP camp, but to stay in Munich. He asked me to wait for him at the museum until he got there.

---

1. Frank Friedman lived in Orangeburg, NY. He and his wife Ruth moved to Saint Louis, MO.

CHAPTER SIXTY-THREE

Frank Friedman

As I mentioned earlier, my friend Frank Friedman survived the Holocaust and he resided in Munich, Germany. When Frank and I met for the first time, he looked at me and I looked at him in astonishment and then we embraced. Both of us have changed; we had not seen each other for about three years. The last time I saw Frank I was only sixteen and I wore Chasidic garb. Now I was nineteen, wearing shabby, but modern clothes. He also had changed; the last time I saw him he had payos and a dark suit, now he wore a nice modern suit and a modern haircut. We spoke for a while and then he took me to his place, where I spent the night. Frank had rented a room for me in another section of the city. It was the same neighborhood where Yanki Rosman lived.[2] The next day he took me to my new residence and I settled into my room. I wasn't too thrilled with it; nevertheless it was a place where I could put my head down. There were many Jewish refugees renting rooms in this neighborhood. I met Yanki Rosman and gave him the German Marks his father had sent him. I was happy to be free of this responsibility.

My life in Munich was less stressful and I no longer suffered from depression, but I still didn't find any purpose in my life; my whole existence seemed to be transitory. I still had no idea what I wanted to do with my life, but I knew for certain that I didn't want to return to live in Romania. There were business opportunities in Munich. I was offered a partnership in a movie-house venture.

My mind was made up that under no circumstances would I consider

---

2. Yanki Rosman settled in Los Angeles, CA in the USA.

settling in Germany. I wanted to settle in a place where I would not be constantly reminded of Auschwitz and the Holocaust.

My friend Frank Friedman was deported to Auschwitz and ended up as a prisoner in the Dachau Concentration camp. This part of Germany was liberated by the Americans forces, and consequently, Frank was liberated by the Americans. He settled in the city of Munich, Germany.[3] I don't know how Frank found out that I survived, but soon after I came home to Dej, he communicated to me via travelers to join him in Munich. He emphasized that life is much easier and pleasanter under the American occupation. His message gave me a spark of hope and brought back some life into my soul. I began to make plans to leave Dej, but I waited until after the High Holidays to finalize my plans.

---

3. After World War II, they created four zones of liberation: the American, the British, the Russian, and the French zones. However, due to competing ideologies, there was very little communication between the Russian and the other zones.

CHAPTER SIXTY-FOUR

Rabbi Feivel Halberstam

Palestine or America was on my mind; I wanted to live in a country where I could be a Jew without worrying. About that time, my cousin (Keshanever) Leitsu was on her way to America and she stopped in Munich to visit me. She received immigration papers from her uncle, who lived in Brooklyn, NY.[1] Keshanever Leitsu and I grew up in Dej, but we did not socialize with each other. In Chasidic Dej, girls and boys did not socialize, even if they were cousins. Her American uncle sent her an affidavit and proper documents, which enabled her to immigrate within a very short time. When she visited me in Munich, I casually asked her to speak on my behalf to her relatives; perhaps they could also send me papers. I didn't expect it to materialize, because it was a complicated matter to prepare the papers. To my surprise I received the papers within four weeks.

In my mind it was like a miracle. The papers were sent to me by her cousin, Rabbi Feivel Halberstam.[2] He was actively working on behalf of Jewish refugees in Europe, soliciting well-to-do individuals in America to sign blank affidavits for the refugees. When Leitsu spoke to him on my behalf, he had papers ready, suitable for any refugee; all he had to do is fill in my name. The proprietor of a feather company had already signed the affidavit beforehand.

---

1. Her uncle in Brooklyn was Rabbi David Halberstam. They are descendants of the great Sanzer Rabbi, Rabbi Chayim Halberstam.

2. Rabbi Feivel Halberstam is the son of Rabbi David Halberstam. He became the Keshanever Rebbe when his father passed away; since then Rabbi Feivel Halberstam, z"l, also passed away.

When I arrived to America, Feivel Halberstam was there at the docks waiting for me; he took me to his house where his family welcomed me. Later on, Leitsu married Feivel Halberstam; they lived in Brooklyn with their lovely family. At that time Feivel was in the diamond business and was a member of the diamond club on Forty-Seventh Street in Manhattan.

CHAPTER SIXTY-FIVE

Eugene Pollack

Eugene Pollack was another good and close friend of mine in Munich. He was originally from Dej, and we knew each from the past. When I arrived in Munich, Eugene and Frank Friedman were already roommates. Very soon the three of us became inseparable. We traveled together all over Bavaria, visiting many interesting places, among them Garmisch-Partenkirchen.[1] We also visited some royal palaces in Bavaria and Austria.

Karl Lindner was a close friend of mine in Munich, but we had different backgrounds; he was a college graduate from the Warsaw University and I studied in a Yeshiva. He came from Poland and I came from Hungary. Also He was 5 years older from me. Our mutual languages were Yiddish and German. We used to spend many evenings just having nice discussions. I admired his broad knowledge and education. We came to America on the same boat, but after a while we lost contact.

Eugene was one of those rare individuals who didn't have a selfish bone in his whole being. He was a great intellect and very well read. He was also idealistic and an ardent Zionist. He had the chance to immigrate to the USA, but for idealistic reasons, he chose to go to Palestine. This was just before the State of Israel was established. A few months after I left for America, Eugene immigrated to Palestine. He was there when the new State of Israel was established. He married, and some years later he passed away in Israel. May his blessed memory live forever and may Hashem grant him a resting place in the Gan Eden.

---

1. Garmisch-Partenkirchen is a resort place in the picturesque scenic Bavarian Alps, near a place called Zugspitze.

The wait to immigrate to America seemed to be so long that I despaired; I began to wonder if I would ever get to see the shores of America. After Frank left it was only Eugene and I still living in Germany. Eugene was due to leave for Italy in a few months from where he was to take a boat to Palestine. I dreaded the prospect of being left all alone in Germany. Finally I was notified by the American consulate to report to their office for a hearing on a certain date. I was very excited and I got myself ready for the interview. I was ushered into the office of a vice consul. He wore a military uniform with the rank of a colonel. He asked me questions in English, which I answered in German, and the interpreter translated the answers into English. He seemed to be pleased with the answers, because after a half hour of questioning he told me, "You are welcome to America."

After I was approved to immigrate, I was referred to the Jewish agencies to provide me transportation to America. At the Agency I was told that my passage would take place within the next four weeks, depending on the availability of transportation. Within a few weeks after that, I was told to report to the Jewish Agency in Munich, where many other refugees were gathered to be transported to Bremerhaven. The plan was that we would stay in Bremerhaven a few days until a boat was available to take us to New York. However, when we arrived to Bremerhaven we were informed that there would be a small delay due to a strike by the Coal Miners Union. Most of the headlines in the newspapers were about a dispute between President Harry S. Truman and John L. Lewis, president of the Coal Miners Union; they were having a disagreement. At that time I did not understand the issues, and I was worried that my cherished trip to America was in jeopardy.

CHAPTER SIXTY-SIX

My Cousin, Erno Judovits

BEFORE I LEFT GERMANY I received a letter from my cousin Erno Judovits,[1] suggesting that I should send him a power of attorney to reclaim for me my father's property in Naprad. Erno survived the Munkaszolgalat[2] camps and returned to Naprad after the war. He was a member of a committee representing absentee landowners reclaiming their property; he also wanted to reclaim mine. At that time the Romanian communists took control of the country under Russian tutelage. I sent Erno the power of attorney. I am not familiar with all the details, but soon afterwards I found out that Erno barely escaped from being exiled to a labor camp in Romania. I was told that he was already on a transport to be shipped off to Maria Negre, but in the last minute, two communist officials, who were his friends, came to his rescue. I think the problem was that some fanatic communist official, who had tremendous power in the new government, did not want private individuals to own farmland properties.

In Bremerhaven they put us up in some military barracks. I was quartered in the Eisenhower barrack. Being a refugee and having been in so many camps, I considered this barrack by comparison, quite nice; the rooms were spacious with plenty of light. Each room had ten bunkbeds with clean bedding, and a maid changed the sheets frequently. There was a huge cafeteria nearby with plenty of food. Judging by the standards

---

1. Erno Judovits is my cousin. He and his wife Eva lived in Los Angeles, CA. Erno and Eva have two children, Tom and Edith. His brother Hugo and his wife Erna lived in New York. Hugo and Erna have one daughter, Dalia.

2. Munkaszolgalat was the Jewish work brigade in Hungary.

of postwar Germany, it was luxurious food. To this day I have no idea who paid for our accommodations, but I am very grateful even to this day. The philanthropic agencies that took care of us did great work and saved many lives. As an aside, during the time I was in Bremerhaven the well-known Klausenburg Rebbe, Rabbi Halberstam,[3] was also there waiting to immigrate to the USA. Originally they told us it will be only a short delay, but on account of the coal strike, we had to stay there for six weeks.

Finally in January of 1947, my friend Karl Lindner and I boarded the liberty ship Ernie Pyle, which brought us to America. It was a troop-carrying ship with few amenities, but I didn't care; all that mattered was that we were on our way to America. We were assigned sleeping places at the bottom of the ship. The first day I felt great. There was plenty of good food in the cafeteria; however I was shocked and amazed to watch the left over food being thrown overboard every day. Coming from a starving Germany it seemed to me to be wasteful and extravagant, almost sinful.

On the second day of our voyage I became seasick; I couldn't hold down any food and my head was spinning. My friend Karl Lindner and I stayed close to each other. I went upstairs to get some fresh air, hoping that it will stop my headache. The fresh air did help and I felt a little better. I noticed that there was an empty room next to the captain's room. It was neither an office nor a compartment, just an empty anteroom without any furniture. The door was open to the room and a lot of fresh air flowed into the room. I sat down on the floor leaning my back against the wall to rest. Since I hadn't slept the night before, I fell asleep immediately. Karl came looking for me and found me sleeping on the floor. He woke me and said, "I looked for you all over, just by chance I looked in here; it never dawned on me that you would be sleeping in the captain's anteroom."

I said to him, "I am not going back to that hole in the bottom of the boat."

He said, "Let's bring up our bedding and see what happens."

And so we did. The captain was kind enough not to say anything; he tolerated us the rest of the voyage. Carl and I had to go for our meals

_____

3. Klausenburg is a city in Transylvania, sixty kilometers from Dej. I had known Rabbi Halberstam before the war; he came to Dej frequently.

in rotation; one of us stayed to watch the space. It took ten days to cross the ocean, and on January the thirteenth, we arrived in New York.

We docked in a pier on Forty-Third Street or nearby. After being cleared by the immigration department, I walked out to a large reception hall. I had no idea what to expect. I had no close relatives in America except my cousin Leitsu Paneth. I had notified her of my arrival, but I didn't expect her to be waiting for me. In Chasidic circles it is not proper for a single girl to do that. To my surprise Leitsu's cousin, Feivel Halberstam, was in the hall waiting for me. He was the one who made it possible for me to come to America; he sent me the affidavit. I will always be grateful to Feivel Halberstam for making it possible for me to live in this great country. Also waiting for me was my friend Frank Friedman.[4] Feivel Halberstam hailed a taxi and took me to the Williamsburg section of Brooklyn. He arranged with his aunts, who lived nearby in Williamsburg, to put me up temporarily for a night or two. Feivel and his parents also lived in Williamsburg.

During our taxi ride from the Manhattan port to our destination in Brooklyn, we had to pass the lower east side of Manhattan. From my taxi window I noticed the various signs on the storefronts, all of them written in Hebrew letters. Having just left Germany, where Judaism was almost completely eradicated, that sight, those Hebrew letters, gave me an exhilarating feeling. I thought to myself, "Judaism in America is alive." It was the last thing I expected to see. It was for me unimaginable that Jews would still have the freedom to display Hebrew signs openly in one of the great cities of the world. That taxi ride felt like a march of triumph.

The next chapter in this book was written by our family as a tribute to my wife Helen, their mother and grandmother. It is a memoir of her life as a child, her experiences in Auschwitz, and her endurances in the labor camps.

Many of the stories were repeated and confirmed to us by Ella, Helen's sister who was imprisoned in the same camps with Helen.

I want to express my gratitude to my children and grandchildren for writing this chapter; it is very significant. A special thanks to my granddaughter Talya for editing this chapter. I know you put a lot of thought and effort into it, and we all appreciate it.

---

4. In those days I called Frank Friedman "Feivel." Coincidentally, both guys who waited for me at the docks were called Feivel.

CHAPTER SIXTY-SEVEN

Helen's Memoir

OUR BELOVED MATRIARCH

It is not an easy task to write about someone you loved, someone you miss, someone whose memory you think should be honored and live on forever. There are so many words to write and stories to share. That's never the hard part. The writer's block comes when trying to put these words and stories together in a way that bring that person to life, so much so that the reader feels like they know her, and love her, too.

This person, as you may have guessed from the title of this chapter, is our family, our wife, our sister, our mother, and our grandmother, Helen Judovits.

We wish to honor and share her memory in hopes to both educate others through her experiences surviving the Holocaust, and inspire through her tremendous acts of generosity, selflessness, and unconditional love.

AS A CHILD

Helen was born on July 28, 1930 in Priekopa, a small village located in Slovakia (then Czechoslovakia), near the border with Ukraine. There were 18 Jewish families in the village. In addition to other businesses, her father, Herman Jakubovits, owned and ran a farm. He, together with her mother, Rose Jakubovits, née Roth, raised Helen and her seven siblings, including four sisters, Ilona, Ella (both older), Yolan, and Tziri, and three brothers, Miksa (Mordechai), Ignatz (Yitzchak) and Moshe Wolf.

She grew up in a traditional Orthodox home, surrounded by woods without end and horses. Although Helen attended public schools in Priekopa, she also took private lessons in Jewish studies.

As a fun-loving girl, Helen would spend long days outdoors, independently climbing trees on her family's property, as well as occasionally trespassing on the neighbor's property to pick the fruit off of their trees. On one such occasion, the neighbor came to speak with Rose to complain about her daughter climbing their trees and picking their fruit. Although Helen worried that she would get in trouble, her parents understood and cherished her independent and playful spirit.

While Helen did not have many recollections from this all-too-brief period in her life, the ones she had were filled with love, warmth, and joy. And they are these precious small memories that remained the essence of her childhood.

AS A DAUGHTER

In the spring of 1944, the authorities in the village of Priekopa ordered all the Jews to assemble in the synagogue. After waiting for many hours inside, horse-drawn wagons arrived. Helen and her family were loaded onto the wagons and taken to the nearest town of Ungvar where they were confined inside a ghetto.

When asked in 2010, what was going through her mind while being taken from her home, Helen responded, "Well, first of all, I was 13 years old thinking, 'What is going to happen to us? Where are they going to take us?' We were worried, afraid for the family."

For six weeks, day after day, the Jakubovits family, together with the other seventeen Jewish families in the village, subsisted in a dilapidated building with no walls to protect them.

At the start of the seventh week, the Hungarian police rode a train into the ghetto that consisted of cattle wagons with not a seat to be found inside – standing room only. Helen and her family were loaded onto the cattle wagons and taken to Auschwitz. The ride took three long days, with no bathroom stops, forcing the elders to publically embarrass themselves in front of each other. The strong smells of excrement surrounded them for the duration of the trip. There was no food to be had and children screamed through the night. Everyone feared for their lives.

As they got off the train at Auschwitz, the authorities made them form a line and ordered them to go in separate directions; men to the right, women to the left, mothers with children, this way, and young girls on their own, that way.

Helen had been standing with her mother, Rose, and her younger sister, Yolan (Rachel Yita), in the line for mothers with their children. As they moved forward, it became apparent that their line was headed for the gas chambers. Helen had the opportunity to get on a different line with younger girls including her older sisters, Ella and Ilona. She ran to join her sisters, without having enough time to realize that that moment would be her last with her mother and Yolan. There was no goodbye.

AS A SISTER
Auschwitz

During her initial days in Auschwitz, Helen was unable to eat after seeing other prisoners in a worse section of the camp than hers with harsher conditions. She would dig a little ditch under the fence to their section and would smuggle the little food she was given to them. Instead of feeling good about the act of kindness she was doing and lives she was saving, she felt embarrassed to be blessed and thanked by these prisoners so profusely for the little she gave them.

After only a few days being in the camp, Ilona heard one of the other prisoners calling out the Jakubovits name. She responded and the prisoner handed her a stone with a small note addressed to the Jakubovits family attached to it. This miraculous delivery was from their younger brother Ignatz, or Itzu, as was his nickname; he was about 12 years old.

He, too, was in Auschwitz, but a tall wire fence separated him from his sisters. In the note he had thrown over the high fence, he inquired about their mother, wanting to know if she was alright. He also warned his family not to drink the water and sent them his love.

The sisters were comforted by the fact that their brother was alive, at least for now, and close enough; they could feel his love protecting them.

In July 1944, Helen and Ella's time with Ilona was cut short. The Nazis took their older sister, age 17, and sent her to a labor camp. Helen and Ella watched on, crying and scared to be separated, yet again, from another member of their family. All they had now was each other.

Her sister Ella recounts, "Every morning they would wake us up at 5am and make us go outside for zehl appel, or roll call. We had to stand in line for hours to be counted, even when it would rain. If the counting revealed that one or more persons were missing, they made us kneel in the mud and sand for hours. Every morning they gave us a ration of bread and black coffee. For lunch, they gave us a soup that occasionally had some horse meat."

The two sisters endured plenty of hardship and close calls together in Auschwitz, coming out with some unique and miraculous stories that are rare amongst Holocaust survivors.

"One time a German officer came to select girls for a labor camp, as they needed girls for delicate work," Ella explains. "He was looking for girls with good eyes and fine hands and fingers. He looked carefully at each one of us and picked me, but not Helen. I was sent to a separate side. I pulled Helen with me, but another German soldier sent her back. I went over to the German officer and asked him with tears in my eyes to let my sister come with me. He looked at me for a few seconds and then muttered angrily at Helen, 'go with her.'"

Helen remembered more details from that day. "In August or September, the German military came to our camp, as they routinely would when they were looking for workers, or when they did not have enough people for burning. They told us that this guy who came from Berlin needed two hundred girls, young girls, but they did not say for what.

"Later, as the selection was going on for the whole camp, there was a German soldier who passed by the fifth row, where my sister and I were standing and he said to his attendants, 'Don't let this one run away,' pointing to my sister, and they came and they grabbed her. But my sister ran back to me, again and again, three times, four times . . . She knew, that if she went, that's the end. Finally, they caught her, but she still came back to me and took my hand.

"Nobody I have ever spoken to that has survived the camps had the guts to go over to the German soldiers with her little sister, saying, 'Please, that's my little sister,' and most of the time the officers would take both of them and just throw them. The officer looked at me and then told me that I could go with my sister.

"At the end of this particularly close call, we both looked up at the black smoke rising from the crematoriums and I remember Ella saying to me, 'Even in there, I will stay with you and G-d willing we will go up to heaven together.'

"When the question was [keeping brothers and sisters together] they always made sure to separate them. Our story is the first time that I know of where they kept us together, and that is actually how my sister saved my life. So I went with her, but of course, it's a long story how we stayed alive . . ."

The initial relief of having miraculously avoided separation from each other was short-lived. The two sisters were off to work. However, they, along with the other girls selected, could not leave. The war Allies had bombed the train tracks. They were quickly sent back to one of the buildings in the area instead, where they were jammed inside together with the other prisoners. There were no beds or bunks, forcing them to sleep on the cold concrete floor.

Two months later, after the train tracks were fixed, the German military was able to remove them from Auschwitz. Helen and Ella were sent to Horneburg, a town southwest of Hamburg, to a small camp to work amongst German civilians in electronics.

Horneburg

Helen had always said to herself while in Auschwitz, "If I ever manage to leave here, I know I could survive." And when this happened with their first stop in Horneburg, she started to have a little hope.

During this time, the war was very slowly approaching the end. As the Allied armies and Russian armies were coming into different parts of Germany, the German soldiers would hastily and cruelly shove the Jewish prisoners onto trains, transporting them from one camp to another. The conditions on the trains were no better than their first one to Auschwitz.

While in Horneburg, their barracks shook during the Allied bombing of Hamburg. It was cold inside of their barracks and even colder outside. Helen and Ella were only given thin workers' dresses to wear on their backs and wooden shoes to put on their feet.

"A German woman soldier came into our barrack," Ella remembers. "She asked us, 'Who spit? If no one comes forward to admit to it, you will all get a beating.' We all had to go outside and lie face down on the ground, dresses up, and they beat us. We had no underwear. I fainted from the beating. Helen told me later that I only woke up once back inside our barrack.

"The next day they took us to work in a factory, threading needles to sew garments. We had to have good eyes and steady hands. After the beating the day before, we could not sit down; our behinds were completely sore. We had to work while standing.

"They would not give us permission to go to the bathroom. When we asked, they would say, 'Come back in 15 minutes.' When we asked again in 15 minutes, they would repeat the same answer. The civilians who also worked in the factory along side us would ask what happened, and we told them. They seemed to be upset about our starvation and beatings."

Porta Westphalia

After three months in Horneburg, Helen and Ella, along with hundreds of other girls, were loaded onto cattle wagons yet again and taken to a big mountain near Porta. There was a tunnel opening, leading to an ammunition factory underneath the mountain. A pulley was used to take them down deeper and deeper underground.

"I never knew if it was day or night," Helen remembered. "Despite everything, it was fairly good there in comparison to other places we had been. They gave us at least a meal a day and we were sheltered from the cold and from the rain.

Ella, Helen's sister, remembered "Our sleeping quarters consisted of a large room with wooden bunks. When the German soldiers turned off the lights, rats would come out and bite us, pulling at the short hairs that had managed to grow since our heads were shaved upon entrance to Auschwitz. We could not sleep on account of the screaming and crying from the rat bites."

Bendorf

As liberation came even closer, Helen and Ella were rushed to leave Porta and found themselves in Bendorf, a salt mine, joining prisoners who had come from other labor camps.

Helen's husband, Martin, recalls hearing the eyewitness account from Ella of what happened one cold day, while being unable to warm up in the mine. "All of a sudden there was an announcement that all prisoners would be transported to another location. Hundreds of us started to line up, everyone picking up pace, tripping on each other in hopes that maybe this next destination would bring freedom. In the midst of people running every which way, Helen spotted one young girl whom she knew named Alice Schlosser.[1] Alice had two sisters there with her in the salt mine, but the crowd managed to separate them. She, like everyone, was malnourished and was trying to run, but could not keep up with the swarm of prisoners. At one point, her legs gave out and she fell. She was immediately trampled on by hordes of other prisoners. Helen, age 14 and malnourished herself, ran to her, picked her up, placed her on her own back, and carried her to safety where Alice was reunited with her sisters."

A Concentration Camp Following Bendorf[2]

Although the end of the war was nearing, the conditions of the prisoners were getting worse and worse.

Helen explained, "We were so hungry already, I and the girls I was with. One was nine years old and she just couldn't take it, so, knowing that there was a kitchen, I decided to go bring some food. As I entered the kitchen, I see on the floor that there are beets; you know, sugar beets, like the ones that you feed to the horses. For us, it didn't matter, as long as it was something. I grabbed one, and then grabbed another one, without realizing that an SS was up there watching me. He shot after me, but he did not want to kill me, because that would be too easy for me. He caught me instead and beat me up. The girls who knew my sister and I, they came to pull me up afterwards. It was really a miracle that I was still alive. When I got up, the first thing I did was look in my clothes for the beets. They were gone, and that bothered me more than the beating!"

Helen lost most of her vision in her right eye as a result of this beating.

Buchenwald

Their next and last stop would be Buchenwald, not in the camps, but rather in the woods.

The Axis powers were about to lose the war, and the Germans knew it. They wanted to dispose of the prisoners they had in their possession and were simply carrying out executions every which way they could.

Upon arrival, all Helen and Ella could see were piles and piles of men

---

1. A photo of Helen and Alice Schlosser is #11 in the photo section of this book.
2. I don't remember its exact name.

shot to death. Prisoners were hanging from the trees, wrists behind their backs. Screams could be heard echoing throughout the woods from the pain and starvation of each prisoner.

When it came time for Helen and Ella's turn to be executed, luck was on their side. The German soldiers ran out of ammunition.

The sisters were sent back to smaller barracks, where the two did nothing except sit and starve; only going out for zehl appel. Their next miracle, however, would be close behind.

AS A SURVIVOR

In March 1945, the Swedish Red Cross made a deal with the Germans to exchange prisoners for food, an operation named "White Buses." As a consequence of this agreement, two months later in May, the Red Cross liberated Helen and Ella and took them to Sweden. They both were skin and bones at this point, pure skeletons.

"The Red Cross nurses told us that we were free," Ella recounts. "They took us by train to Denmark and from there to Sweden by boat. We had to stay outside on the deck because we had lice. When we arrived to Sweden, we were deloused and showered before they let us into a cleaned-out school building. They gave us dog tags; my number was 1913 and Helen's number was 1914."

"They brought us into a room full of mattresses on the floor. They fed us light food to avoid getting sick; our stomachs were not yet ready for heavy food," Ella explains.

Helen remained forever grateful to the wonderful nurses and doctors who took such good care of her, and would always speak fondly of her time in Sweden and of the kindness of the Swedish people for taking her in as an orphan and bringing her back to life.

After Helen and Ella gained back their strength in Sweden, they wrote a letter home, to Priekopa, addressed to their gentile neighbors, hoping to find out which other members of their family were still alive. By the time the neighbors received the letter, their older sister, Ilona who had been separated from them while they were in Auschwitz, was back home.

Ilona had gotten word after her own liberation, that their father, Herman, had come back to Priekopa, so she had come back to look for him. To her dismay, it turned out to be someone else. However, Ilona would still leave with good news. Just upon her departure, the neighbor who had received Helen and Ella's letter called after her, "Your sisters are still alive!"

The neighbor gave Ilona the letter from Helen and Ella, and Ilona wrote them back to Sweden, letting them know that she had survived, but the rest of the family was not as fortunate.

Helen explained what she felt after the liberation. "Well, when we were liberated and we sort of came to ourselves, my emotions were terrible, because that's when we realized that we had lost everybody," she said. "Month after month, we had been suffering, hungering, in the cold and rain, you name it. Even in the summer time, when it was hot and we were standing in the C-lager with shaved heads while people were falling like flies, somehow, I was rooted better with my nerves.

"But for me, it was very difficult when I realized everyone was gone. My father was only 37 years old, and my mother was 36. They were young people, the whole family . . . It was a very hard time for me."

Helen and Ella remained in Sweden for two years during which time Helen was enrolled in school. Ella eventually chose to leave Gutenberg, having received papers from their paternal aunt to come to the United States. Ella then immigrated to America in 1947.

Meanwhile, Helen had dreamed of making Aliyah, to live in Israel, and was awaiting papers to immigrate there. However, before she received the papers to travel to the Holy Land, Ella sent her papers to come join her in America. And that's exactly what she did.

Helen was fluent in several languages; in addition to the Hungarian, Yiddish, Hebrew, German, Swedish and Slovak languages she already spoke, as well as the Russian and the Polish languages she understood, Helen quickly learned to fluently speak the language of her new country, English.

She was on her way to putting the dark behind her and lighting a bright path towards family and future.

AS AN ESHET CHAYIL (WIFE OF VALOR)

Up until the end of her days, Helen remembered everything about the first meeting with her husband, Martin Judovits, and their courtship. They met on January 29, 1950 at a Holocaust survivors gathering in New York City. Whenever her family would ask about their early dates together, she would laugh and retell a specific story.

It was Valentine's Day in February. And, to be expected for a winter in New York, it was extremely cold outside with snow falling rapidly on the ground. Rather than stay home, Martin came to the apartment where Helen was staying with a box of chocolates and flowers. She opened the door and just looked at him with a frustrated face. "What are you, completely crazy?" she exclaimed. "It's freezing outside and you are going to catch a cold!" But the truth was, she was completely in love.

Martin and Helen married[3] on June 25, 1950.

The two complemented each other incredibly well. Helen loved to be outdoors, and Martin loved to be indoors with his books and studies. He was always very cerebral and methodical, thinking things through, while Helen was always very spontaneous, emotional, simple, and direct. But when she decided to do something, you knew it was going to get done and get done right.

While Martin was the designer and builder, Helen made everything come to life in the home she shared with her family. She was very proud of her husband and his accomplishments, especially with regard to support for Israel, the Jewish community, and the synagogues to which they belonged. Martin and their children are the first to admit that their family would not have worked without Helen and her constant support.

Their love and caring for each other was even stronger during their last years together.

Martin recounts another story of Helen's kindness. "A few years ago, in 2009, Helen was attending services in the Boca Raton Synagogue; it was during a holiday when they recite Yizkor (memorial prayers). A young lady, about 20 years old, was nearby praying. Helen noticed that she was sobbing and crying bitterly. Helen approached her, asking her what was wrong. The girl replied, 'It is the first memorial for my father; he died last year from cancer. I miss him so much.'

"Helen put her arms around her and told her, 'I know it hurts. I lost both of my parents in Auschwitz when I was only fourteen years old.' She continued to talk to her and to console her. A week later, Helen received from her the most beautiful thank you letter."

Helen and Martin were frequently giving to both Jewish and non-Jewish causes throughout their marriage. Helen volunteered as a substitute teacher for the Hebrew school of the Orangetown Jewish Center, as well as for the Blauvelt public school system. The two would speak

---

3. A photo of Helen and Martin on their wedding day is #9 in the photo section of this book.

often together at different schools, both public and private, about their experiences during the Holocaust, in spite of the painful memories this brought each of them.

AS A MOTHER

Although the memories of the Holocaust often intruded on her daily life and made it difficult for her to sleep at night, Helen was committed to shielding her family from these horrors.

She believed that the best revenge against Hitler and the Holocaust was to raise healthy, self-confident, Jewish children. So she devoted herself entirely to raising normal children, without adding the burden of her life experiences.

ROBERT

My earliest and most frequent recollections of my mother are her laughing and playing with me. She would do something to get my attention, get me excited, smile, and then laugh. And her laugh was just infectious.

Being happy and enjoying the simple things in life was not a philosophy with my Mom, it was who she was. She had fun going food shopping and enjoyed cleaning her house. Her level of satisfaction and fulfillment from seeing her home in order and all of us happy and productively engaged was immeasurable.

The Bronx

Similarly to my mother, who had a few vivid recollections of her early life in Priekopa laying the foundation for her own childhood, I, too, visualize my younger years through pieces of scattered memories with my mother.

I'm seven years old. We're at Seal's and Claire's Bungalow Colony in the Catskills. We are walking along a country road. There is a tall crab apple tree with many branches. Mom scrambles to climb up the branches, all the while laughing. Then she starts tossing them down to me.

We're in our Bronx apartment. A neighbor is coming over and Mom tells me she has a lot to do and can only talk for ten minutes to the neighbor. They are sitting in the kitchen. I am in the hall leading to the kitchen. The neighbor is sitting with her back to me. I've learnt to tell time. Ten minutes pass. I begin to frantically point to the clock trying to get Mom's attention. Finally the neighbor hears the commotion, turns around and sees me pointing to the clock. Mom breaks down in hysterical laughter.

We are in our Bronx apartment. Mom is angry at me. I am sad. I decide to leave home and tell Mom. She says "Okay," and packs clothes and a bag with food and gives it to me. I go outside and sit on the landing steps not sure where to go. After a while Mom comes out and says that it is getting late and it is best if I leave tomorrow.

We are playing cards; usually gin rummy. She is a good card player. Then she is playing with her friends. I can see she is enjoying the game. She plays with enthusiasm. They are talking and laughing.

Mom is on the other side of the street. I run across to join her. A car comes to a screeching stop an inch from me. The look on Mom's face is indescribable, and remains a permanent image engraved in my mind. I heard afterwards that she bit down so hard that she lost a tooth.

Mom loved songs and loved to sing, specifically these songs:

"Que Sera Sera, whatever will be will be" was her favorite,

"You are my sunshine" was not far behind,

"My Bonny Lies over the Ocean,"

"How Much Is That Doggy in the Window."

Mom was always proud of our family, her husband and each of her children. She was proud of our grades in school and never stopped telling us how well we did. She loved to hear me play accordion and then piano, asking me to play songs over and over again. Considering the fact that I was never quite able to carry a tune in any form, I know her love was endless.

As much as she loved us, she didn't hesitate to expect the highest standards of behavior. If I didn't walk straight, she would yell at me and say that if I didn't walk straight, I would grow up to be like the dinky doinky man, a character in our Bronx neighborhood. If Lawrence or I left off doing some task in the middle, or didn't do something at all, she would yell at us and say, "Look at you two big horses and look at me. Aren't you ashamed of yourselves?" And we most certainly were.

From the Bronx to Blauvelt

Mornings were Mom's time. She was an early riser, usually the first one up, smiling, happy, bright, and a ball of energy. She loved to do things, to be busy and active. She was always in motion, having absolutely no patience for people that did nothing or sat around all day. If she got up after my father, she was still the first in the kitchen cleaning and straightening up. She would always say to us, "Look at the floor, it is so clean you can eat off of it." And it was.

In Blauvelt, I remember her waking us up on school days. She made breakfast for my father in the morning while he showered. She then made Lawrence and myself breakfast, and sent us off to school with a lunch that she would pack for us daily, usually a sandwich with one of the following: balonga, corned beef, pastrami, roast beef, homemade tuna salad, sardines, or peanut butter and jelly.

I never recall her walking us to school in Blauvelt. We lived nine tenths of a mile from the elementary school and therefore weren't eligible for bus service. She never worried. She expected us to be independent and stand on our own two feet. In fact she kept telling us this, and we did.

On the weekends, especially on snow days, there would be piles and piles of pancakes layered with sticks of butter and maple syrup. Usually she would make us "coffee-for-children," comprised of a drop of coffee, mostly milk, and a few teaspoons of sugar – a very sweet latte without the espresso.

For dinner, there were standards. Her specialties included:

Stuffed cabbage – I never appreciated it. However, my friends did. When I went off to college, after bringing some up with me the first time, my apartment mates were always asking me to bring more.

Hamburgers – When I went with her to the butcher, the hamburger would start with her getting a piece of chuck steak and having it ground in front of her. At home she would add onions, eggs, and matzo meal to the ground meat and then fry the burgers. I'm sure there were other spices added besides the onions, but I no longer remember. I remember the onions because both Mom and I would tear up while peeling them.

Cucumber salad – Comprised of cucumbers, vinegar, salt, and sugar, this salad was famous across most of the western hemisphere. Unbelievably delicious! She loved salt and vinegar, eating herring with relish. She also liked gefillte fish, which will always be an eternal mystery to me.

However, given all of the above, when it comes to food, the strongest memory I have is of my Mom making coffee in a percolator pot and enjoying a good cup of coffee either with my father or with friends. Mostly though, I don't recall her eating as much as I recall her enjoying watching her family eat the food she made.

From Blauvelt to Boca

I never remember doing laundry. I assume that I just thought it was a phenomenon of nature that when I opened my drawers, all my clothes were clean and neatly folded. It wasn't until I left home and went to college that it actually occurred to me that someone had to have had actually been doing this.

Mom loved to garden. In Blauvelt, she would tend to her rose bushes on the side of the house, fertilizing them with eggshells and coffee grinds. I have made a career of buying unsuccessful gifts for friends and family, however, one year, I struck gold. The best gift I ever bought was a compact specialty gardening tool set from Brookstone for Mom. She loved it from the word "go." Forever after when I went down to Florida, I would see her tending her garden using this tool set.

She was always talking about the importance of helping others, and she did continually, running errands for neighbors and friends, befriending those in need in our community who she deemed worthy. She had one friend that must have been at least 20 years older than her, Mrs. Felberbaum. She was unable to drive. I remember Mom taking her everywhere, picking her up, and bringing her to our house to spend time with us while Mom took care of us as well. It wasn't enough for my Mom to help Mrs. Felberbaum; she wanted her to have fun as well, and she would take her places and shopping. There are many more tales that I am familiar with and I'm sure even more about which I don't even know.

My parents were always very involved in the Jewish community; whether it was leading food drives at the temple or sending care packages to Israel. While they didn't go out together much with their close circle of friends, they certainly stayed in together, each family hosting parties taking turns in their own home. Although I don't remember the parties much, I do remember that the house always sparkled, and my mother would sparkle even more, totally enjoying the preparation process and the party.

Her Heart in Israel

On one of the final trips to Israel with my parents, just Mom and I drove from Jerusalem where they were staying, down by way of the Dead Sea, to the apartment I owned in Arad. It was a wonderful trip with a stop at the Dead Sea, and then back up to Arad for an inspection of my apartment and meeting with the realtor that rented the apartment for me. Afterwards, we decided to drive back to Jerusalem via Hebron and stop at the Cave of the Machpelah. I recall army checkposts and a stark barren and dry landscape under a brilliant blue sky.

We got out of the car somewhere before arriving in Hebron. I took a photograph of Mom. She is standing proudly in the photograph with a great big smile on her face with this stark landscape in the background. She is happy to be there. Happy to be standing in the Land of Israel, and I imagine her thinking that she has contributed to the continuance of the Jewish people and their living in their own country in the Land of Israel.

Lawrence

As my sister Joyce writes so well in the article below, my mother did not share, to any extent, her Holocaust stories with me either. She always told me that it was to spare me the horror of it. I do remember the incident of the "selection" process, when alighting from the cargo train at Auschwitz she was told to go to a separate line away from my grandmother, Rose, and my aunt, Yolan, who were with her at this time. She did not want to go at first but was urged on by another woman, and I suppose she realized that she was choosing an opportunity to survive. After separating from them, she never saw her mother or younger sister again.

Another story I remember was the pact my mother made with her sister, my Aunt Ella; that they would not separate even if it meant to take one last walk to the crematorium. My Aunt Ella told me that this pact was tested when, in late 1944 (maybe November), slave labor was needed in a factory. A hundred fifty or so girls were selected, but of the two sisters, only Ella was picked. My mother was not. Ella then begged the person in charge of the detail to take her sister. He relented with a quick yes that was not contested by the other guards.

My final story is one of which I'm not very confident, but I do remember my mother relating it to my wife Nancy and me. Being young, fourteen, she was still a child and curious. Not long after coming to the camp, she saw a group of fellow prisoners marching, so she decided to march with them. The march took her to the entrance of the death camp (Auschwitz was divided into two parts: a work and a death camp). As she approached the gates, a German guard told her (as best as I can remember my mother's words), "Go back little girl, you do not want to come in here."

Finally I would just like to add one of the lessons I learned from my mother, and that would be – when you are staring down into an abyss, life has gotten tough, be true to yourself and work through it.

Joyce

My mother did not share a lot of her Holocaust stories with me. Perhaps this was her way of protecting me, or trying to make sure I was insulated from her horrific experiences. The one story that she did repeat over and over, especially as her time drew toward an end, but while she was still able to speak, was her deep regret over the way she separated from her mother.

As referenced earlier in this chapter, upon arrival at Auschwitz, my grandmother, Rose, was placed in a line with other mothers, carrying or holding the hands of young children. My grandmother was with my aunt, Yolan, or Lolica (Rachel Yita), as my mother fondly called her. There was an unspoken awareness of the fact that this line was headed for the Nazi gas chambers. Mom had an opportunity to get on a different line – one of those who were deemed fit enough for labor. My mother was only fourteen or so at the time, and she seized the chance to separate herself and run to join this group. She did not take the time to say goodbye to her mother or sister. She chose life.

Her recurring need to tell me this story was to express her sorrow about how quickly she left her mother and how she did not have any parting words or gestures for her. And each time she did I would try to help her place herself in her mother's shoes. "Okay, Mom – you are standing in that line holding my hand, knowing that you will go with me to our death. Lawrence or Robert are there and have a chance to run and live; do you want them to delay and miss their chance?"

Her answer was always the same – she of course most emphatically would want her child to live. And that is what she did; she lived an exemplary life and was the most devoted of mothers.

She loved me with the depth of her being and that abundance of love was lavished upon me, whether I was deserving of it or not – regardless of my words or actions.

I knew that my mother was in my corner instinctively and immediately throughout my life. At no time was this more apparent than in her care of my younger son, Jonah. Jonah is quadriplegic and profoundly mentally disabled. He needs assistance for the most basic of his needs. Many would be put off, scared, feel not up to the task of caring for such a grandchild. Not my mom. She was incredible with all her grandchildren, but with him, her youngest grandchild, she was exceptional.

My parents would spend the summers away from the Florida heat with us in Seattle. My mom would begin each day waiting for Jonah to wake so that she could feed him his breakfast, walk with him in the garden, show him the cat hiding from the wheelchair, and read him a book. She would shoo away his caregivers – "I think there is laundry to fold," "Why don't you unload the dishwasher?" She wanted this child to herself. Her dedication was apparent.

You might assume that she had an affinity for people with disabilities, that perhaps she was acclimated to this population. This was not the case. My mom loved Jonah with intensity because her immense love for me was so great that it spilled onto all that I created and touched. My children to her were an extension of me and, therefore, cherished, and yes, unconditionally loved.

I can only pray and aspire to be such a wonderful mother. The example is set for me, but the bar is so very high.

AS A GRANDMOTHER
Mayah

One of my earliest and happiest memories of my childhood is sitting under the apple tree in my grandparent's backyard in Rockland County, New York. I am three years old, and Savta is lovingly feeding me pieces of chicken while we sit on the lush green lawn. She loved to be outdoors, especially exploring or tending to plants.

Twenty-five years later, my son Mordechai, her great-grandchild, would also remember his Savta-Raba vividly during a visit to Boca Raton when he was only four years old. Savta took him outside to the front lawn where there was a large palm tree. She picked him up so he could grab a red looking berry with his hands, and Mordechai screeched in pain when he felt the prickly thorns on his skin. Savta felt so badly. She also touched the thorns to see how they felt, consequently hurting herself, as well. She couldn't let her great-grandson suffer without feeling his pain, too. She removed the thorns from his hand and kissed him. Her curiosity and love of plants and nature was so much fun to me and to Mordechai, who also shares her passion for the outdoors.

Savta was constantly in motion, enthusiastic about every project. As an early conservationist and environmentalist, she would collect the vegetable peels from her cooking and carry them together with heavy buckets of dishwater out to the garden to be used as compost for the soil; she did this even in her later years.

She kept her house sparkling clean, always. Once after we had left her house following a visit, she was cleaning a mirrored wall in the dining room with Windex. She noticed at her knee level several tiny handprints of Mordechai, her great-grandson, on the mirrored glass. She lovingly could not bring herself to wipe them clean and kept them there, as is, for several weeks after we left.

All her life she was an avid Zionist and devoted to Jewish causes, especially charities that supported the State of Israel. Savta's warmth and kindness was truly exceptional and exemplary. She could strike up a conversation with anyone and often had people she had just met opening up and telling her their entire life stories.

She treated every person with the same respect and attention, always saying hello and how are you to the cashier at the checkout or to her neighbors. When someone was sick or homebound in her Boca Raton development, she took it upon herself to cook and deliver meals. These activities were done privately, out of the public eye. Acts of loving-kindness were her daily purpose. When her family visited, she would squeeze oranges in the morning to make fresh juice for everyone. She was devoted to her husband, children, and grandchildren.

We miss her every day. Her moral compass, courage, kindness, and generosity serve us as a guiding light in our lives.

Talya

My grandmother's day would start around 4–5am. It was great. If you had trouble sleeping, took an early flight, made aliyah (me), you just picked up the phone, dialed Boca, and Helen Judovits was on the other end, bright and cheery, as if she had been up for hours. She would be in the kitchen, drinking her first cup of coffee (mostly "just water") before sunrise and reading the paper that she had just brought in from her driveway. Her right hand would tremor ever so slightly as she picked up the coffee cup to her mouth; I always assumed a lasting scar from the war. Reading glasses would be on, but as soon as she began a conversation with one of us, they went down on the paper with excitement in her face. Her focus was on the voice coming through the phone.

You could talk about anything – she always had great reactions, good advice, and such an infectious, body-jerking laugh. You would start laughing, too, from wherever in the world you happened to be making the call. While you would want to be on the phone for hours with her, she would cut you off after twenty minutes saying, "Well, I don't want to keep you." Although she really did love hearing the sounds of our voices, we probably talked her ear off. No worries, she would hear from us again soon.

We involved her in every aspect of our lives, except illness. That, though, I have to say, we learned from her. You don't tell anyone in the family you're sick or suffering unless you end up in the hospital and the situation is not looking good. You only reestablish contact after you have recovered and can then explain what happened with a clean bill of health.

I remember telling her about all these weird guy experiences, school experiences, Aliyah experiences . . . She was my number one fan, my cheerleader. She was my source of strength, and voice of reason. She had words and expressions of wisdom my family and I quote frequently, simply because they are so true and embody the values and morals by which we choose to live.

She never felt sorry for herself; she was never worried for her own health or future (and if she was, she never showed it). She dedicated her entire life to her family. She survived the Holocaust, but never changed her day-to-day behavior because of it. She would often say when I was little and would start to get tired of walking, "G-d gave you two legs, da'ling, walk on them." It would actually work. "That's true," I would think. "I can walk a bit more."

Helen, or Savta, as we endearingly call her, was in on every joke going on inside the house or wherever we were together. She was so playful and loved to laugh with us . . . and I still laugh with her to this day, as she continues to be the voice guiding me towards my happiness.

Amelia

My best memory of my grandmother is not a single memory, but rather the overall memory of her nature, who she was as a person. This memory of her overall being remains forever embedded in my mind as a personal yardstick between right and wrong.

She always stood her ground; her path was clear as to what justice was. If something didn't sit right with her, she made it known and did something about it. Friends that wronged her or had questionable morals did not remain her friends.

At the same time, she gave everyone a fair chance. Everyone was good to her and had something to offer until proven otherwise. She could strike up a conversation with anyone and bring even the shyest wallflower out of his or her shell. She made the best of any situation and made it a natural priority to get to know the people around her in any place – the supermarket, the park, the doctor's office, the plane, the sidewalk, anywhere. There were no limits to where you could meet someone interesting.

What was amazing was how at ease you could feel around her and how willing you were to open up to her. She had the most youthful of spirits. She had a permanent sparkle in her eyes. They would glisten like ripples of water do when they catch the light of the sun. She had a lust for life and fun, and found it in even the saddest of moments. She stood for life. She lived through the most horrific of atrocities, the Holocaust, and it was as though she spent the rest of her life showing G-d that she didn't take it for granted.

She rose early with infectious enthusiasm and went to sleep late as though to squeeze every last drop out of her days. Whether it was cleaning her home, tending to her garden, or making one of her delicious apple cakes, she did each job to its fullest, not cutting any corners. She also used all her power not to waste anything in the process. She would use leftover egg yolks from her baking and add them to shampoo, and she would collect water after washing the dishes to water the plants.

By that same token, she would never hoard and only liked to have in her home what she truly needed. She easily would give away or throw out objects collected or her children's old belongings, deeming it junk. She didn't place any importance on material objects or form an attachment to them; to her the most important thing in life was her family. She made this known to the world, letting the love she had for her children and grandchildren leap out of her skin.

Benjamin

Savta. Her life is true inspiration for how one should live. For someone who saw great tragedy, to find the willingness to continue moving forward in life is a miracle in itself. That's what I admire most about her. She didn't look back, but rather kept moving forward and found new hope, love, and family.

That's what Savta taught me. To keep moving forward, always be willing to take the next step in life. And also, most importantly, keep people in your life who appreciate you just as much as you appreciate them.

She was a very outspoken and strong-minded individual. If you believed something that was contrary to her belief, you were going to hear it. If you did something she just didn't like, you were going to hear it. If she was proud of you for the littlest thing in the world, everyone else was going to hear about it.

I love her and I miss her. And I know for sure she loves us and misses us more than any of us can fathom.

Emily

My grandmother was part of my life. I loved my Savta and she loved me. Every morning when I would be visiting at her house in Boca, I would wake up to find her in the kitchen having coffee. She would get out her USA puzzle map and teach me about the states, and then she would make me scrambled eggs.

She used to take me on walks all around the neighborhood. We would put on some hats and walk around in our flip-flops and sunglasses. When I was just a year old, and Savta was staying at our home in Pennsylvania, she took me outside to play in the snow, dressing me up in a snowsuit. When she was not looking, I crawled into a pile of snow and then popped out. She laughed when I did that.

She has given me so many things that I still have, including her straw hat and her earrings. But she is not around anymore to read me stories, let me play with her dolls, or to hold my hand, though now that I am older, I don't need any of that. It doesn't get easy when everything just slips away and bothers you for the rest of your life, does it? I hope no one needs to face the same suffering of losing someone that I had.

Noah

As a kid, the summer meant freedom from school, trips to friends' cabins, and basketball camp. But it also signaled the arrival of my Saba and Savta, who would come and stay at our house every summer. Amidst the late mornings and long days of lounging by the pool, my Savta was there, either laughing at one of my poorly constructed potty-humor jokes, or unintentionally making a hilarious comment of her own.

We used to do a lot together. We would go on long walks around the neighborhood where we would pick fruits from our neighbors' trees and eat them as snacks on our way to getting a slice of pizza. We looked at people's flowers and she would tell me what kind they were, and if we liked them enough we would pick them too!

As I grew older, we would still treat the world like our little Garden of Eden, but Savta's recounting of her experiences in Europe and the Holocaust would highlight our walks more. I remember most of her stories – some of the details have become more faint to me – but the thing I took away most about what she told me was the amount of perseverance and determination a person can have. My grandmother was in Auschwitz, starving, being abused, and on the verge of death, yet she still had the presence of mind to share her food with others. She not only didn't give up herself, but she wouldn't let others succumb either. I like to think that my desire to never quit came from her. After all the horrible things she saw, she could still enjoy the beauty of life and share nothing but happiness with me.

It's been nearly four years since my Savta passed away. I couldn't be there for the funeral. I was in my freshman year of college and it was a hard time for me; I was very distracted. When I was first told to write of a moment I shared with Savta I couldn't think of something specific. This made me sad at first, but I was comforted by the realization that my memory of her is manifested in who I am, not what we used to do. I wish I could hear Savta's broken English again, or her songs that she used to sing to my brother. I so wanted to tell her the story of when I got thrown out of Oktoberfest for no reason by large, German security guards only to sneak back in when they weren't looking; I know she would have loved that.

Until that point in time when we can do all these things again, I preserve Savta's memory in my heart by trying to emulate her kind-heartedness, determination, and perseverance.

Jonah

> Savta, you knew, right? From my ear-to-ear smiles and
>   how I would pick up my knee?
> Every time you touched a curl on my head, I could
>   feel your strong love for me.
> Savta, I looked forward to your Seattle summer arriv-
>   als. I loved the sound of your voice.
> You gave everything to be with me, Noah, my par-
>   ents, Rick, and Joyce.
> Savta, how you sang to me, I remember, and how you
>   would feed me, I still get excited.
> I remember your face at my birthday parties . . . You
>   were absolutely delighted.
> Savta, you had a special relationship with me that I
>   did not share with anyone else.
> You understood my enthusiastic sounds to be words,
>   and your translations were never false.
> Savta, I miss the time we shared together with your
>   arms wrapped around me, as if forever.
> I love you, Savta. Your soft skin, warm heart, strong
>   spirit, I will forget never.

AS A BELIEVER IN HASHEM

There is always the question a Holocaust survivor gets, after experiencing such horrors and witnessing the very worst of which humanity is capable: How is it possible to believe in G-d, in Hashem?

And Helen's answer to this question would always be centered on the love she had for her family.

"I really believe more now in miracles because we experienced so many miraculous events, and so our beliefs became even stronger. Can you imagine me having three beautiful children, beautiful, wonderful grandchildren . . . and great grandsons, all wonderful people with love and so giving of attention?

"I have a granddaughter who graduated college and she picked herself up and she made Aliyah. There is not one Friday that she should not call us to wish us Shabbat Shalom.

It is so hard to explain . . . I go to my daughter's in Seattle for the summer, and my grandson, no matter where he is, calls me up and asks, "Savta, did you drink?"

He would make sure that I was drinking water because he knows I have to keep hydrated.

"I'm just saying, the attention I get from my family, and love, it's incredible. So really, Hashem blessed us."

*

This concludes the memoir chapter written by the family.

אמונה – Faith

As a Holocaust survivor, I am often asked the following question:

Do you still believe in God? You lost your parents and your entire family in the Holocaust for the sole reason that they were Jewish. And you yourself endured enslavement by the Nazis because you were Jewish. Did that affect your belief in God? Do you ask yourself, "Why did God allow this to happen?"

Answer:

With regards to the question, "Why did God allow this to happen?" I cannot answer for God; that answer can be given only by God himself. "The hidden things are known only to God."

With regards to the question, "How could I still believe in God?" After I was liberated, I was an angry man, and many years afterwards I was still angry. I was depressed and I had many doubts. I thought a lot about it. I was looking for answers and these are my thoughts about this question:

Thought 1

While I was a prisoner in the labor camps, I experienced numerous personal miracles. I survived many close calls with death, as described earlier in this book. There is no question in my mind that it was the hand of God that saved me in all of those close calls. There were times when I was already very sick and without any strength; I thought that it is the end – that I would die. There were no doctors, no hospitals, but there was God who kept me alive.

Thought 2

My parents believed in God, and they showed me the way to believe in God. They learned it from their parents and grandparents, all the way back to Abraham, our patriarch.

Anyone who denies the existence of God is merely expressing an opinion. Therefore, Heaven forbid, if I should express such an opinion I would be boasting, "I am smarter than my parents and I am smarter than my ancestors." Expressing such an opinion would be blasphemy and spitting in the faces of my parents.

Thought 3

As a child of martyred parents I consider myself a lucky person, and I am proud that I was born to my wonderful Jewish parents. Heaven forbid, had I been born to a Nazi murderer, would I be proud of my parents? Would my offspring be proud of their grandparents? Or would any decent person be proud of their behavior?

Thought 4

If a Holocaust survivor excludes God from his life because he or she is angry at God for allowing this to happen, that person is only adding to his or her losses and loneliness. The parents are already murdered, the brothers and sisters are gone, and now God is also gone.

Thought 5

After liberation I was able to come to America; God was good to me, and blessed me with a new good life in this new country. Coming to America was in itself a miracle. I had no one in America who would send me papers, but somehow someone, who was a stranger to me at that time, sent me papers. God was good to me.

Then I got married; God blessed me with a wonderful and beautiful wife.

Then we had children, God blessed us with wonderful and healthy children.

Later on God blessed us with beautiful and gifted Grandchildren,

In later years God blessed us with wonderful great-grandchildren.

God has granted me a long life, blessed me with productive good years.

God has been good to us all these years. For all those blessings I thank God and I believe and trust in him.

My Life after the Holocaust

T HE FIRST TWENTY YEARS OF MY LIFE I lived in Europe. My years spent in Europe ended in tragedy; I lost everything that was dear to me. I lost my parents, I lost my brothers and sister, I lost numerous uncles and aunts, and I lost so many cousins that I can't even count them. I lost my home and all my personal belongings and even all the photographs of my parents, brothers, and sister. I was able to find some photos of my mother and photos of my family at relatives who were not deported. Thank G-d I didn't lose my sanity and I didn't lose my humanity. The past is sad and irreversible, but the future looked bright and promising. And so it was.

My new life in America began on a happier note and has been wonderful for all those years, with a few exceptions, like major illnesses.

In 1950 I married my beautiful and wonderful wife, Helen.[1] The Chupah of our wedding was in the Williamsburg section of Brooklyn, in the home of my cousins Rabbi Yosef Moshe Meisels, the Ujvar Rabbi, and his Rebetzin Feigish. The wedding was arranged and sponsored by Rabbi Feivel Halberstam, the same wonderful person who sent me the papers enabling me to come to America.

My wife Helen was also a Holocaust survivor with many horrific stories of her own. At her deportation to Auschwitz, she was only a fourteen years old child, but she had a strong will and spirit and she survived.

Helen and I were blessed with three beautiful and wonderful children: Robert (Shlomo), Lawrence (Yosef Tzvi), and Joyce (Nechama Reizl).

---

1. See photo #9 in the photo section of this book.

Robert was married to Shifra, and they have three wonderful children: Mayah, Talya, and Amelia. Lawrence is married to Nancy, and they have two wonderful children: Benjamin and Emily. Our daughter Joyce is married to Rick Israel, and they have two wonderful children: Noah and Jonah.

In 1952, I went into my own drapery business. It was located in a small loft on Broadway and 18th Street, in New York City. In 1963 I received a patent from the US Government Patent Office, #3,082,818. The patent was for a drapery device. In 1964 I received a second patent, #3,132,686. This was a pleating device for draperies.

In 1970 I became interested in art, and I began to study painting in the Rockland County Art Institute. I have continued to paint ever since, and since I retired I devoted a lot of time to this hobby. Regretfully, I didn't have a chance to study in a real art school.

In 1974, I moved my factory to 130 Fifth Avenue, at the corner of 18th Street in New York City.

In 1978 I retired from business entirely.

In 1983 we sold our home in Blauvelt and we moved to Boca Raton, FL. We joined the newly formed Boca Raton Synagogue; soon afterward I was elected a member of the board.

In 1985 the synagogue bought a five-acre parcel of land on which we planned to build a sizable synagogue building. We started first with a small synagogue building to serve us temporarily.

In 1989 I was appointed building committee chairman and I began planning a new larger building; I submitted the plans to the board. After the board approved the plan, we hired an architect, and in 1992, under my direction and supervision, we began building the new Boca Raton Synagogue[2] and Mikvah.

In 1992 I became president of the Boca Raton Synagogue, but I also continued as chairman of the building committee.

The buildings[3] were completed and dedicated in 1994. In my dedication speech to a large audience I declared, "My labor of the past five years was a labor of love, which I have dedicated to the memory of my

---

2. The groundbreaking for the Boca Raton Synagogue is #12 in the photo section of this book. In the picture is my wife Helen and I.

3. Photos #13A and #13B in the photo section of this book are pictures of the Boca Raton Synagogue, exterior and interior.

parents, and to the parents of my wife Helen, and to my family who perished in the Holocaust."

In the year 2000, Helen and I celebrated our 50th wedding anniversary in the Boca Raton Synagogue at a Shalosh Seudos; many of our friends attended.

In 2009, I published my first book titled *Sages of the Talmud*. The book is about the authors of the Talmud; it lists almost 400 biographies of the great Sages of the Talmud.

In 2014, I published my second book titled *Find it in the Talmud*. The book contains over 6000 entries. Most of the entries are about ethics and proper conduct advocated by the Talmud.

In 2010, a Holocaust memorial[4] was erected in front of the Boca Raton Synagogue, which I planned and designed. The memorial consists of six black granite pillars, each measuring eight feet tall and thirty inches wide; the pillars are shaped like candles split in two. Engraved on the flat side of the pillars are the names of many martyrs who died in the Holocaust. On the curved side of the candles are engravings of maps with names of Holocaust labor-camp sites. At the dedication, Rabbi Lau, former Chief Rabbi of Israel, was the keynote speaker.

There is a separate chapter in this book, memoirs of my wife Helen. She died Friday evening, on September 9, 2011, in Seattle in the home of our Daughter Joyce, and son-in-law Rick Israel. She was my lifetime partner; we were married for 61 years. Most of the family was present and gathered in her room just before she died, and we sang the traditional Friday evening chant Eishes Chayil song ("A woman of valor"), and we made the Shabbat Kiddush in her room. A short while after that she was gone.

---

4. Photos #14A and #14B in the photo section of this book are pictures of the Holocaust Memorial that stands at the entrance of the synagogue. It was planned and designed by Martin Judovits, the author of this book.

APPEAL!

An Appeal
From a Holocaust Survivor

To the Jewish Leaders
In every country of the world

To address an urgent problem:
Namely, the declining Jewish population

Let us convene a meeting
in Jerusalem!

Let us propose plans for how to
solve this problem! Please, let us do
something!

In this chapter I propose several ideas how
To solve this urgent problem

Bring your ideas and proposals to this
convention and let us decide what to do.

The goal shall be

6,000,000 more Jews
in the world

APPEAL!

An Appeal
From a Holocaust Survivor

To the Rabbis
In every country of the world

To address an urgent problem:
Namely, the declining Jewish population

Let us convene a meeting
in Jerusalem!

Let us propose plans for how to
solve this problem! Please, let us do
something!

In this chapter I propose several ideas how
To solve this urgent problem

Bring your ideas and proposals to this
convention and let us decide what to do.

The goal shall be

6,000,000 more Jews
in the world

אור חדש על ציון תאיר

A Survivor's Ideas for a Jewish Rebirth:
The Rebirth of 6,000,000 More Jews
in the World

As a Holocaust survivor I am deeply concerned about the declining Jewish population in the United States and around the world.

Before WWII, the Jewish population of the world numbered about eighteen million. After the war was over and after we lost millions in the Holocaust, that number was reduced to about twelve million. Today, seventy years after the Holocaust, we are still only about twelve million and the numbers are further declining.

This steady decline is an intolerable situation.

At the same time the entire world population in 1945 – after WWII ended – numbered about two billion people. Today in 2014, the world population is close to seven billion people, which is a 350% increase.

My great concern is that we are facing a creeping physical and spiritual holocaust. For thousands of years we held on to our heritage in spite of persecution, poverty, and hostility. This heritage, which held us together as one people and was so dear to our parents and grandparents, is being discarded as so much extra baggage.

In Israel, the demographic picture is also alarming. Israel could lose its Jewish identity within a few decades if nothing is done to increase the Jewish population.

Our inaction in this regard is actually causing a new silent holocaust; there are no gas chambers, no mass killings, but the ultimate result could be just as devastating.

What can be done to reverse this urgent situation? The status quo is unacceptable; something must be done.

Here are my ideas and proposals:

Let us convene a meeting in Jerusalem!

The convention in Jerusalem shall establish a new organization specifically for the purpose of implementing a plan of action to stop the declining Jewish population.

The new organization shall be named:

עם ישראל חי
שמור שארית ישראל
Protect the Remnant of Israel

The organization shall implement a plan to restore the Jewish population of the world to the level it was prior to the Holocaust.
The goal shall be:

6,000,000 more Jews in the world

The task of the organization shall be to find sponsors and donors to finance the restoration of the Jewish people. The funds for the program shall be raised from the following sources:

From wealthy individuals,
From middle income individuals,
From Germany,
From Israel bonds,
and
From various other sources.

Incentives to Parents to Have Larger Families

To accomplish our goal, the organization shall offer significant monetary subsidies to parents in the categories below.

Donors will pledge to subsidize parents who already have two children with a subsidy to bring to this world a third child. Additional subsidies will be given for each additional child thereafter.

The subsidy will be in annual installments. The first annual subsidy will be when the child is born; this sum will be given to the parents of the child. The balance of twelve annual subsidies will be towards the child's education.

The donors will undertake to pay a substantial annual amount to a trust fund in the name of the designated family or child. I have in mind an amount of $20,000 annually for thirteen years, however the exact amount shall be established by the board of this future organization. It shall be enough to cover the cost of the tuition or a large portion thereof. The recipients will be given the funds starting after the child is nine years old and depending on verified needs and eligibility.

It will be the aim of the organization to help parents bring up a new generation that is highly educated, able to contribute to the spiritual and economic strength of the Jewish people and Israel, and imbued with love for the Land of Israel.

The organization shall form a loose partnership with schools that have a strong Jewish curriculum and also a good secular curriculum.

The parents of such children will have to be cleared for eligibility by a proper committee.

To reach the number of six million may take one hundred years, but historically, 50 years or 100 years is not considered a long time.

How to Fund the New Organization

It will be the task of the organization over the long term to find thousands of individuals to underwrite the subsidy for one or several children. Each donor will be asked to subsidize one or more newborn children with a subsidy for thirteen years.

It is my opinion that there are many Jewish philanthropists who would be receptive to invest in the Jewish future. This urgent problem of the declining Jewish population needs to be brought to the forefront and to be made a priority. We need to sound the alarm to this urgent problem.

All the worthy causes will be for naught if our numbers keep declining; all the investments in the other worthy causes are very useful for the present, but they do not stop the decline.

will be in twelve annual installments, starting after the child is nine years old and depending on verified needs and eligibility.

It will be the aim of the organization to help parents bring up a new generation that is highly educated, able to contribute to the spiritual and economic strength of the Jewish people and Israel, and that is imbued with love for the Land of Israel.

Subsidies for School Budgets

The task of the organization shall also be to find individual donors who will undertake to subsidize 50% of a designated school budget in a Jewish community. Any school that will receive a 50% budget subsidy will reduce the tuition by 50% or even offer free tuition to students in need. For this subsidy the donor will receive proper recognition from that school for the donation, like naming a building in the donor's name.

A Jewish Teaching Museum

We must address also the needs of our existing Jewish population. How do we introduce Judaism to secular Jews who never learned to appreciate their heritage?

Today we have many Jews, young and old, who are ignorant of their Jewish heritage; some are still in their formative years. According to the statistics, 85% of the Jewish population is unaffiliated with any synagogue.

The declining Jewish population and assimilation should be of great concern to all of us. **The declining Jewish population will affect not only those families whose children assimilate, but also our children and grandchildren who remain Jewish.**

With a shrinking Jewish population, what will the Jewish world be like for our children and grandchildren? Jewish schools and Jewish institutions will surely decline, and smaller Jewish communities will have even greater difficulties maintaining themselves.

How do we turn this around? How do we bring our heritage to them?

I have thought about this problem for many years, and I have formulated a few ideas how to turn this around.

It is unlikely that the unaffiliated would suddenly decide to visit or join a synagogue or join a Jewish organization; it is more likely that they would visit a museum of interest. Therefore it would make sense to establish a Jewish Teaching Museum.

The museum will exhibit subjects like:
Jewish Traditions,
Jewish Ceremonies,
Jewish Culture,
Jewish History,
Jewish Achievements,
Jewish Art
and a Children's Museum.

The museum I have in mind will open the eyes of adults and children alike to our rich heritage, our colorful traditions, and our amazing culture. The museum will show the viewer every facet of Judaism. By establishing this museum, we will open the eyes of many and they will discover a heritage they never knew was theirs.

People differ in their interests; therefore the museum I have in mind would also have exhibits of different interests, like an art gallery, and historical and cultural exhibit sections. A museum of such diversity would attract a variety of people. We need to motivate the parents to want to bring their children to the museum. The best way to accomplish that is to have a museum that is attractive to children and adults alike. New converts to Judaism will also benefit from the museum by learning not only from one teacher, but from a multitude of teachers about all facets of Judaism.

EXHIBIT ROOMS

A Shabbat Room

This room shall be dedicated entirely to the day of Shabbat. A table shall be set for a Friday night meal with Shabbat candles, a beautiful tablecloth, and fine dishes and glassware, as it is practiced in many Jewish homes. In addition, a video will show the candle lighting at sunset before the Shabbat starts, parents and children participating and enjoying a family meal together with lively chatter, the Kiddush, zemirot, and blessings after the meal.

Instead of parents wondering where their children hang out on Friday nights, they will have them at their table enjoying a family night together.

The video will also show how the rest of the Shabbat is observed during the entire day.

It will show a kitchen on Friday full of activities preparing for Shabbat: baking Challah, cooking special foods.

A Pesach Seder Room

For Passover, the Seder room will have a table set for a Seder, displaying all particular items traditionally used at a Seder. In addition, a video will show on a screen how a Seder is conducted, from the beginning to the end. It will show the interaction of children and grownups, singing together and discussing freedom and the Exodus.

A Sukka Room

An actual walk-in Sukka will be displayed, with ornaments. In addition a video will show how the Sukka is used and explain its observance. The video will also show how to perform the Mitzvah of the Lulav and Ethrog.

Rooms for Other Holidays

There will be exhibits for Yom Kippur, Rosh Hashana, and others.

Modern Israel

A room will exhibit sites of modern Israel.

Jerusalem Room

A replica of the Temple will be on display and other pertinent facts about the city.

A Holocaust Room

Historical data about the communities lost will be on display.

The Shtetel room

A replica of a typical Eastern European Shtetel will be on display.

A Jewish Music Room

Cantorial music, Kletzmer, Yiddish songs, and other Jewish music will be heard and displayed.

Jewish Achievements Room

Jewish achievements in all fields, like science, medicine, music, literature, etc. will be displayed.

The Prophets Room

The history of the Prophets and their prophecies will be displayed.

The Kings of Judea and Israel

The history of the Jewish kings will be displayed.

The Talmud Room

The era of the Talmud, its authors, and the academies in Babylonia and Judea will be on display.

Biographies of the great Talmudic teachers: the Tannaim – Rabbi Hillel, Rabbi Shammai, Rabbi Akiva, Rabbi Gamliel, Rabbi Eleazar ben Azaryah; The Amoraim – Rav and Shemuel, Rabbi Yochanan, and many more.

Chasidism Room

The way of life, The Rebbe, the various Chasidic courts, and communities will be on display.

Ceremonies and Blessings Room

The ceremonies of a wedding, Bar and Bat Mitzvah, Bris, mourning, and Havdala will be exhibited. The practice of saying blessings before eating bread, fruit, etc. will be on display, and also the prayer after leaving the toilet will be explained.

The Great Jewish Personalities Room

The personalities of Rashi, Rambam, and of other great Jewish personalities will be on display.

The Art Gallery

Jewish art or art by Jewish artists will be on display. The subjects displayed will have to be approved by a panel of rabbis. Modesty is the keyword.

Art from other museums on loan, like the Israel museum, can also be exhibited

Lecture halls

The lecture halls will have movable walls to be able to convert the large hall into smaller lecture halls.

Children's Museum

The Children's Museum exhibits should be presented in a format of games and puzzles; a place for children to feel at home.

Young Children's Room

This room will be a place for young children to play and learn, with hands-on educational toys. This room should be a large, comfortable room to accommodate many children of different ages.

Room of the Righteous

The history of Raoul Wallenberg, Chione Sugihara, Emil Zola, etc. will be shown. The exhibit rooms should be user-friendly and entertaining.

The greatest experts in each field should be used, and every detail should be scrutinized.

The Gardens

In front of the museum there shall be beautiful gardens with Biblical themes. The main museum building shall be in a large metropolitan city where many Jews reside.

MUSEUM ON WHEELS

We need to introduce Judaism to every Jew who is interested, including those who live in small communities. Therefore the Museum should also have a traveling museum, a "Museum on Wheels." The Museum on Wheels will be on several trucks and will visit smaller communities, communities where they have no access to such an institution. The trucks will travel from one end of the country to the other end. Since the Museum on Wheels will be an event usually not seen in smaller communities, it should be of great interest and attract many of the locals.

Admission to the museum should be inexpensive for adults and free for children.

The Museum should have lectures and classes on all subjects of traditional Judaism. In addition, it should have a list of schools and teachers it could recommend to students interested in learning more about Judaism.

TEACHERS

After more exposure to the teachings of Judaism, there will probably be a demand for more study, therefore the museum should keep a list of teachers who are available in every community in the United States for students who want to further their Jewish education.

AWARDS AND RECOGNITION

We need incentives to be given to the generous donors. It is very important to honor and give recognition to the generous donors who will sponsor the education of one child or several children, and it is also important to give recognition to the museum donors. Perhaps we can combine the two and give recognition in the museum building to all donors.

Meaningful awards should be established for donors and solicitors. There shall be a variety of awards: awards for solicitors and donors. Very generous donors will have an entire room in the museum named for them; others will be inscribed on plaques or tablets. It would be a great incentive if the awards were given out by the President of Israel.

SANHEDRIN

As was pointed out previously, we are confronted at this time in our history with many difficult problems and challenges. One of those challenges is that we are fragmented and pulling in different directions. There is no central Jewish religious authority to decide for all of Judaism important questions and Halachic decisions.

We need innovative ideas; we need new approaches to bring unity to our people.

At the same time, we also live during a period in which we have in our hands great historical opportunities to change the status quo. We live in an historical time in which the Jewish people have their own sovereign country; this is the first time in 2,000 years that we have our own country. We should use this great opportunity to make changes of far reaching consequences.

Therefore I am proposing the idea of reinstituting the Sanhedrin.

The Sanhedrin was functioning in ancient Israel during the existence of the Temple and also after the destruction of the Temple. In the Tannaic period, after the destruction of the Temple, it helped revive Judaism. The Sanhedrin was the Supreme Court of Judaism and, at the same time, it was also the legislative body on Halachic matters. The great sages Rabbi

Hillel, Rabbi Gamliel, Rabbi Yehuda Hanasi, to name a few, were the leaders (Nasiim, presidents) of that body.

Let us bring back the institution of the Sanhedrin to serve as the unifying authorized Central Religious Authority for the Jewish people all over the world.

The function of the new Sanhedrin will be:
- To render great Halachic decisions
- To speak out on world issues
- To be the teachers of the Jewish people
- To be role models
- To work for the cause of Jewish unity

To start the process of reinstituting the Sanhedrin, a worldwide Jewish conference shall be convened. All the great rabbis of our time, all the great Talmudic scholars, all the great lay leaders, should be invited to this convention. The ultimate goal of the conference shall be to elect 71 qualified people as members of the Sanhedrin.

The first step is that the conference shall appoint a committee of 9 eminent persons to choose 36 nominators. The 36 nominators shall consist of eminent rabbis and lay leaders, and they shall be approved by a majority at the conference. The 36 nominators shall put 100 candidates in nomination for the Sanhedrin, of which only 71 will be chosen. The entire Sanhedrin body will consist of 71 members.

The nominees for the Sanhedrin will be chosen from rabbis all over the world. To qualify as a nominees for the Sanhedrin, the candidate must be an outstanding rabbi and have ordination from an Orthodox yeshiva, approved by the conference. Each candidate will need two-thirds a majority of the nominators to be placed in nomination as a candidate. Each candidate will have to give his approval in writing to be nominated.

The Sanhedrin itself, after it is elected, will choose a Nasi (president) and other officers. The election of the 71 members of the Sanhedrin will be by a two-thirds majority of all those attending the conference and will take place once every ten years. The Sanhedrin will be elected for a term of ten years.

The idea of reinstituting the Sanhedrin is a thought I had a long time ago and I have been talking about it with friends. In 1988 I wrote down my ideas and gave them to my friend Jerry Hahn, *z"l*. He took the ideas to Jerusalem and showed them to some rabbis in the Old City. Regretfully it did not attract any interest at that time. I am revisiting the idea now; I still think it will do a lot of good.

It is my opinion that if the Sanhedrin is elected by the Jewish people from all over the world, and the nominees for the Sanhedrin are chosen from people all over the world, then the Sanhedrin will receive wide acceptance and will eventually bring Jewish unity.

JEWISH SUMMER CAMPS

In discussing my ideas with my son Robert (Shlomo), he mentioned to me that he discussed some of my ideas with a friend of his. This friend suggested that Jewish summer camps would be a good device to be used in inculcating our children with Jewish values, Jewish practices, and Jewish observances. I think the idea has a lot of merit and I am adding it to my list of suggestions.

We should establish an organization that will subsidize parents who can't afford to send their children to a Jewish summer camp. Exposure to a Jewish summer camp may change many young children into a generation that is educated in Jewish tradition and values, and into children who are imbued with love for the Land of Israel.

It will be the task of the organization to solicit thousands of donors to subsidize children who want to spend a summer in a Jewish summer camp. It would be for children whose parents can't afford it.

In conclusion to what I have written in this book, we have **two choices:**

We can do nothing, and continue to have a declining Jewish population that may lead, God forbid, to extinction,

Or we can act and bring a rebirth of the Jewish people that are vibrant and are contributing to the betterment of mankind, inaugurating a great future for our children and grandchildren.

עם ישראל חי

APPEAL!

This is an appeal
to every Jewish person
reading this book

Join me! Let us all be partners
in this undertaking

Please call or write
to the Jewish Leaders, and ask them

To convene a meeting
in Jerusalem

to address these urgent issues

6,000,000 more Jews
in the world

Picture 1: My mother Nechama Reizel Judovits,
Daughter of Dejer Rabbi Moshe Paneth

My Father

Salamon Judovits

ר שלמה בן מרדכי יודאויטש

Was martyred in Auschwitz

in June of 1944

Corresponding to the month of

סיון תשד

Picture 2: My father Shlomo Judovits
(I was unable to find a photo after the Holocaust)

Picture 3: My grandmother Rebetzin Chayah Sarah Paneth,
wife of Rabbi Moshe Paneth

Picture 4: My mother, my brother Moshe, my aunt Frieda Margoshes, Rebetzin in Dorna, front row children; my sister Matel Leah, my cousins Mendi and Fogerl Margoshes

Picture 5A: My cousin Sarah Paneth, my sister Matel Leah, my cousin Rivkah Paneth

Picture 5B: Photo of the author Martin Judovits, at age 11 years old

Picture 6: Rabbi Yechezkel Paneth Rabbi of Dej, my mother's brother

Picture 7: Rabbi Yaakov Elimelech Paneth, Rabbi of Dej, my cousin and teacher

Picture 8: Rabbi Elisha Horowitz, my cousin and teacher

Picture 9: My wedding picture

Picture 10A: The great synagogue of Dej, interior

Picture 10B: The great Synagogue of Dej

*Picture 11: My wife Helen with Alice, the girl she saved from being
trampled in the labor camp*

Picture 12: Martin & Helen Judovits at ground breaking for the Boca Raton Synagogue

Picture 13A: The Boca Raton synagogue, exterior

Picture 13B: The Boca Raton Synagogue, interior

Picture 14A: The Holocaust memorial at the B R Synagogue, designed by Martin Judovits

Picture 14B: Holocaust Memorial, view of the martyr's names

חכם בא לעיר

תנו כבוד לתורה

▪▪▪▪▪▪▪▪▪▪▪▪▪▪▪▪▪▪▪▪▪▪▪▪▪▪▪▪▪▪

בזה דנודיע בקול 3 ▪▪▪ יען בסדר ליד קדשו ת"ו

יד יב שאל זו זקדית ישמיי באר ויחיד והיה חיש

ב"ד ד טיפ"וחא רב: נשיאה ממשפחת רם

א ד מ ו " ר כ ק ש ' ת

מ ← **יעקב אלימלך פאנעטה** [שליט"א]

לש אברהן שנד לא ובלל רש מדברא וחשכו תהלה משכת

נשא אברכל וכלל דבענבדתק וסיאר באהרם ת"ז
(ותד שד אבחד הק בודי קדש (וכמו)

כל מבד ידוח ומקד חחס דבן מדבקסם

לבוא בהמונים לקברת פני קדשו

תקבלת עם תדי בשער בתי כולל דבענבירגן

תהלת כולל דבענבידעק וסיגארי
בקרוב ישרים תנבא

Picture 15: Poster announcing visit of Rabbi Paneth to Jerusalem.
(The poster was given to the author by Mr. Eli Genauer from Seattle;
he found it on the Internet.)

```
                   Mauthausen No. 71908 Jude Ung.
Date 22.6.50/D.R.                            OCC15/145/
Name  J U D O V I T S ,  Mozes  File  -IA/1-
BD  6.3.22      BP    Des              Nat  Hung.Jew.
Next of Kin
Source of Information Photoc.of orig.Mauth.Nummernbuch
Last kn. Location                      Date
CC/Prison Mauth/Gusen Arr.             lib.
Transf. on              to
Died on   1.2.45        in     Gusen
Cause of death
Buried on               in
Grave                          D.C.No.
Remarks
```

Picture 16: Certificate of my brother's death in Mauthausen labor camp
(found at Yad Vashem)

Picture 17: Grave of Rabbi Yechezkel Paneth, author of the Sefer Mareh Yechezkel

Picture 18: Grave of Rebetzin Chaya Rachel Paneth, wife of Rabbi Yechezkel

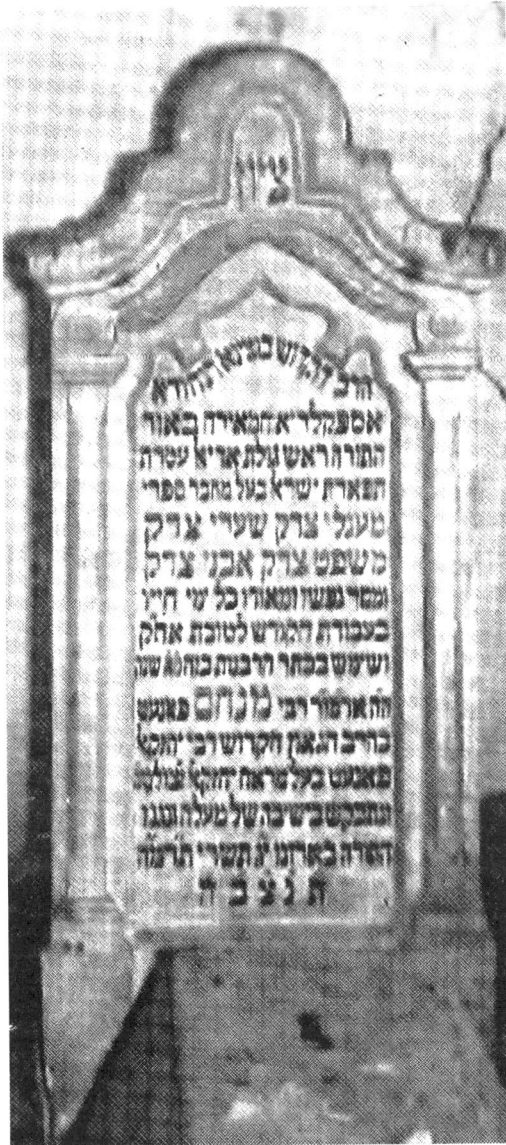

Picture 19: Grave of Rabbi Mendel Paneth, first rabbi of Dej

Picture 20: Grave of Rabbi Moshe Paneth, rabbi of Dej